Business cycle theory as a basis for economic policy

This book aims to start a debate on the relationship between economic theory – and more precisely business cycle theory – and economic policy, emphasising the diversity of views on economic policy which characterised older periods, in contrast to the homogeneity of the analysis and diagnosis provided by current business cycles developments.

Since the 1970s, economic theorists excluding economic policy interventions and favouring supply-side economic policies have gained a growing influence. The development of Equilibrium Business Cycles theories coincides with the collapse, at least in academic circles, of the Keynesian consensus favouring stabilization policies. The alternative approach which emerged was based on an *a priori* hypothesis about the stability of the economy – or at least on its remarkable ability to stabilize itself. The direct consequence of this approach is that any stabilization objective for economic policy is not only misguided but also inefficient. There are many reasons why Keynesian policies ceased to be dominant in theoretical circles, but paraphrasing Harry Johnson, one must recognize that the most helpful circumstances for the rapid propagation of a new revolutionary theory is certainly the existence of an established orthodoxy, clearly inconsistent with the most salient facts of reality.

This book offers a sample of different theoretical approaches to business cycles, examining their respective views on economic policy with the objective of understanding business cycle theories that have been lost, and identifying those views which explain fluctuations and the way we conceive economic policy.

This book was originally published as a special issue of *The European Journal of the History of Economic Thought*.

Pascal Bridel is Professor of Economics at the University of Lausanne, Switzerland. He has published in various fields including the history of economic thought and monetary theory.

Muriel Dal Pont Legrand is Professor of Economics at the University of Nice Sophia Antipolis and GREDEG CNRS, France. She has published in various fields including the history of economic thought.

Business cycle theory as a basis for economic policy

Edited by
**Pascal Bridel and
Muriel Dal Pont Legrand**

Routledge
Taylor & Francis Group
LONDON AND NEW YORK

First published 2016
by Routledge
2 Park Square, Milton Park, Abingdon, Oxon, OX14 4RN, UK

and by Routledge
711 Third Avenue, New York, NY 10017, USA

First issued in paperback 2017

Routledge is an imprint of the Taylor & Francis Group, an informa business

British Library Cataloguing in Publication Data
A catalogue record for this book is available from the British Library

ISBN 13: 978-1-138-10665-9 (pbk)
ISBN 13: 978-1-138-93881-6 (hbk)

Typeset in Garamond
by RefineCatch Limited, Bungay, Suffolk

Publisher's Note
The publisher accepts responsibility for any inconsistencies that may have arisen during the conversion of this book from journal articles to book chapters, namely the possible inclusion of journal terminology.

Disclaimer
Every effort has been made to contact copyright holders for their permission to reprint material in this book. The publishers would be grateful to hear from any copyright holder who is not here acknowledged and will undertake to rectify any errors or omissions in future editions of this book.

Contents

Citation Information   vii
Notes on Contributors   ix

Introduction: Business cycle theory as a basis for
economic policy   1
Pascal Bridel and Muriel Dal Pont Legrand

1. Economics of the crisis and the crisis of economics   6
   Axel Leijonhufvud

2. On the importance of institutions and forms of organisation
   in Piero Sraffa's economics: the case of business cycles,
   money, and economic policy   21
   Richard Arena

3. Mr Keynes, the Classics and the new Keynesians:
   A suggested formalisation   47
   Rodolphe Dos Santos Ferreira

4. Three macroeconomic syntheses of vintage 1937:
   Hicks, Haberler, and Lundberg   85
   Hans-Michael Trautwein

5. Lange's 1938 model: dynamics and the "optimum
   propensity to consume"   117
   Michaël Assous and Roberto Lampa

6. Toward a non-linear theory of economic fluctuations:
   Allais's contribution to endogenous business cycle
   theory in the 1950s   145
   Alain Raybaut

7. The "Treasury View": An (un-)expected return?   166
   Pascal Bridel

   Index   189

Citation Information

The chapters in this book were originally published in *The European Journal of the History of Economic Thought*, volume 21, issue 5 (October 2014). When citing this material, please use the original page numbering for each article, as follows:

Introduction
Special issue: Business cycle theory as a basis for economic policy
Pascal Bridel and Muriel Dal Pont Legrand
The European Journal of the History of Economic Thought, volume 21, issue 5 (October 2014) pp. 755–759

Chapter 1
Economics of the crisis and the crisis of economics
Axel Leijonhufvud
The European Journal of the History of Economic Thought, volume 21, issue 5 (October 2014) pp. 760–774

Chapter 2
On the importance of institutions and forms of organisation in Piero Sraffa's economics: the case of business cycles, money, and economic policy
Richard Arena
The European Journal of the History of Economic Thought, volume 21, issue 5 (October 2014) pp. 775–800

Chapter 3
Mr Keynes, the Classics and the new Keynesians: A suggested formalisation
Rodolphe Dos Santos Ferreira
The European Journal of the History of Economic Thought, volume 21, issue 5 (October 2014) pp. 801–838

Chapter 4
Three macroeconomic syntheses of vintage 1937: Hicks, Haberler, and Lundberg
Hans-Michael Trautwein
The European Journal of the History of Economic Thought, volume 21, issue 5 (October 2014) pp. 839–870

Chapter 5
Lange's 1938 model: dynamics and the "optimum propensity to consume"
Michaël Assous and Roberto Lampa
The European Journal of the History of Economic Thought, volume 21, issue 5 (October 2014) pp. 871–898

Chapter 6
Toward a non-linear theory of economic fluctuations: Allais's contribution to endogenous business cycle theory in the 1950s
Alain Raybaut
The European Journal of the History of Economic Thought, volume 21, issue 5 (October 2014) pp. 899–919

Chapter 7
The "Treasury View": An (un-)expected return?
Pascal Bridel
The European Journal of the History of Economic Thought, volume 21, issue 5 (October 2014) pp. 920–942

For any permission-related enquiries please visit:
http://www.tandfonline.com/page/help/permissions

Notes on Contributors

Richard Arena is Professor and Director of the *Maison des Sciences de l'Homme et de la Société Sud-Est*, a cooperative Research Federation including all the main research groups of the university in human and social sciences at the University of Nice, France.

Michaël Assous is a Senior Lecturer in Economic Science at the Université de Paris 1 – Panthéon Sorbonne.

Pascal Bridel is Professor of Economics at the University of Lausanne, Switzerland. He has published in various fields including the history of economic thought and monetary theory.

Muriel Dal Pont Legrand is Professor of Economics at the University of Nice Sophia Antipolis and GREDEG CNRS, France. She has published in various fields including the history of economic thought.

Rodolphe Dos Santos Ferreira is Professor Emeritus of Economic Science at the Bureau d'Economie Théorique et Appliquée, University of Strasbourg, France.

Roberto Lampa is based at CONICET (National Scientific and Technical Research Council) and the University of Buenos Aires, Argentina.

Axel Leijonhufvud is Professor Emeritus in the Department of Economics at UCLA, Los Angeles, California, USA. His research interests include high inflations, alternative monetary regimes, computable economics, and the evolution of modern macroeconomics.

Alain Raybaut is based in the Groupe de Recherche en Droit, Économie, Gestion (GREDEG) in the Institut Supérieur d'Économie et Management at the University of Nice Sophia Antipolis, Nice, France.

Hans-Michael Trautwein is Professor of International Economics in the Department of Business Administration, Economics and Law at Carl Von Ossietzky Universität, Oldenburg, Germany. His research includes the evolution of macroeconomics, monetary integration and international financial markets, and transnationalism and transnational governance.

Introduction

Business cycle theory as a basis for economic policy

The editors are pleased to present this special *European Journal of the History of Economic Thought* (EJHET) issue collecting a selection of papers given at a workshop organised in Southern France on 12th–17th September 2011 and bringing together historians of macroeconomics and macroeconomists interested in the evolution of modern macroeconomics. This week-long meeting was hosted by the Treilles Foundation. Organisers and participants alike are deeply indebted to the Foundation Scientific Committee for its generosity and to the local staff for making our stay in their beautiful surroundings a memorable occasion. We also wish to address our grateful thanks to the international Hubert Curien programme (Procope and Germaine de Staël sources of funding) which provided financial support for the development of this project at an earlier stage.

The main theme of the conference was organised around business cycle theories and their aftermaths in terms of economic policy. In contrast to the homogeneity of the analysis and diagnosis provided by current business cycle theoretical developments, and far from aiming at providing a complete analysis of economic policy debates, the idea of the project is to emphasise the diversity of views on economic policy which characterised older periods.

As a paraphrase of a book edited by one of the participants (Leijonhufvud 2001), the title of this special issue – *Business cycle theory as a basis for economic policy* – reflects rather accurately the common concern that motivated the various papers proposed here. Most of them strive to understand how various business cycle theories perceived and determined the role and shape of economic policy. However, this workshop never intended of course to produce an exhaustive presentation of the numerous and sometimes very different business cycle theories, but more modestly to start a debate on the relationship between economic theory – and more precisely business cycle theory – and economic policy.

Since the 1970s, economic theorists excluding any economic policy interventions and favouring strictly supply-side economic policies have gained a growing influence. Indeed, the development of equilibrium business cycles theories coincides with the collapse, at least in academic circles, of the Keynesian consensus favouring stabilisation policies. The alternative approach which emerged extremely quickly was based on an *a priori* hypothesis about the stability of the economy – or at least on its remark-able ability to stabilise itself. The direct consequence of this approach is that any stabilisation objective for economic policy is considered as not only misguided but also inefficient. There are many reasons why Keynesian policies ceased to be dominant in theoretical circles but, paraphrasing Johnson (1971), the most helpful circumstances for the rapid propagation of a new revolutionary theory is certainly the existence of an established orthodoxy which is clearly inconsistent with the most salient facts of reality. The purpose of this special issue is to offer a sample of different theoreti-cal approaches to business cycles, to examine their respective views on eco-nomic policy, with the objective of identifying the explanatory elements for the understanding of business cycles that have been lost, and, finally, to identify those which today mainly explains fluctuations and how this can affect the way we conceive economic policy.

The debate is opened by Axel Leijonhufvud's contribution, the title of which "Economics of the crisis and the crisis of economics" echoes that of his famous 1968 book (Leijonhufvud 1968) in which he already emphas-ised strongly the major importance for macroeconomics of coordination issues. In his paper, he reassesses his belief that the stability-with-impedi-ments approach on which the current business cycle models are based, the so-called DSGE (Dynamic Stochastic General Equilibrium) models are misguided in the sense that they do not capture elements which may explain recent events, and that, ultimately, they logically fail to suggest the correct policies. The author then identifies the economic fundamental features macroeconomic models should capture and how they should deal with related policy issues. The six following papers deal then with different episodes of macroeconomic theory, which were of fundamental impor-tance both for the development of business cycle models as well as for the economic policy debates.

The purpose of Richard Arena's paper concerns the importance given by Piero Sraffa in his published and unpublished works to social conflicts, institutions, and types of organisations in his approach to economic analy-sis. The first part of the paper illustrates this viewpoint in relation with the problem of price formation and offers hence a general outline of Sraffa's broad approach. The second part of the contribution focuses on the rela-tion between monetary theory, business cycles, and economic policy. It especially shows that in various periods of Sraffa's economic investigations, his emphasis on institutions and forms of organisations were always very much present in his theoretical approach.

In the spirit of Leijonhufvud's coordination failure approach, Rodolphe Dos Santos Ferreira offers a remarkable synthesis of his long-standing attempt at devising an alternative new Keynesian formalisation of the

General Theory. This is of course not obtained by a simple and literal translation of Keynes's verbal argument but by designing a convenient instrument (fitting of course Keynes's own methodology) to interpret and assess Keynes's theoretical contribution. The paper suggests a reduced form model, which entails a diagram with three curves relating employment and the real wage, which represent the two fundamental classical postulates and the principle of effective demand. This diagram illustrates better than IS–LM the generality of Keynes's theory, clarifying the distinction between voluntary and involuntary unemployment. Other significant features are the role of the distribution of expected interest rates among heterogeneous agents, whether dispersed or concentrated, in shaping the LM curve, as well as the role of wage competitiveness constraints as a foundation of Keynes's relative wage hypothesis. By logically concentrating on the methodological choices of Keynes's Book II concerning the treatment of expectations and aggregation issues, the author brings back to the forefront of the debate the new role and shape of economic policy in such a synthetic model.

Serious investigations in History of Economic Thought tend to demonstrate that far from having produced a single (neo-classical) synthesis between "Keynes and the Classics", macroeconomists have shown regularly a tendency towards synthetic theorising. Embracing a very large literature, Hans-Michael Trautwein succeeds in offering a very comprehensive survey of three such syntheses: those offered by Hicks, Haberler, and Lundberg. An analytical comparison between these three syntheses of 1937 vintage is particularly interesting because they suggest a revealing contrast on the causes of market failures as well as on the capacity of those systems to be self-stabilising. More specifically, the paper analyses why and how the shift of focus from imperfect intertemporal coordination to imperfect wage or price flexibility took place. This leads the author to compare the content, method, and impact of these three different syntheses in particular by evaluating the extent to which the New Neoclassical Synthesis has led "structural characteristics of imperfect information as well as coordination [to be] largely lost out of the sight" of most modern literature.

The next two papers deal with particular episodes in the history of endogenous business cycles. The objective of these approaches was to provide deterministic dynamics that would capture the inherent instability characterising market economies. Today, research in this area has practically disappeared, but during the interwar period and in the following decades, the interest for endogenous dynamics was part and parcel of the debate opposing *laissez-faire* to interventionist proponents – a fundamental antagonism that led to divergent views on the necessity and role of economic policy.

Michaël Assous and Roberto Lampa's paper explores potential dynamic implications of Lange's 1938 paper that have not been explored so far (despite Samuelson's 1941 initial investigations). Building on Lange 1934 and 1942, the authors provide a model, which encapsulates two fundamental features for the time lag between investment orders and actual investment, as well as for the implication of Lange's non-linear investment function (which differ both significantly from those proposed by Samuelson). They then suggest a model that clarifies first the role of the propensity to consume in Lange's approach and second, allows a better understanding of the role of the propensity to save. The model exhibits an intrinsic instability that corresponds to the way Lange perceives capitalist dynamics; it also captures Marx's main ideas about cycles and growth, which are the outcome of the interaction between income distribution and savings.

Using a completely different theoretical background, in his contribution, Alain Raybaut focuses on the impressive, although little known, contribution to non-linear business cycle theory made during the 1950s by Allais. In this framework, the existence of a limit cycle is mathematically proved and its existence confirmed by empirical evidences. The mathematical tools are similar to Keynesian pioneering non-linear macrodynamic advances but the theoretical framework is obviously totally different. In particular, for Allais, the origin of endogenous cycles is monetary, and explained by the interplay between two key elements: the agents that hold the desired money balances and the banking system that can create money. However, Allais says very little on the connections between his model and possible economic policies to smooth such cycles.

Finally, Pascal Bridel completes that set of papers with a contribution on the (un?) expected resurrection of the old Treasury View. Indeed, the author shows – if still needed – that the recurrence in these types of debates proves the necessity for a serious knowledge and training in history of economic thought. Indeed, to be conversant with the historical roots and theoretical developments of one's models is the only way to evaluate possible progresses or "repetitions under different guise" which are sometimes difficult to identify. It also helps to understand the current economic controversies showing for instance that "the simplified version of the Treasury View has (fortunately) very little to do with decision-making processes in economic policy but is a purely academic dispute linked to modelling preferences" (p. 20). Finally, and perhaps more important, Pascal Bridel questions the operational function and also the respectability of social science models, which do not seriously feel concerned by the link(s) between their formal constructions and their interpretative content.

4

All the papers selected for this special issue have been subject to the same refereeing process as all other contributions published in EJHET. The editors are grateful to the anonymous referees who helped them in selecting the papers and to the authors for revising and improving their contributions. We believe that this set of papers reflects particularly well the scholarly and friendly atmosphere of this September 2011 workshop. In particular, in addition to the interest raised by each individual paper, we hope that this selection has the merit to offer the reader a broad reflection on recent and less recent developments of macroeconomic theory and more specifically on business cycle theories.

References

Johnson, H. (1971, May). The Keynesian revolution and the monetarist counter-revolution. *The American Economic Review*, 61 (2), 1–14.
Leijonhufvud, A. (1968). *On Keynesian economics and the economics of Keynes*. New York: Oxford University Press.
Leijonhufvud, A. (2001). *Monetary theory as a basis for monetary policy*. In association with the International Economic Association. London: Palgrave.

Pascal Bridel
Centre Walras-Pareto, University of Lausanne

Muriel Dal Pont Legrand
CLERSE CNRS, University of Lille 1

Economics of the crisis and the crisis of economics

Axel Leijonhufvud

1. Balance sheet troubles

This is not an ordinary recession. The problems unleashed by the financial crisis are far more serious and intractable than that.

The United States and the Eurozone countries are in the midst of a *balance sheet recession*. The concept is due to Richard Koo[1] who used the term to summarise his diagnosis of Japan's economic troubles in the wake of its 1992–1993 crisis. A balance sheet recession is fundamentally different from the garden variety and the usual countercyclical policies are not adequate to cope with it. The questions to be discussed below all pertain to the extraordinary nature of balance sheet recessions in general and, of course, the present one in particular: What makes them different from ordinary cyclical recessions? How do they come about? What makes them peculiarly intractable? What policies are effective or less effective in dealing with them?

Apart from these substantive questions, there is one further question worth considering: What kind of economic theory helps us understand these matters better and what kinds do not?

2. Stability and instability

How did we end up in our present unpredicted predicament? A short answer would be: by not being alert to the symptoms of instability. Almost all bankers, regulators, policy-makers and (of course) economists disregarded the possibility of serious systemic instability. But the widespread assumption that a system of "free markets" is stable needs re-examination.

---

1 Koo (2003, 2009). See also Leijonhufvud, "No Ordinary Recession", VoxEU, 13 February 2009.

2.1 Markets for produced goods

The beginning student's first introduction to economics tends to be the supply and demand model for a produced good. Two negative feedback loops are supposed to guarantee that the equilibrium is reached (*ceteris paribus*). If supply exceeds demand, price will rise so as to reduce the discrepancy in quantities. If marginal cost exceeds the demand price, output will decline so as to decrease the discrepancy in values. Both feedbacks *reduce the deviation* from the market equilibrium which is why they are termed "negative feedbacks".

In principle, it is possible that the interaction between the two feedback controls will generate persistent fluctuations in both output and price but theoretical reasons and practical experience both tell us that this possibility can most often be disregarded. So the conclusion is that we are safe in presuming that the market for any particular produced good will home in towards its equilibrium neighbourhood, which is to say, that the market is stable.

This presumption has been carried over to general equilibrium systems with an arbitrarily large number of goods. This is the case even though theoretical proofs of the stability of general equilibrium exist only for some special cases of limited interest. But as far as I know – and my knowledge is limited – the economists who in the last 20 or so years have based their macroeconomics on GE constructions have shown little interest in investigating their stability properties. Stability has been taken "on faith".

This faith may have some merit as long as what is being discussed are: (i) *non-monetary* GE models lacking fractional reserve banks and in which lending and borrowing are intertemporal barter transactions and (ii) budget constraints are always binding and never violated. These conditions are assumed in real business cycle theory, for example, which pretty much dominated high-brow macrotheory just a few years ago. But obviously these assumptions remove us altogether from the world of our experience.

Suppose we take stability on faith and trust that "market forces" will always tend to make output and consumption move towards a coordinated equilibrium state. How then explain recessions? Well, there might be conditions that interfere with markets and prevent them from doing their beneficial work. The "wage rigidity" postulated in conventional Keynesian theory as an explanation of unemployment would be an example. The recently dominant dynamic stochastic general equilibrium (DSGE) theory has pursued this logic. But a single "rigidity" does not take us very far in making the models "fit" the data. So we now have large-scale DSGE models with more than a dozen "frictions" and "market imperfections" – with more to be added, you can be sure, when the models do not fit outside the original sample.

It is my belief that this *stability-with-impediments approach is quite wrong, that it does not explain recent events, and that it fails to suggest the right policies.*

2.2 Financial markets

For more than a hundred years the instability of fractional reserve banking was the dominant topic in what came later to be called macroeconomics. Traditional banks had (i) large liabilities in relation to own capital (high leverage) and (ii) liabilities of very short maturities relative to their assets (maturity mismatch). High leverage and maturity mismatch remain the keys to financial instability today.[2]

The Great Depression of the 1930s provided the ultimate lesson that taught us how to control traditional banks. Deposit insurance removed the incentives for depositors to run on banks and thereby also the "contagion" that had characterised the banking panics of the past. Reserve require-ments served to limit the leverage ratios of banks. The limits on leverage meant that banks by and large were earning the same rate of return on own capital as other industries.[3]

2.3 Leverage dynamics: The build-up

In the last 20 years, financial institutions have not been satisfied to earn a rate of return no higher than that of other industries. The big investment banks, in particular, have learned to set themselves rate of return targets two or three times what is earned in the "real economy" – and the markets have learned to expect that such returns are actually achieved.[4] The only way in which such returns can be achieved is by operating at high leverage.

In retrospect, the piling up of leverage not just by financial institutions but also by other firms and notably by households has been the key to American prosperity since the early 1990s. It was an oft-repeated cliché among American economists that the American economy performed

---

2 Many observers would add *fraud* to the causes of recent instability. They are not without reasons. See, for example, Wray (2011).

3 Note that this stands in dramatic contrast to recent years when large banks have aimed for – and often achieved – rates of return above 20% while returns in manufacturing, for example, have remained in the single digits.

4 These rates of return, however, are not returns to shareholders – or capital would flow into the banks from every corner of the world. Bank executives appropriate enough of the profits of financial institutions to maintain the returns of shareholders at "normal" levels.

better than Europe in the 1990s because of its "flexibility". The simpler truth is that when more or less everybody spends more than he earns this will keep the "good times rolling". But it leaves a legacy of debt.

The arithmetic of leverage is simple enough. A bank with a leverage ratio of 30, which can invest in assets earning just $\frac{1}{2}$ of a per cent more than its liabilities, will earn a rate of return of 15%.[5] (And if the central bank supplies funds at a rate hardly different from zero, it might be able to do a lot better than that!)

Such a handsome return, however, will attract competitors and competition will narrow the margin between rates earned on assets and rates paid on liabilities. To keep its rate of return up as the margin shrinks, the individual bank can pursue one or more of several strategies. First, it can increase its leverage further. Second, it can move parts of its portfolio into riskier asset classes where the rates earned are a bit higher. Third, it can acquire assets too risky for its own portfolio, securitise them in bundles, and sell them off to investors that know no better. Fourth, it may be able to issue shorter term liabilities on which it pays less, such as overnight repo loans.

Competition will push all the major financial institutions in this same direction even as the risks they take on keep growing and their margins keep shrinking. As Charles Price, former CEO of Citigroup, famously quipped: "As long as the music is playing, you've got to get up and dance. We're still dancing". *So the boom ended in 2007 with leverage ratios at historic highs, risk premia at historic lows and maturity mismatches all around.*

2.4 Instability and economic logic

The economic analysis taught in universities everywhere tends to presume that markets are stable. Leverage dynamics exemplify instability – *positive feedback* processes. Instability often turns economic logic on its head. *Much that is true when the economy is stable ceases to be true when it is not.*

The analysis that I just went through provides an example. Normally, we approve of competition. The more the better. It produces socially desirable results. But the competition that drives leverage dynamics, pushes the competing firms into positions that will suddenly prove untenable – and the crisis that results has severe and adverse social consequences. Moreover, it also has the undesirable result that an already oligopolistic industry sees some of its member firms go under so that industry concentration increases. In the United States, financial institutions that were "too big to

---

5 A leverage ratio of 30 is quite high, of course, but in 2007 all the big American investment banks had ratios hovering around that number. Some European big banks have operated with higher ratios than that.

fail" to begin with are now *"much to big to fail"* – although they may not yet be quite in the novel category of "too big to save" that we have seen examples of in Iceland and Ireland and which at one time posed a looming threat in Switzerland.

Similarly, macroeconomic policies that ordinarily are prudent become dysfunctional, even reckless, in conditions of severe instability. Conversely, unconventional policies become necessary. We have seen a lot of unconventional policies in the last few years. Unfortunately, not all unconventional measures will be helpful.

2.5 Leverage dynamics: Unravelling

In a process analysed by Hyman Minsky[6] many years before the recent crisis, high leverage builds up slowly in an economy. Those tend to be years of prosperity. Eventually, the system ends up in a highly fragile state such that some relatively small shock will have enormous consequences.

To lend this statement some concreteness, consider that losses on US sub-prime and AltA mortgages were at one time estimated[7] at about $235 billion. Not pocket money, to be sure! But the loss of income in the United States over the first two years of the recession was on the order of $6 trillion. A very strong endogenous *amplification!* The corresponding (approximate) figures for the United Kingdom and for the Eurozone added together would amount to somewhat more than 6 trillion in dollar terms.

This striking disproportion between "cause" and "effect" is to be explained by several interacting *positive* (deviation-amplifying) feedback loops. High leverage means small losses will render an institution technically insolvent. To avoid failure it will then try to shorten its balance sheet. The knowledge among banks that their counterparties are in the same position freezes interbank markets. The institutions will then find themselves unable to roll over their short liabilities so as to refinance their positions. The ensuing scramble to meet short liabilities and to reduce leverage puts pressure on asset prices and strangles lending. When some banks are forced into "fire sales" of assets, the balance sheets of all are impaired. Growing unemployment and falling incomes undermine the ability of non-bank sectors to service their debt. The quality of bank assets deteriorates. If the general price level begins to fall, the economy is threatened with a true debt-deflation.

---

6 See, e.g. Minsky (1986). Minsky's (1977) is an excellent short introduction to the work for which Minsky is best remembered.

7 The figures I am giving here are by now quite dated and may not be accurate. But the point I am trying to make concerns *relative*, not absolute magnitudes.

2.6 Network structures and instability

This deleveraging dynamic is today even more dangerous than it used to be. The reason is that the structure of the financial industry, nationally and internationally, has evolved into a network of much higher connectivity than it had in the past. The United States provides the most clear-cut example.

The (second) Glass–Steagall Act (1933) embodied the lessons drawn from the Great Depression. One particular aspect of its strategy for curbing financial instability is especially noteworthy. It partitioned the American financial sector into a number of industries and industry segments. Each industry branch was defined by the liabilities that the financial institutions within it could issue and the assets they were allowed to acquire. A firm in one branch could not trespass into another. In some vital respects, the industries were similarly segmented geographically by the states in which the institutions in question were located and licensed.[8]

My metaphor for this Glass–Steagall architecture is that it sought to turn the financial system into an "unsinkable ship" by dividing it into numerous "watertight compartments". In this it was successful. In the late 1970s and early 1980s, the United States went through the crisis of the savings and loan industry. The assets of the savings and loan industry were basically 30-year mortgages which were financed by short term deposits. The industry was ruined by the inflation in the 1970s which raised the rates it had to pay on deposits high above what it was earning on old mortgages. (This is a *very* abbreviated version of the story.)

The point of this historical episode is the following. The losses in the collapse of the savings and loan industry were of roughly the same magnitude as the losses on sub-prime mortgages a quarter century later (and the US economy was significantly smaller, of course). Yet, only this compartment of the financial ship was flooded. The disaster did not engulf the other segments of the American financial sector, nor did it spread to the rest of the world.

We are now in an era of *conglomerate banking* in which few watertight compartments of any significance remain. The giant banks are engaged in virtually every financial market and not just in their home country but around the world. Also ordinary banks are trading in many more types of

---

8 Financial regulation in the United States was formed on the template of this organisation of the financial sector. Each "box" in the organisation chart has its own regulatory agency (although overlapping responsibilities were common). This regulatory structure has *not* kept pace with the changing structure of the financial sector. The crazy-quilt of regulatory agencies is utterly ill-suited to deal with present-day conglomerate finance.

assets and liabilities than they used to. The financial system is now a *very highly connected network.*

It seemed at one time a safe assumption that allowing financial institutions to diversify both their assets and their liabilities would surely make them safer. As it turned out, the highly connected network in which they thus became embedded exposed them to risks that they could not assess and some of which they did not even recognise. Financial economists believed – or so I believe! – that letting individual institutions diversify risk would make the system of such institutions more robust. But this was a fallacy of composition. The opposite turned out to be true.

High connectivity of a network means that a disturbance arising somewhere in the system will not be confined to some small part of it. Instead it will percolate through the entirety of it. The question is whether in so doing it will dissipate more or less harmlessly or cumulate, perhaps disastrously. The answer depends on several properties of the network. It will depend on whether agents in general carry high or low leverage. It will depend on the volume and distribution of "toxic" assets in the economy. It will depend on whether the network has critical nodes the failure of which would make large segments of the net collapse.

The properties of our modern financial system with its interdependent *conglomerate institutions* have proved to be unfavourable in all these respects.

3. Corridor stability and bifurcation

In a paper that is now 40 years old,[9] I advanced a "Corridor Hypothesis". The basic idea was that the dynamic properties of the macroeconomy depended on the extent of its displacement from a (hypothetically) perfectly coordinated state. In particular, the ability of "market forces" to bring the economy back towards "equilibrium" without the aid of policy interventions would be very much weaker, if not entirely absent, outside the Corridor.

The early 1970s were a period of much heated contention between quite simple versions of Keynesianism and of Monetarism and my paper was argued at a correspondingly simple level. But the general idea was right. Allow me to modernise it a bit.

3.1 A complex dynamical system

The economy is a complex dynamical system. In tranquil times, economic agents may make coherent plans up to some fairly distant horizon. In

---

9 Leijonhufvud (1973).

times of financial distress or of high inflation, decision-making becomes for the most part very short-term in both the private and the public sector. Short-sighted adaptive behaviour leads easily into complex system dynamics. The resulting volatility reinforces the tendency for agents to make frequent, short-term decisions. Another positive feedback loop![10]

In the present context, we are interested in the balance between deviation-counteracting and deviation-amplifying (unstable) processes. The former are the familiar market processes that keep departures from equilibrium prices and outputs within more or less stringent bounds. Unstable processes are cumulative but, in the cases of interest here, do eventually converge even if at a great distance from the original position of the system. So these deviation-amplifying, positive feedbacks are *bounded*. It is possible to make some conjectures about the qualitative dynamics of the complex system.

Imagine first a state space representation of its private sector divided into three regions. Over the *first region* of the space the market sector would show "normal" behaviour. Equilibrating market tendencies dominate and "stabilisation policies" in the conventional sense are not useful. In the *second region*, destabilising adaptive feedbacks occur but are fairly tightly bounded. Keynesian multiplier and accelerator processes are examples. The economy goes through more-or-less normal "business cycles". Monetary and fiscal policies may be useful to change liquidity or directly affect aggregate demand. In the *third region*, we find dangerous instabilities such as default avalanches. In this region, we find the interacting positive feedback loops discussed above. The worst outcome in this region of dangerous instability is the "black hole" of a Fisherian debt-deflation catastrophe.[11]

In this third region, balance sheet disequilibria tend to dominate the dynamics of the economy. Analysis must correspondingly concentrate on balance sheet magnitudes and not get trapped into conventional income–expenditure theory. The policy recommendations drawn from income–expenditure analysis tend to mislead – as I think Japan's experience with almost two decades of deficit spending illustrates.

---

10 I like to think of this endogeneity of decision horizons as the "accordion effect". It is of considerable importance in understanding credit crises and high inflations. As far as I know, it is missing from intertemporal general equilibrium models.

11 I have a similar schema for inflation theory but it has to be left aside here. Major stylised facts drawn from high-inflation experiences have to be regarded as anomalies from the standpoint of general equilibrium theory. See, e.g. Heymann and Leijonhufvud (1995) and for a brief summary of the anomalies, Leijonhufvud (1997).

3.2 Financial bifurcation

In the previously mentioned "Corridor" paper of 40 years ago, I also had a section on financial bifurcation. A financial crisis tends to divide the economy into one set of safe, solvent and liquid agents and another set of illiquid agents that are more or less threatened by insolvency and some of which are already bankrupt. Agents in the solvent set will avoid lending to agents in the insolvent set.

Looking (40 years ago) on the 1930s through quantity theory glasses, the solvent economic units would have a low propensity to spend out of money balances while the units in the second set would have a very high propensity. (Think of the unemployed in the 1930s or American state governments, like California's, in this decade!) The money stock would drain out of the second set and pile up in the first and aggregate velocity would then be observed to fall. Monetary injections would go into the first set and never reach the second.[12] So, monetary policy would be unusually ineffective.

This reasoning will sound even more simplistic today than it did 40 years ago and the two situations are dissimilar in various respects. Central banks no longer attempt to control the stock of money. American agriculture and large US corporations are in far better health now than in the 1930s. The federal government, unfortunately, is in much worse fiscal health than during the Great Depression and most American states have become "drags" on the economy through their self-imposed balanced budget amendments. And so on.

But it is still true that monetary stimulus on the whole does not reach the parts of the economy that are in trouble. In the United States, solvent households get the privilege of refinancing mortgages at never-before-seen low interest rates, while households with mortgages "under water" do not get that opportunity even when they are able to keep up their payments. The ineffectiveness of monetary policy in present circumstances has just about nothing to do with the "zero lower bound" to interest rates that so many economists have agonised about.[13] The reason lies rather in the ages-old maxim of bankers: "Never lend money to people who need it!"

---

12 I recall Karl Brunner waxing contemptuous of economists who thought that the Fed was "pushing on a string" in the 1930s, but I believe something of the sort *was* going on.

13 Note also that "liquidity trap" is a rather inadequate characterisation of this state of an economy. It refers at best to only that half of the bifurcated system that has a very low propensity to spend out of cash balances and neglects the half with a very high such propensity.

4. Macroeconomics and financial economics: In crisis?

There are so-called "heterodox economists" of many stripes some of which have useful things to say about our present predicaments (while others do not). But when people debate the question of whether economics is or is not in crisis it is the dominant orthodoxy they have in mind. DSGE theory is that orthodoxy today. It comes in several blends it is true – real business cycle theory, new Keynesian economics, etc. – but such distinctions would take us too far afield. I will confine myself to some comments about DSGE in general.

4.1 Unemployment in DSGE: An example

Unemployment will, of course, fit into GE models only if interpreted as an equilibrium phenomenon. As such it has not attracted any particular interest in this literature. But some recent papers have introduced unemployment in DSGE models.

Two alternative hypotheses to explain it have suggested themselves to DSGE practitioners, namely, either unemployment is due to "labour market frictions" or else to "market power in labour markets".[14] So the issue seen in this context becomes: *Are changes in unemployment due to shocks to the labour market mark-up or to "preference shocks that shift the marginal disutility of labour"?*

When I was a student (half-a-century ago, alas!), GE constructions were often referred to as models of "general interdependence". What is striking about these two hypotheses is that both treat unemployment as a *partial equilibrium* problem confined to the labour market. Moreover, this literature excludes any alternative hypotheses.

It was one of the lessons of an older brand of Keynesian economics that a disequilibrium arising in one part of the economy will disequilibrate also markets where *ruling prices are exactly at the levels that would obtain if the economy were in general equilibrium*. In particular, if the rate of interest were above its GE level, one result would be unemployment even at the "right" (GE) level of real wages.[15]

---

14 My arguments in this section are largely taken from "Axel in Wonderland" a comment on Jordi Gali, Frank Smets, and Rafael Wouters, "Unemployment in an Estimated New Keynesian Model" at a research workshop on "Analyzing the Macroeconomy: DSGE versus Agent-based Modelling", Central Bank of Austria, 15–16 June 2011.

15 This old piece of analysis might be of particular interest to people preoccupied with the *zero lower bound* to the interest rate as a serious problem in our current situation. (But interest targeters had better think twice about assuming the natural rate to be negative.)

Note that downward wage flexibility is unlikely to help in this situation. As long as intertemporal prices are wrong, lower wages will not clear the labour market. If wages were to be *very* flexible, it would make matters worse. Falling wages and prices would disequilibrate balance sheets in Fisherian debt-deflation fashion.

The point applies with multiplied force if intertemporal markets are not just disequilibrated by a market rate higher than the natural rate of interest but are thoroughly disrupted by a financial crisis.

Now, if you are willing to believe that the recent financial crisis *either* increased the market power of labour *or* made workers in general lazy, please feel free to stick with GE as the way to interpret the world around you. General interdependence of equilibria is a lot easier to analyse than general interdependence of disequilibria!

4.2 Representative agent models, fallacies of composition, and instabilities

Representative agent models will not admit fallacies of composition. Keynes taught the paradox of saving: if households try to save more than the business sector invests, they will not succeed; instead income will fall. Milton Friedman had his own favourite version of the fallacy: if everyone tries to add to their money balances when the money supply is held constant, most will not succeed; instead, incomes will fall. The fallacy of composition for our times might be called the fallacy of deleveraging: if everyone tries to deleverage, most will not succeed; instead asset prices and incomes will fall all around.

"The representative agent will not be puzzled by paradoxes of saving; he will not suffer involuntary unemployment; and he is not likely to be gripped by financial panic or to get caught in the maelstrom of debt deflation".[16] *Models that do not admit fallacies of composition leave us blind to the major sources of instability in the economy.*[17]

---

16 Quoting my "Keynes as a Marshallian", in Backhouse and Bateman (2006).
17 One reaction to the charge of ignoring instabilities that I have heard from one distinguished DSGE practitioner is that the system "cannot be unstable" because then it would either have already exploded or imploded. This argument is supposed to justify ignoring the possibility of instabilities. As pointed out by Willem Buiter, however, this mistaken view of the matter seems to be due to the practice of assuming linearity around the solution point as a supposedly harmless way of making DSGE models easier to solve. See, e.g. Buiter (2009).

4.3 Stable GE with "frictions" versus instability

It is true, of course, that the DSGE literature has moved beyond single-agent models. In so doing, has it reintroduced the most relevant fallacies of composition? I do not know. But I believe it is true to say that the DSGE school has paid little attention to unstable processes. The diagnoses of our current problems that we get from DSGE practitioners tend all to run in terms of *stable GE systems beset with "frictions"*.

A somewhat more plausible argument in favour of DSGE is that these models can accommodate multiple equilibria and that, when this is the case, some of these will be unstable. So, it is argued, the criticism that DSGE theory generically ignores instabilities is false. But this defense is not without problems.

One such problem, of course, is to determine which of the multiple equilibria the system will settle on. Here, theorists have often resorted to coordination by "sunspots". In astronomy, sunspots are empirically observable apart from their consequences. In macroeconomics, that is not so and the scientific status of the sunspot literature, therefore, dwells in a darkness where no sunshine ever penetrates.

But the basic stability problem with GE models is rather different. Recall Walras' problem with the possibility of "false trading". The simplest illustration assumes pure exchange in an Edgeworth–Bowley box. If some trade were to occur at a price different from the equilibrium price, the exchange process will not terminate at the solution point determined by the Walrasian equilibrium conditions. The disequilibrium trade shifts the initial endowment.

In a financial crisis, this problem becomes *infinitely worse*. Not only do defaults shift the endowments about, but they keep changing the dimensions of the box. Furthermore, a great many agents will suffer Knightian uncertainty about what their endowments may be and what they may end up being. The probability that the system would settle in *any one* of its multiple initial equilibria is basically zero.

Macromodels that ignore problems of instability are dangerous to the health and welfare of untold millions of people.

4.4 Violations of budget constraints and their consequences

Intertemporal general equilibrium models have solutions that coordinate saving and investment decisions over an infinity of future periods. They do so without fail because they assume the trading plans of all its members to be tied together by a *transversality condition* way out there at the end of time. This kind of model has figured prominently in recent monetary policy debates.

A brief attempt at perspective: one or two centuries ago, the price level was supposed to be governed by the demand and supply of gold while central banks used the bank rate to manage the volume of credit. Today, central banks use the repo rate to manage the price level and trust in the transversality condition to control credit.

If reliance on the gold standard meant putting your faith in a "barbarous relic", trusting in the transversality condition is surely nothing but pure and utter superstition. *This figment of economic imagination simply has no counterpart in the world of experience.* Every bubble that ever burst is proof of this fact. It should be removed from our models.

From the standpoint of the DSGE tradition, the consequences would of course be drastic. If you remove the capstone from a Roman arch, everything crumbles. Remove the transversality condition from DSGE models and everything unravels. Without it, there is nothing to guarantee that individual intertemporal plans are consistent with one another. The system lacking an empirical counterpart to the mathematical economist's transversality condition is likely to experience periodic credit crises. Such crises reveal widespread, interlocking *violations of intertemporal budget constraints.* Walrasian constructions, even those of recent vintage, take for granted that budget constraints are binding. To do GE without binding budget constraints is not easy!

My personal conclusion is that *Walrasian equilibrium models are hopelessly inadequate for dealing with financial crises and their aftermaths.*[18]

The more important conclusion, however, is that our conventional macroeconomic policies are not adequate to deal with the aftermath of a financial crisis. They do not fit the problem. It is true, of course, that we have seen a plethora of quite *unconventional* measures by central banks and by Treasuries. But being unconventional, when conventional will not do, does not guarantee being right.

4.5 An external critique: Ontology

So far I have attempted an *immanent critique* (as Gunnar Myrdal might have said) of the presently dominant theory. An immanent critique uses the terms and concepts of the theory itself to show that it harbours contradictions or is otherwise inadequate. But we should recognise that our problems may lie deeper and affect not just the class of economic models that

---

18 The reader should know, however, that this conclusion does not command widespread assent in the economics profession.

happen to be in fashion today but also the broader tradition of economic theorising of which DSGE is just one branch.

More than a decade ago I read a book by Tony Lawson, *Economics and Reality*. I found it intelligent and interesting at the time but did not realise how often I would recall some of Lawson's arguments and how they would grow on me.

Lawson looks at economics from an ontological perspective. His main message is that one must understand the nature of the subject matter to be addressed and adapt one's methods of investigation to it. If that makes sense − as I think it does − *economics has gotten it backwards*. We insist on forcing our subject matter into the frame set by our preconceived methods of analysis, mainly optimising behaviour and equilibrium analysis. By so doing we create for ourselves − and our students − an utterly distorted image of economic reality. Thus, for example, we treat the evolution of an economy as if were a fully determined (albeit stochastic) process accurately foreseen by all inhabitants.

The main distortion, Lawson maintains, stems from treating an "open" system as if it were "closed". For concreteness, think of a controlled experiment in a natural science as an example of a closed system. The conditions of an experiment controlled in this sense are *never* met or approximated in macroeconomics. (Adding more variables to the right-hand side of our regression equations will never get us there). But in constructing intertemporal models − such as in DSGE − we insist on the make-believe that the macroeconomy is a closed system in Lawson's sense.

The case that Lawson makes has important implications for how we should and should not do economics. From my thumbnail sketch of his position, you will realise that to follow his lead requires us to give up much of the technical equipment that economists have invested so heavily in. So, it is not popular. But I cannot go further in arguing Lawson's case in the present context. I can only recommend his work as worth my readers' time and effort to understand it, at least in outline.

References

Backhouse, R.E. and Bateman, B.W., 2006. *The Cambridge companion to Keynes*. Cambridge: The University Press.

Buiter, W., 2009. *The unfortunate uselessness of most 'state of the art' academic economics*. Mavrecon blog. Available from: http://blogs.ft.com/maverecon/2009/03/the-unfortunate-uselessness-of-most-state-of-the-art-academic-monetary-economics/#axzz33JWY8rO1.

Heymann, D. and Leijonhufvud, A., 1995. *High inflation*. Oxford: Clarendon Press.

Koo, R.C., 2003. *Balance sheet recession: Japan's struggle with unchartered economics and its global implications*. Singapore: Wiley.

Koo, R.C., 2009. *The holy grail of macroeconomics: lessons from Japan's great recession.* Rev. ed. Singapore: Wiley.

Leijonhufvud, A., 1973. Effective demand failures. *Swedish economic journal*, 75 (1), 27–48. Reprinted in 1981. *Information and coordination.* Oxford: Oxford University Press.

Leijonhufvud, A., 1997. Macroeconomics and complexity: inflation theory. *In:* W.B. Arthur, S. Durlauf and D.A. Lane, eds. *The economy as an evolving complex system II.* Reading, MA: Santa Fe Institute and Wesley Addison.

Minsky, H.P., 1977. A theory of systemic fragility. *In:* E.J. Altman and A.W. Sametz, eds. *Institutions and markets in a fragile environment.* New York: Wiley.

Minsky, H.P., 1986. *Stabilizing an unstable economy.* New Haven and London: Yale University Press.

Wray, L.R., 2011. *Lessons we should have learned from the global financial crisis but didn't.* Working paper. Annandale-on-Hudson, NY: Levy Economics Institute.

Abstract

The macroeconomic instability revealed in the recent deep recession steams from the condition of balance sheets. Generally high leverage and strained maturity mismatches build up slowly but generate a financial structure so brittle that the impulse that eventually sends it crashing is hard to identify. The US financial system had been rendered more vulnerable by the financial reforms that swept away the Glass-Steagall regulations. The crisis made the inadquancies of the ruling macroeconomic paradigm painfully obvious. DSGE models generally did not include a financial sector and did not take the possibility of dramatic instability seriously. Unanticipated violations of budget constraints do not fit easily into general equilibrium models.

On the importance of institutions and forms of organisation in Piero Sraffa's economics: the case of business cycles, money, and economic policy

Richard Arena

1. Introduction

The opening of the *Sraffa Archives* to the general public in the late 1993 facilitated the emergence, during the last two decades, of a range of contributions dedicated to the study of the intellectual and analytical materials left by Piero Sraffa after his death and now available in the Wren Library (see e.g. the recent Special Issue of the *Cambridge Journal of Economics* on "New Perspectives on the Work of Piero Sraffa"; cf. Blankenburg *et al.* 2012). Twenty years on, some commentators on Sraffa's economic analysis still do not consider that this new material has modified the interpretation which prevailed before the opening of the *Archives* and many remain convinced of the views expressed prior to the Sraffa Archives becoming publicly available by authors as different as Robinson (1965), Walsh and Gram (1980), and Hahn (1982). These views consist of two propositions: (i) Sraffa's essential contribution is to be found in his 1960 publication *Production of Commodities by Means of Commodities (PCMC)*, and this is primarily a *contribution to price theory*; (ii) this contribution can be considered *either as a special case of* or as *an alternative to* the Neo-Walrasian and the Paretian theory of general economic equilibrium. Other commentators develop the opposite idea, namely, that the discovery of materials from the *Sraffa Archives* changed this initial interpretation of Sraffa's contribution substantially, extending its reach far beyond the price theory. This is also our view. However, this paper is not primarily concerned with this wider debate on the meaning of Sraffa's contribution since the opening of the *Sraffa Archives*. It addresses this only indirectly and focuses on the importance attributed by Sraffa to institutions and forms of organisation in the *Archives* but also in his published work. The role of institutions and forms of organisation in Sraffa's contributions to economic theory has sometimes been emphasised, but only partially so. Section 2 of this paper suggests that this aspect of Sraffa's work should be considered an integral aspect of his overall contribution to economic theory, *including* his contribution to price theory.

Section 3 of the paper then turns to the topics of this Special Issue, namely, business cycles, money, and economic policy. We suggest that for Sraffa, the analysis of business cycles, money, and economic policy is not related to the benchmark of the equilibrium or the equilibrium path of a given economy, as is the case in the so-called "neoclassical" analytical tradition. Rather, for Sraffa, business cycles, money, and economic policy cannot be properly understood, so long as economic analysis does not take serious account of the fact that the economic system is not self-contained but is embedded in a given "society" (according to Sraffa's own terminology, e.g. Sraffa 1960, p. 3) which is historically defined. This embeddedness is primarily related to the prevailing rules about income distribution that encapsulates some form of social inequality between core groups in society. This, in turn, is reflective of the institutional and organisational settings that prevail in society and that Joseph Schumpeter considered in his own way to be the object of *economic sociology* (Arena 2008).

Two further methodological remarks are in place here. First, the *Sraffa Archives* include materials dating from different time periods, and this may imply that Sraffa changed his mind in regard to specific issues he considered over time. This is certainly true, and the meaning and dates of these changes are still debated in the literature (see, for instance, Garegnani 1998, 2005; part III of Cozzi and Marchionatti 2001 including, for instance, De Vivo 2001; Pasinetti 2001; Salanti and Signorino 2001; Kurz and Salvadori 2008). However, this observation is not incompatible with the point of view we will embrace, namely, that during his academic life, Sraffa *always* stressed the importance of institutions, forms of organisation, and the social context and *of their influence* on the working of economic systems. Moreover, Sraffa *never* considered the economy as a closed and self-contained system, but as an open system connected with what he called the "society" in his 1960 publication.

Second, our point of view also emphasises the necessity of a consistent analytical reconstruction of Sraffian economics as yet to be achieved. This paper does not pretend to provide any such complete reconstruction but should be understood as a first step in paving the way towards this reconstruction, in what is, for the moment, an open field of inquiry. Yet, it is also far from being mere archaeology. Some of the "bricks" for this reconstruction are already there and, in this paper, we draw attention to these. Other building blocks remain elusive and will need to be provided to complete the picture, as best this is available from the *Sraffa Archives*.

2. Institutions, social conventions, and forms of organisation in Sraffa's contribution to economics

As we argued in Blankenburg *et al.* (2012), the *Sraffa Archives* contain many materials and developments dedicated to the study of the institutional framework of the economic system and of organisational devices or social conventions relevant to its working. These developments do *not* constitute a specific and separate theme of Sraffa's work, but are *present in most of* his writings. In line with the point of view we mentioned in our introduction and in order to illustrate the *permanence* and the *predominance* of the role of institutions and of forms of organisation in Sraffa's economics, we have chosen three significant examples from *different* periods of his writing and on *various* but crucial themes. The purpose of this first section is, however, more general than the purpose of the second since it concerns the core of Sraffa's economics.

2.1. The "given quantities assumption"

The first example we will consider is included in *PCMC* and is related to what Roncaglia called the "given quantities assumption" (Roncaglia 1978, Chapter 1, Section 8, and Chapter 2, Section 4; 2001). This assumption became the subject of intense discussions and was largely misinterpreted, immediately following the publication of *PCMC*. Some time had to pass for its meaning to be fully understood. For Sraffa, the "given quantities assumption" excluded the constancy of returns to scale, at least in the case of single-product systems, even if some commentators continue to this day to include fixed coefficients, adopt price/quantity dual systems, and argue that this assumption is natural or even necessary in a Sraffian framework (Bidard 2004; Benetti *et al.* 2007, for instance) for price theory as well as for steady-state growth. As early as 1962, Newman (1962, pp. 59–60), however, specified and stressed the importance of "the given quantities assumption", noting that instead of an assumption of constant returns to scale, it only amounted to a "recipe", that is, a mere description of the various quantities of commodities necessary to produce a "given quantity"; therefore, it excluded the use of "a model of fixed coefficients *à la* Walras–Cassel–Leontief" (Newman 1962: pp. 59–60). If matrix calculus is used, then each quantity of output j is assumed to be equal to 1 and each quantity of input i used in industry j is conventionally represented by the *proportion* of the total quantity *i* used in this industry. The relevance of the "given quantities assumption" is not, however, mainly formal but *analytical*. If quantities are given, this obviously means that in Sraffa's system, technology *but also the historical, social, and organisational conditions that prevailed during the last processes of production – and the previous ones –* are *both* given (see, for instance, Chiodi 1993; Chiodi and Ditta 2008, pp. 12–3): the given quantities – and not the given productive coefficients – sum up the past and present organisational and social conditions of production and not only the given technological proportions. Therefore, the debate about the room to be afforded to the assumption of constant returns to scale within *PCMC* is *not mainly formal* or pertinent only to the nature of the relation between technology and prices. It is *theoretical* and highlights two different views concerning Sraffa's message.

This is the context in which, in 1931, Sraffa discusses the relationship between the notion of surplus and the concept of "necessity":

> The study of the "surplus product" is the true object of economics (…).

> This notion is connected with that of "necessity"; & "necessity" has only a definite meaning from a given point of view, which must be explicitly stated, & then adhered to consistently.

> The surplus product goes all to expenses which are not "necessary" for producing a given commodity.

> What is necessary are the given circumstances, i.e. the known one (whether natural or social), of a given subject: the surplus is what belong (remains) to the subject himself. It must be mentioned at once that the boundary between the subject & his surroundings is by no means clearly defined; the subject himself may be doubtful as to where he himself ends & his circumstances begin. E.g. when one takes the classless human standpoint, he should regard all wages, rents & profits as surplus; but then always (e.g. Ricardo & Marshall) it is recognised that a part of wages are necessary for production, i.e. a worker is in part looked upon as a natural circumstance, an animal to be fed, & in part as a subject who participates in the distribution of the surplus (see especially Marshall's confusion as to the surplus which he says would not have to be distributed in a slave economy).

> Therefore, according to what an economist selects as the "subject" of his economy (usually identifying himself with it), the "surplus" will be different. The standpoint of capitalist society itself, is that of the ruling class, & therefore the surplus is composed of rent, interest & profit. (Sraffa Papers, D 3/12/7 (161), 4, dated August 1931)

In other words, if quantities are given – and in contrast to the first position mentioned above that excludes this problem – Sraffa refers to *necessary* quantities and differentiates these from other quantities. Obviously, as in the first view, technological inputs are *necessary costs*. But what about wages, interest, speculative gains, or profits? Sraffa dedicated some of his writings to these incomes, and this gave him the opportunity to investigate *which are the social agreements or the institutional arrangements* that are technically *or socially necessary* (that is, *conform to social norms*). The definition of the surplus, its size, and the characterisation of the "society" (Sraffa 1960, p. 3), as defined by a specific type of income distribution, directly depend on this analysis.

In regard to *wages*, for instance, in *PCMC*, Sraffa presents two "societies" or "systems" (Sraffa 1960): one in which wages only include the payment of social subsistence costs in the classical sense and, therefore, socially necessary costs (case where wages are included in the production advances), and another in which at least some part of wages is paid *post factum* as a share of the surplus. In this second system, therefore, a part of wages is not *a priori* necessary. It only becomes *socially necessary* if wage-earners have sufficient bargaining power to impose this. Labour enters the analysis furthermore in regard to another perception of necessity, and not only with regard to its role in sharing a part of the surplus. As Sraffa also noted in the 1940s:

> There are many other such socially necessary costs which appear as technical necessities. Thus, the work of a ticket collector on a bus or a railway: obviously, the railway would run equally well if no tickets were collected; but, if everybody travelled without paying, the shareholders would stop it; the work of the ticket collector prevents the shareholders from stopping the railway; the shareholders would be as effective in stopping trains as lack of coal in the engine. The ticket collector is therefore as productive as the fireman. (Sraffa Papers, D 3/12 18/11)

It is clear in this example that, for Sraffa, labour can be productive even if it is technically useless, strictly speaking. Therefore, the social organisation and rules of society *can* play their role in the definition of what is a part of *necessary* costs and what is not. In the second of the two approaches mentioned, we therefore face a problem that is meaningless in the first interpretation of Sraffa's contribution: fixed coefficients only reflect the state of technology prevailing in the economy *in a specific* society *at a given point in historical time*.

Concerning incomes other than wages, Sraffa was much more sceptical. Concerning interest, Sraffa (Sraffa Papers, D 1/15 6) considered the justification of the necessity of interest or of its inclusion within "real costs" based on "abstinence" or "waiting" as an "absurdity" (Sraffa Papers, D 1/15 2). In his *Lectures on Industry*, Sraffa reinforced and reiterated these arguments stressing how the justification of interest was arbitrary and therefore why its "necessity" was highly disputable.

Sraffa also discussed the case of *speculative gains* in the *Archives* and espe-cially in his *Lectures on Industry*. He considered them as the reward for a gambling activity (Sraffa Papers, D 1/18 17) and, therefore, related to pure "risk" (ibid.). The *Lectures on Industry* further developed this view by taking into account the introduction of the separation of ownership from control in the governance system of firms and considered two types of games of chance. However, Sraffa clearly did not, therefore, regard enter-prise and speculation as interchangeable or similar phenomena. He was in fact critical of speculation since this was based solely on a technique of risk evaluation in a specific but pure gambling activity. By contrast, individual enterprise entailed a different form of risk (requiring technical skills and therefore distinct from a pure gambling activity). Moreover, and, in terms of ethical requirements, Sraffa considered Robertson's "golden rule" to be consistent since it attributed the right to profit to those who accept to bear the risk associated with business ability.

These remarks on the "necessity" of costs and incomes support the view that the "given quantities assumption" is not only formal but also theoreti-cally a crucial assumption requiring substantial attention. It shows that the Sraffian system is not a standard linear model but an economic model of society in which this assumption introduces the embeddedness of the economy in a given context of social and organisational history and of socially prevailing inequalities. The consideration implies in its turn a reflection on the nature and the size of the surplus and, therefore, on its frontiers formed by technically but also by *socially* "*necessary*" *costs the inclu-sion of which requires a preliminary and thorough reflection*. Economic institu-tions and forms of organisation, but also social conventions or conflicts, thus clearly contribute to the formation of economic magnitudes, and these magnitudes reflect a given social "form of life", to use a term that highlights the intellectual relationship between Sraffa and Wittgenstein in this regard (see Arena 2014, p. 92). As noted in the introduction to this paper, this conclusion shows that even *PCMC*, undoubtedly Sraffa's *major published* achievement, was not only a contribution to price theory but rather one that shows how we can define a price model in which the eco-nomic system is open and connected to "society", namely, to its institu-tional and organisational foundations.

2.2. *Price entrepreneurial decisions and real-world competition*

The second example we will consider here has received much less atten-tion in the literature. This concerns Sraffa's reflections, in the *Archives*, on the pricing of entrepreneurial decisions and "semi-monopolistic" competi-tion. Much of the literature on Sraffa takes it for granted that the price theory developed in *PCMC* is a comprehensive summary of Sraffa's thoughts on the role of prices in the economy. However, Sraffa's price theory in *PCMC* had only two purposes: (i) to provide a "surveyable" or a "perspicuous representation" of surplus-based societies, to again use a terminology that highlights the Sraffa/Wittgenstein connection (see Arena 2014, part 3); and (ii) to demonstrate the existence and the positivity of production prices in this context. It, therefore, does not, for example, provide any information about the stability of production prices or about the process of their formation. For insights on some of these issues we, once again, need to consider the contents of the *Archives* and, in particular, the manuscripts dating from *before 1928* and dedicated to the analysis of the "practice of business life" (Sraffa Papers, D 1/29) and to "semi-monopoly" (Sraffa Papers, D 1/32). We, thus, return to the mid-1920s, considering a new theme and a different period of Sraffa's contribution to economics, for which forms of organisation are relevant.

In these manuscripts, Sraffa extensively quotes from and comments on Marshall's *Economics of Industry* as well as *Industry and Trade* (Sraffa Papers, 1928, D 1/36), based on his careful reading of both works, that, as he specifically emphasises, contain "illuminating suggestions" (ibid.), in particular with regard to the themes of competition and price formation. These comments by Sraffa on Marshall do not, of course, mean that Marshall's views on organisation and the social division of labour are the only ones that Sraffa took into account. The perspective of classical political economy undoubtedly was another crucial influence, that is not contradictory to Marshall's conception of a national system of production (Arena 1998). However, it is clear that there are striking analogies between Marshall's and Sraffa's emphasis on the necessity of taking into account organisational aspects of the economic system to understand agent coordination within the process of social division of labour. Sraffa's major role in the dismantling of Marshall's "symmetric theory of value" is very well known. Sraffa pinpointed its core inconsistencies with precision, specifically the incompatibility of the assumption of increasing returns with the framework of perfect competition, of the assumption of decreasing returns with the framework of partial equilibrium, and of the assumption of constant returns with the idea of the "symmetric forces" of supply and demand (Sraffa 1925, 1926). The last pages of the 1926 paper contain, however, a further contribution that has later been interpreted as laying some of the foundations of the theory of imperfect competition. As we will argue, this is not an interpretation that can be maintained in any serious sense.

To begin with, the reflections contained in Sraffa's manuscript on "semi-monopoly" show that, far from having in mind the construction of a theory of imperfect competition, Sraffa intended to build a *general* theory of "*semi-monopolistic*" *competition* characterised by both the existence of a tendency to competition *and* of a tendency to monopoly, based on continuous entrepreneurial efforts to create what Marshall referred to as "private markets", through a form of product differentiation. This viewpoint, therefore, excludes the possibility to consider semi-monopolies as cases of "imperfect" competition. On the contrary, for Sraffa, semi-monopolies are the predominant case, that is, the case that prevails in the real world. Thus, commenting on John Maurice Clark's analysis of "overhead costs", Sraffa importantly remarked that the case of "semi-monopoly" does not correspond to some imperfection of the market but – quite the contrary – to its "normal operation" (Sraffa, pre-1928, D 1/32, p. 14).

This perspective is entirely compatible with the classical view according to which there are only two types of competition – free competition and "monopoly" – with *the latter* including all cases in which competition is restricted by natural as well as legal, technological, or strategic obstacles (see Arena 1992). It also foreshadows the theories of economists, such as Edith Penrose or George Richardson, who considered what conventional economics refers to as "imperfections" of competition as the very conditions that allow the *real working* of a market economy. Moreover, the *Archives* show that Sraffa worked on this theory for a very long period of time, trying to channel this into a precise and rigorous general theory of competition in the real world. It is clear that the origin of the concept of semi-monopolies is prevalently Marshallian. In the notebook dedicated to Marshall's *Industry and Trade*, Sraffa carefully annotated all the developments which announced the theory of semi-monopoly. He especially quoted this passage from Marshall:

> It will in fact presently be seen that, though monopoly and free competition are ideally wide apart, yet in practise, they shade into one another by imperceptible degrees: that *there is an element of monopoly in nearly all competitive business.* (Marshall, *Industry and Trade*, p. 397, copied and quoted by Sraffa, pre-1928, D 1/41)

The theory of semi-monopoly, therefore, implies that semi-monopolistic entrepreneurs favour this *industrial form of specialisation and organisation* by increasing the differentiation of their products. This attention paid to the real forms of the organisation of markets and industries also surfaces in the second part of the 1926 article when Sraffa criticises the theory of perfect competition because of its inability to take into account two main empirical features of modern concentrated capitalism: the fact already noted that, in the real world, entrepreneurs are generally price-setters and not price-takers, and the existence of firm-internal economies.

Finally, the theory of semi-monopoly also captures another fundamental feature of modern capitalist forms of organisation, namely, the *a posteriori* division of labour, which characterises them. Market economies are decentralised. Therefore, entrepreneurs take their decisions *ex ante*, thereby also putting into place a specific division of labour between them that is not necessarily validated by consumers in the markets since markets only validate *a posteriori* the *a priori* division of labour decided by entrepreneurs. This is the reason Sraffa refers to the prices fixed by semi-monopolistic entrepreneurs as "prospective prices" (Sraffa Papers, pre-1928, D 1/33), and why, furthermore, pricing in a semi-monopolistic framework is subject to the constraint of a structural form of uncertainty (see Sraffa Papers, pre-1928, D 1/32/6).

The importance that Sraffa attributes to the notion of semi-monopoly is also confirmed by a letter from Sraffa to Keynes, written in Milan on 6 June 1926.[1] In this letter, Sraffa announced to Keynes what he intended to include in his forthcoming paper in the *Economic Journal*, referring explicitly to the theory of semi-monopoly. He provides an interesting summary of the state of his research at the time, stressing that "reality must be somewhere between" monopoly and competition (Sraffa 1926, D 3/6, p. 2).

The notion of semi-monopoly illustrates the contents of Sraffa's general research programme on *forms of industrial and market organisation* and their impact on price formation.

First, Sraffa's approach clearly demonstrates his rejection of the standard theory of competition. He did not only criticise the "Marshallian" symmetric theory of prices, but also criticised the methodological device used to differentiate perfect from imperfect cases. For Sraffa, the real world can never be a source of "imperfections" contrasting with the "perfection" of the theory of pure competition. Instead, the theory of competition must use semi-monopolies (or monopolies) as the prevailing case since it better reflects what *forms of organisation* are dominant in the real world. Therefore, at least during the 1920s and 1930s, for Sraffa, free competition did not represent a kind of necessary or indispensable point of reference for a satisfactory theory of the workings of a market economy.

Sraffa's rejection of conventional economic theory also explains why he tried to eliminate any subjective elements inherited from Marshall. He, first, interpreted semi-monopoly pricing as a form of "full-cost" pricing (Sraffa, pre-1928, D 1/29/1). Second, he attempted to develop a concept of demand freed from any subjectivist foundations. Demand had to be represented by *monetary demand elasticities* that could be observed rather

---

1 A first draft of this letter is present in the Sraffa papers but the original letter is included amongst the Keynes papers held in the Marshall Library in Cambridge. Its discovery is owed to Roncaglia (1978, Chapter 1).

derived from microeconomic foundations (cf. Sraffa, pre-1928, D 1/44 or D 1/68/29).

Finally, Sraffa's approach also had a Marshallian flavour insofar as it stressed *the importance of real market organisation as a crucial element of the social division of labour* (Arena 2008). Thus, Sraffa's view of semi-monopoly puts at its heart entrepreneurs seen as the "integrating force" he referred to in the *Archives*. They take the production and pricing; they try to influence consumers through advertisement and product differentiation; they try to reduce uncertainty by organising their own "private markets"; they sometimes also coordinate their activities with those of their competitors within the industry. In sum, they assume the major role of *organising and coordinating* production and exchange activities; they thus constitute the "integrating force" of the social division of labour.

2.3. Ownership, management, and control

Our third and the last example is to be found in the *Lectures on Industry*. In these *lectures*, Sraffa analysed how limited liability and the separation of ownership from management changed modes of the *control* of firms and industries (Sraffa, *Lectures on Industry*, Sraffa D 2/8 3)

Again, Sraffa poses the question whether under corporate capitalism the agent who controls the firm is still the same agents who bore the risk prior to the introduction of the rule of limited liability, namely, the owner or, instead, a new agent who has a "business ability", i.e. the manager. Sraffa insisted that the interests of company directors generally overrule those of shareholders (Sraffa, 1941–1943, pp. 22–4), and he clearly regarded this predominance of company directors as excessive. Hence, raising the spectacle of a general assembly of shareholders, Sraffa noted that the latter are "somewhat in the position of elector in a fascist country, where there is only one party; even if he is quite free to vote, and even to nominate a candidate, it is clear that if he has no party organisation, his vote will count not for little but for nothing at all."(Sraffa 1941–1943, p. 21). Therefore, shareholders' and directors' interests are not only different but they can, more often than not, be opposed (Sraffa, 1941–1943, p. 26). However, here again, Sraffa suggested that the solution to this conflict consisted of a *social convention*, interpreted by the members of a firm as an objective and shared reality:

> It appears that in practice some sort of compromise is achieved [...] between the conflicting interests of control and shareholders. [...].

> This [is done] has been done through the gradual, but now widespread, acceptance of the belief that there is an *interest of the company*, as distinct from both the interest of

the individual shareholders and of the control. This is purely *mythical entity*, much like the Hegelian State, but business men, however hard boiled, have a firm belief in it. (Sraffa Papers, 1941–1943, p. 29–30)

Therefore, the economy is not a pure and self-contained reality, entirely autonomous from society. It is embedded in a *social convention* that, in this case, is considered by Sraffa to be a "purely mythical entity". This entity is not the result of an explicit contract or of a tacit compromise between the managers and shareholders. It is the result of a *collective belief* which allows managers and shareholders to envisage a third interest they both serve either spontaneously or strategically. This third interest is the result of a *self-organisation process* that produces a solution of convention to a potential social conflict between managers and shareholders, and that can be either provisional or long term. This final example shows how the definition of some conventional entity avoids this type of conflict through the construction of an *organisational device* or *collective belief*: the interest of the firm. It also shows how it is impossible to consider Sraffa's system of prices as a closed system where income distribution would imply that the rate of profit and the rate of growth are determined simultaneously as two dual unknowns.

3. The role of economic institutions, forms of organisation, and social inequalities in Sraffa's conception of business cycles, money, and economic policy

Sraffa did not develop a complete, systematic, and unique theory of money and economic dynamics. Quite the opposite, he developed different theories starting from the old Fisherian version of the quantity theory of money and building progressively a theory incorporating conventional and institutional components (see Panico 2001; De Cecco 2008). Here too, he gives substantial space to the consideration of economic institutions, political or social conflicts within these institutions, and to their effects on the workings of the monetary and financial system. In the remainder of this paper, we will illustrate this point for a range of contributions and contexts from the *Archives*, but also for aspects of Sraffa's published work.

We begin with Sraffa's early writing on monetary theory and policy.

3.1. Sraffa's early contributions to monetary theory and policy

As De Cecco (1993) and Panico (2001) have argued convincingly, economic and political conflicts and institutions already played a major part in Sraffa's honour thesis on inflation in Italy. In this thesis, Sraffa "placed himself squarely in the camp of orthodoxy. This was the Ricardian view of inflation, and in Turin and elsewhere in Italy it was accepted by the great majority of economists." (De Cecco 1993, p. 2). However, as Panico emphasises, even if Sraffa is mainly influenced by Keynes's *Tract* and his conception of quantity theory, he adopts a "conventionalist" standpoint "according to which the *level* of the economic variables under examination is not determined by natural or material forces, such as the availability of the factors of production in the neoclassical theory of distribution, but can establish itself at any level considered *normal* by the common opinion and can be affected by the decisions taken by the monetary and other authorities." (Panico 2001, p. 287).

More precisely, Sraffa was interested specifically in the relationship between inflation, deflation, and income distribution, and his approach to the analysis of income variables was entirely different from marginalist theory. As Keynes, he emphasised the asymmetrical effects of inflation and deflation (Panico 2001, pp. 286–7) but focused in both cases on *income distribution* and *social inequalities*.

For instance, Sraffa noted that, during the First World War, inflation negatively affected wage-earners since their money wage increases lagged behind those of the general price level (Sraffa 1920, p. 25). Within a conceptualisation of income distribution based on social conflict rather than primarily on productivity constraints, this fall in real wages contributed to the increase of entrepreneurial profits. Moreover, inflation was associated with an expansion of the money supply and a fall in interest rates owed by entrepreneurs. (Sraffa 1920, pp. 25, 36–7). Entrepreneurs were, therefore, the only agents who benefited from inflation since they earn variable incomes. Pensioners and rent-earners on fixed incomes were also negatively affected by the rise of monetary prices. Shareholders were in a position which benefited from entrepreneurial extra-profits but, overall, they too earned a fixed income, and suffered from the combined effects of inflation and of the fall in the rate of interest (Sraffa 1920, p. 36).

Deflation could, in principle, provide an opportunity for a revenge of fixed-income earners on entrepreneurs. But this was true only in the very short-term period. Eventually, the reduction of entrepreneurial profits would have negative implications for wage-earners as well, since persisting deflation and a concomitant fall in profits would likely result in lower demand for labour, possible plant closures, and thus an increase in unemployment. In Sraffa's analysis, deflation can incentivise entrepreneurs to postpone investments and in the wake of reduced access to bank credits and a possible credit squeeze. The state cannot extend a helping hand in this context since a contraction of production entails an increase in public debt (Sraffa 1920, pp. 40–1).

Finally, in Sraffa's honour thesis, inflation and deflation are not only considered in relation to monetary crises, monetary policies, and the international monetary systems. They are also analysed in terms of their effects on income distribution, monetary institutions, and social conflict. This angle is obviously original since it tends to disconnect income distribution phenomena from pure economic realities such as technology and productivity. Quite the reverse, it *connects* problems of monetary disturbances with *social and institutional conflicts* and emphasises their role in economic dynamics. Following his honour thesis, Sraffa wrote several papers on the nature and the evolution of monetary systems.

In the *Archives*, we first find some notes on money (Sraffa, pre-1928, D1/18), most likely written during Sraffa's stay in London to study monetary economics at the London School of Economics (cf. Panico 2001, p. 287). Sraffa here considers the institutional context of possible applications of the quantity theory of money or of a monetary policy based on it. For instance, he compares the quantitative equations in Fisher and in Keynes's *Tract*, not so much for their respective analytical merits but above all to assess the extent to which these capture the *institutional characteristics of the monetary system* both authors have in mind (Sraffa, D 1/18 2). To turn to another example, Sraffa also examines different ways in which a quantitative monetary policy can be used in an open economy, and stresses the impossibility of implementing "a ruthless policy of high bank rate, which would cause a fall in the general price level" (Sraffa, D 1/18 7). Such a policy would be "impracticable" since the Central Bank "would not feel itself justified, nor would public opinion tolerate, deliberately to bring about a further depression of trade" (Sraffa, D 1/18 8). These remarks are particularly interesting, and we will return to them further below. They show how, for Sraffa, the *average opinion* and the *state of institutions and social conflict* must be taken into account even in the context of conventional quantitative monetary policy.

Sraffa's papers published in the *Economic Journal* and the *Manchester Guardian Commercial* (Sraffa 1922a, 1922b) make related points (see Panico 2001, esp. 228). These contributions constitute a first expression of Sraffa's interest in studying the complex relationships between the industrial sector and its entrepreneurs or managers, the financial sector and the shareholders, and the political world and its actors, deepened later on in the *Lectures on Industry*. For Sraffa, the state, entrepreneurs, and shareholders are not mainly individual or representative agents taking rational and independent decisions. They are interdependent actors using conflicting strategies and considering mainly *group interests* that cannot be reduced to conventional Marxist class interests, but that have direct and substantial impacts on income distribution. These *conflicting* interests also affect the evolution of *economic institutions and policy* and, therefore, economic dynamics, such as, business cycles. From this point of view, Panico's remarks about the concept of a "mixed banking system" is also important here because it is at the centre of the *Lectures of Banking*: once again, *institutions matter* and there is no unique optimal way to determine the best allocation of resources. Various paths are possible, with *the historical and social context* often providing a better guide to the choice of any particular path than rational choice. Obviously, one of the main features of the relationship between industry, banking, and finance is what Sraffa referred to as:

> the general tendency (...) towards the (...) formation of large 'groups' of companies of the most varied kinds concentrated around one or more banks, mutually related by the exchange of shares and by the appointments of Directors common to them. Within these "groups" the various interests are all equally subject to the interests of a few individuals who control the whole group (...). Very little is known (...) about these groups (...). What the public knows and feels (...) is the enormous financial and political power which they have and the frequent use they make of it to influence both the foreign and home policy of the government in favour of their own interests. Each group keeps several press organs which support its policy, and some of the accusations made against certain Ministries of being actuated by the interests not of a class, but of private concerns, and of favouring one financial group against another, have no doubt a basis of truth" (Sraffa 1922a, p. 196, quoted by Panico 2001, p. 289).

We will not enter here in Sraffa's characterisation of the events leading to the banking crisis (see Sraffa, 1922a, pp. 191–2). For the present discussion suffices to note that he explained the 1921 crisis of the Italian banking system and the run on one of the four major Italian banks, the *Banca Italiana di Sconto*, at the end of 1921 by analysing the underlying mechanisms. He thus focused on how *conflicts between different and rival groups of interrelated firms and banks* led the Italian government to support some of these selectively, and therefore, to adopt economic and monetary policy measures that did not favour the Italian general interest. Sraffa thus provided an historical example of how economic and, specifically, monetary policy was precisely not the result of purely technical and economic decisions taken by a representative agent called the state and inspired by some form of rational choice. Rather, economic policy resulted from *social and political conflicts* but also from *institutional arrangements* which could lead the state to favour particular interests over the national interest.

The implication is, however, not that Sraffa revived a rudimentary Marxist dichotomy of capitalist versus working-class interests. Thanks to the correspondence between Sraffa and Angelo Tasca in August 1926, it is possible to show that Sraffa defended a much more *complex view of the relationships between social groups and the state*, whereas Tasca argued that in a capitalist regime, "every single action of the fascist government (and of any capitalist government) is *directly* dictated by the *immediate* interests of the banks and of the big industrialists." (Sraffa 1927, p. 1089; italics in the original; *our translation from the Italian*: "che ogni singolo atto del governo fascista (e di ogni governo capitalista) sia *direttamente* dettato dagli interessi *immediati* delle banche e dei grossi industriali" – *RA*). According to Tasca, faced with a long-term devaluation of the Lira, the main objective of Mussolini's government was the stabilisation of the Italian economy and the revaluation of the Italian currency in favour of the upper class ("la grande borghesia" in Tasca's language; cf. Tasca 1927, p. 187). Sraffa objected, first, that since speculators would see through this policy of revaluation, they would in fact neutralise it. Second, Sraffa considered that *the political and administrative institutions and organisations* were in a position to influence the choice and implementation of economic policy. This suggested a considerably more complex picture than that suggested by Tasca. In particular, Sraffa argued that the Fascist government's stance in favour of a revaluation of the Lira was also directed at gaining the support of middle classes and of a part of the working classes with a view to strengthening its political and societal bases.

Two wider implications follow from this analysis. First, Sraffa insists *that the state, the government, and their institutions and organisations* constitute a complex set of relationships with a *limited but real autonomy* of decision-making in matters of economic policy. State and governmental actors and organisations are thus not representative rational agents with a unique set of objectives. Second, the presence of complexity as well as degrees of autonomy in the public sector does not entail a view by which decision-making in this sector becomes independent from the interests of the various social groups. Rather, it stresses the possibility that the respective influence of each of these groups can change with the wider social and political setting.

3.2. Sraffa on business cycles

A recent paper by "Nerio Naldi provides an interesting analysis of Sraffa's early views, in 1924, on the nature of business cycles (Naldi 2007, p. 131). Naldi begins by referring to Sraffa's visit to Keynes on 31 October 1924 and his subsequent thank-you letter to Keynes, dated 6 November 1924. Sraffa's position here is largely influenced by his more general and positive reaction to Keynes's *Tract on Monetary Reform*.

Most importantly for us,

the core of the social policy depicted by Keynes to Sraffa in Autumn 1924 and that the latter wished would "direct progress in the near future" could lie in the idea that State intervention in monetary management and in directing investment through a programme of public works could remedy the most dissatisfying features of a capitalist

> economy and was supported by a broader philosophical and political approach which
> justified that intervention and stressed the possibility of reforming the basis of capitalist
> society without yielding to a suppression of individual liberties. (Naldi 2007, p. 137)

Therefore, Sraffa's sympathy for the theory of business cycles developed by Keynes in the *Tract* was not only based on analytical considerations pertaining to the realm of economic theory, but also reflected *social and political* views informed by Sraffa's wider philosophy of capitalism, with this, in turn, being strongly influenced by his past political activities and his friendship and exchanges with Antonio Gramsci. It is uneasy to decide if Sraffa's sympathy for the theory of business cycles developed by Keynes in the *Tract* expressed a real change of view in relation to his past Marxist political convictions or if it only implied concessions in his relationship with Keynes. In both cases, however, and here again, and as early as 1924, we find in Sraffa a view of economic analysis *embedded in a more general conception of history and society*. In other words, for Sraffa, the theory of business cycles could not be seen as a pure technical construction but had to be related with the historical circumstances of his application and the type of economic policy which it implied.

This critical sympathy for Keynes's contribution to the theory of money and business cycles is also present in Sraffa's reactions to the *Treatise on Money* even if they include Sraffa's attention paid to *forms of market organisation*. Thus, in his "Notes on the causal sequence of events in the Treatise on Money" (Sraffa, D 1/71, 1930, 1931), Sraffa characterises "the causal sequence of events according to the Treatise" as "(a) savings exceed investment, (b) the general-price level falls, and finally, (c) the fall in prices brings about a trade depression" (Sraffa, D1 / 71.1). Even if Sraffa appears convinced by the general dynamics as depicted in the *Treatise*, he has doubts about the way, in which the *Treatise* constructs a sequential connection between (a) and (b). He does not accept as obvious the fact that "the *direct* effect of a fall for consumption goods will be an immediate and proportional fall in their price; while an increase in the effective demand for stock exchange securities will not appreciably raise their price". He regards the market for consumption goods as a typically "imperfect" market with "sticky" commodity prices, whereas the market for securities is "perfect" with asset prices being "fluid" (Sraffa, ibid.). Sraffa also contests "the identification of machinery & securities, under the ambiguous name of "new investment goods" (ibid.). The prices of machines depend to a large extent on demand by entrepreneurs and the prices of securities vary with the demand by financial investors. It is not straightforward to eliminate this difficulty. If saving exceeds investment, the fall of consumption goods prices will be slow, given the possibility of inventory adjustments and output reduction. By contrast, the price of securities will increase fast and pronouncedly. An equilibrium *could* therefore emerge, in principle. However, the bulk of firms will underestimate their profits on securities and therefore limit their supply to the financial market: "Instead of considering the rise in price [*in the market of securities* – RA] as a source of profits (equal to premiums) they would merely regard it as reduction in the rate of interest" and "the trouble is that companies should (quite wrongly) not regard themselves as producers of securities, as well as of goods. Thus, ceasing to issue securities, they go on making losses on goods, and restricting output, while failing to make the profits of issuing securities." (Sraffa, D1/71 3). This reaction to the *Treatise*, as well as related notes in the *Archives* (e.g. Sraffa D 1 72 and D 1/73), shows that even in a macroeconomic framework, Sraffa *did not believe* in a theory in which "perfect" markets with perfectly flexible prices are a useful point of reference. Instead and in contrast with a conception of economics based on traditional economic equilibrium, he argued that *markets also operate via a range of institutional devices* and that their *organisational features* – such as price rigidities – must be given serious consideration. Furthermore, and again even in a macroeconomic framework, Sraffa maintained micro-relations that need to be considered primarily in terms of the emergence of *organisational* economic interdependencies between firms and industries, in particular with regard to arguments about market-based adjustment processes and the formation of expectations. Traditional views based on the assumptions of individual economic rationality and self-adjusting markets are considered to be inappropriate. Therefore, recessions (and more generally, business cycles) cannot be analysed independently from general organisational inter-firm and inter-industry interdependencies, with these providing the relevant "micro-foundations" for the analysis of the macroeconomic system of production and distribution.

These same insights also arise from Sraffa's notes made in preparation of his critical comment on Hayek's *Prices and Production* (Sraffa, D 3/9 and D 3/10). Sraffa considered that both Hayek's *Prices and Production* as well as in Keynes's *Treatise on Money* rested on microeconomic assumptions about business cycle dynamics that were problematic. As Kurz (2000) and Zappia (1999) noted, Sraffa was critical, in particular, of Hayek's explanation of forced saving and of business cycles generated by inflation. During the process of capital accumulation and in a monetary economy, firms producing capital goods can finance their investments via an expansion of credit underwritten by banks. However, to avoid inflation and economic fluctuations, this expansion must be backed by an increase in saving deposits. This increase can be voluntary, implying a fall in the demand for consumption goods, or it can be "forced", that is based on an inflationary transfer to purchasing power from consumers to producers. Referring to Hayek, Sraffa notes that:

> The true difference between the two cases is, according to him, that the change in the structure of production brought about by saving is permanent, being due to the 'voluntary decisions of individuals' whereas the same change, if due to inflation, is 'forced' and therefore the consumers, as soon as inflation ceases and their freedom of action is restored, will proceed to consume all the capital accumulated against their will, and re-establish the initial position. (Sraffa 1932, p. 47)

Sraffa had no major objection to the case of voluntary saving but objected to the case of forced saving:

> When the robbery comes to an end, it is clear that the victims cannot possibly consume the capital which is now well out of their reach. If they are wage-earners, who have all the time consumed every penny of their income, they have no wherewithal to expand consumption. And if they are capitalists, who have not shared in the plunder, they may indeed be induced to consume now a part of their capital by the fall in the rate of interest; but not more so than if the rate had been lowered by the 'voluntary savings' of other people. (Sraffa 1932, p. 48)

Moreover, in a footnote to his 1932 paper, Sraffa also highlighted *another weakness* of Hayek's business cycle theory, relating to Hayek's *conception of individual agents*. Sraffa noted that, according to Hayek, consumers and entrepreneurs had to be simultaneously identical and distinct:

> For only if they are identical can the consumers' decisions to save take the form of a decision to alter the "proportions" in which the total gross receipts are divided between the purchase of consumers' goods and the purchase of producers' goods; and only if they are distinct has the contrast between "credits to producers" which are used to buy producers' goods, and "credits to consumers" which are used to buy consumers' goods, any definite meaning. (Sraffa 1932, p. 45, note 1)

This contradiction raised a number of concomitant analytical problems and derived from Hayek's view of the role played by individual agents and their rationality. Differently from Hayek, Sraffa clearly thought that entrepreneurs and consumers constitute *heterogeneous* agents belonging to *different* social groups. Thus, at the time, Hayek clearly (still) assumed that the economy could and should be analysed as a self-contained and closed system of individual rational agency, whereas Sraffa is already opposed to this approach.

Here again, as in his mentioned comments on Keynes', Sraffa emphasises the limits of the micro-foundations Hayek's theory of business cycles adopts. Thus, he highlights, for example, how Hayek's vertical capital theory prompts him to take on board a number of logical requirements that underpin the *theory of general interdependence* between agents Hayek still accepted at the time. Furthermore, and in line with a more Keynesian inspiration, Sraffa also makes it clear that saving was not a necessary condition of capital accumulation: "In Mr. Robertson's expression, saving may form the 'inducement' but not the 'source' of accumulation" (Sraffa, D 3/9 1) (see Section 2.1).

Moreover, Sraffa criticised Hayek's conception of money. According to Sraffa, Hayek's well-found objections against the concept of an aggregate price index led him to reject the quantity theory of money (Arena 2002) and, therefore, to limit the use of the concept of money to the perturbations it could generate between monetary and relative prices. However, Sraffa also pointed out that Hayek's rejection of the quantity theory of money led him to defend the view that the role of money in the economy is limited to that of a medium of exchange, and to neglect its role as a store of value. He, furthermore, insisted on the role of money *as a social unit of account*, as emphasised by Keynes in his *Treatise on Money*, that is, money as "the standard in terms of which debts, and other legal obligations, habits, opinions, conventions, in short all kinds of relations between men, are more or less rigidly fixed" (Sraffa 1932, p. 43). Sraffa thus clearly accepted and shared Keynes's views on the *institutional* nature of money, developed in Volume I of the *Treatise*. He also pinpointed the role of money as a social unit of account as the source of some of the inevitable rigidities (already noted) that are characteristic of modern market economies, and that he then extended to the analysis of the role of different income variables, such as rents and wages, in these economies.

Finally, Sraffa insisted on the close link of monetary valuation with habits, opinions, and conventions, which *transform inter-individual relations into social rules or institutions*. This idea of monetary valuation reflecting primarily social conventions could not ignore Keynes's *General Theory* and its "two different lines of research, which are not perfectly integrated (and may be not integrable): the first one is a classical analysis in terms of demand and supply, the second one is a much more heterodox analysis in terms of conventional and institutional factors" (Ranchetti 2001, p. 315). The first line of enquiry refers to the theory of liquidity preference of which Sraffa was highly critical (cf. Kurz 2000), whereas the second line of enquiry refers to a conventionalist approach to the formation of the rate of *interest based on market conventions and monetary policy*. It is clear that Sraffa preferred this view over the "first", once more stressing the importance of the role played by institutions, social conventions, and forms of organisations in the working of markets.

3.3. Sraffa on banking, finance, and industry

This last section of our contribution concerns two sets of lectures given by Piero Sraffa: the *Lectures on Continental Banking* (1929–1930) and the already mentioned *Lectures on Industry* (1941–1943). We will not enter here into a detailed analysis of either of these lectures (see De Cecco 2008 for the former and Arena 2010 for the latter). Rather, our focus here is on a brief evaluation of these *Lectures* in regard to the importance accorded by Sraffa to the need to *consider economic system within their historical context of given organisational and institutional settings.*

In the *Lectures on Industry*, Sraffa raised the issue of the "personification" of companies that characterises modern capitalism and changes the conventional economic conception of an economy driven and controlled by impersonal interactions between individual agents. He argued that conceptualising companies as persons or individuals was reflective of an increasingly predominant collective belief within firms as to the existence of a separate "interest of the company". As mentioned above, this interest is distinct from "both the interest of the individual shareholders and of the control" (see p. 13). In the long run, however, and in spite of this collective belief, the "interest of the company" tends to coincide with that of the directors. Sraffa notes that this need not always be the case and that no such tendency prevails in the short term (Sraffa, 1941–1943, pp. 30–3), but even so this development undermines the strictly individualistic thought that dominated classical capitalism:

> The ideology of laissez faire, of the beneficent results of leaving individuals to their own devices in economic matters without interference from the State, was based on a conception of a society composed of competing individuals, each of whom was independent of the others and free in his actions. There is nothing in that conception that could apply to vast organisations, employing hundreds of thousands of men, governed dictatorially and more powerful that the Government of a fair-sized country. These great companies had come into being as the result of the development of mechanical techniques, which have specialised the work of production and made it necessary to conduct it on such a large scale, that individuals could no longer operate it by themselves.

> Nothing could stop the progress of such organisations and therefore, in order to fit them into the accepted ideology, make them tolerable, [it became necessary] to reconcile the contradiction, and people had to pretend that companies were individuals. (Sraffa, 1941–1943, pp. 30–3)

Sraffa thus contrasts an ideal individualistic economic society inherited from a, broadly speaking, liberal tradition of thought, with real market economies that, while still decentralised are also increasingly subject to growing centralised control structures, due to a combination of *organisational and institutional changes*, such as the separation of ownership from control and the principle of limited liability. Sraffa is perfectly aware at the time of his writing that there still is no coherent or dominant theory capable of explaining the workings of this latter type of economy. If companies are not individuals, then standard microeconomics ceases to be useful, and this lack of an alternative explanation or economic analysis of an "organised" market economy persists to this day. Moreover, numerous additional problems arise simply because a purely individualistic ideology of laissez-faire continues to be upheld and to collide with legal rules and norms emerging from the real world of joint companies (Sraffa, 1941–1943, pp. 34–7). Again, Sraffa stresses in these *Lectures* how institutions and forms of organisation strongly affect the workings of a market economy, showing once more why we have to consider the economy as an open and not as a self-contained system.

In the *Lectures on Continental Banking*, another example of *the importance of self-organised institutions or forms of organisation* emerges in the form of the concept of a "banking system". Thus, Sraffa makes a distinction between the "evolutionary" British banking system and the "planned" German system (e.g. De Cecco 2008). Sraffa pays specific attention to the German system that he finds to be close to a mixed system. As in the *Lectures on Industry*, Sraffa analyses the concentration process characteristic of modern capitalism, focusing here on banks rather than firms. He also studies forms of competition within the German banking system prior to World War II and, specifically, varied forms of diversification that further highlight his interest in real-world forms of market organisation. Sraffa furthermore stresses the importance of "mixed systems" – referring to the essential role played (at the time) by central banks – stressing how and why from this point of view British and German systems differ (see De Cecco 2008). In these *Lectures*, Sraffa emphasised how the British banking system "arose in an evolutionary fashion, and developed in the 19th century as a clear example of the law of unintended consequences, as banks of issue were repressed by Peel's Act and deposit banking was invented in their stead, giving rise to the circulation of cheques" (De Cecco 2008, p. 351). By contrast, the German and the French modern banking systems "arose as the practical realisation of a social dream by some of the dreamer's disciples. Saint Simon was the dreamer, and the Pereire brothers the men who tried to make it come true. The dream was to create an organic link between banks and industry. This was in nuce the concept of 'active banking', a closed circuit between banks and industry by which banks became able to create deposits" (De Cecco 2008, p. 352).

This opposition between an evolutionary and a planned type of banking system provides another example of Sraffa's interest in institutional context, but also of the processes of innovation and change within these. Moreover, it is rather straightforward to point to the importance of the *organisational and institutional* specificities of banking systems for our

understanding of economic dynamics, including the role played by monetary policy-making. Unsurprisingly, by now, Sraffa focuses on the regulatory aspects of monetary economic activities and policies, as these arise in
the context of different types of banking systems and the role of central
banks as potential lenders of last resort.

4. Concluding remarks

Our core concern in this paper was to provide evidence and support for a
point of view, by which Sraffa's economic writings cannot simply be
reduced to a contribution to price theory alone. This said, our discussion
in this paper need not necessarily contradict some of the early interpreta-
tions of *PCMC*.

Thus, paradoxically enough, our above discussion potentially lends
some support to the notion of "core" developed by Garegnani (1981), *so
long as this is considered independently of debates concerning the notion of a long
period position of the economic system*. Hence, Garegnani emphasised the concept of "a 'core' in the surplus theories" (Garegnani 1981, p. 9), differenti-
ating its components, that is, the "net product", "necessary consumption",
and the "part of the social product which differs from wages" (Garegnani
1981, p. 10). He used a well-known diagram to depict the general relations
between these magnitudes, referred to as the "scheme of the 'core' of the
surplus theories" (Garegnani 1981, p. 14, Figure 1). Moreover, he stressed
the independence and the separate determination of the "core": within
the core, wages, the social product, and the techniques of production are
already known and determined. Now, for Garegnani, as for us, these components are determined by historical and institutional factors, or more
generally, by their "embeddedness" in a wider society. Quite the contrary,
the determination of the relative prices of commodities and of the shares
other than wages only depends on the inside part of the core and is, therefore, related to the *economic logic* stricto sensu, even if it is embedded in a
social and historical context.

We also know that in his 1960 book, Sraffa mentioned the possibility that
the rate of profit could be determined by the rate of interest. This is, by the
way, one of the origins of what Panico (2001) has called a conventionalist
theory of the determination of the rate of profit. This reference to the rate
of interest cannot be, however, interpreted as the indication that Sraffa was
in favour of a mechanical relation between both rates through a purely economic mechanism. He pointed out this view in a letter to Garegnani:

> I am convinced that the maintenance of the interest rate by the bank and (or) the
> stock exchange has had its part in the determination of income distribution among

social classes (…). I did not want to commit myself much, and in general I only wanted to signal something in order to avoid the belief that the system is presented as 'foundation' for a theory of relative supplies of capital and labour! It is what is denied that seems important to me: as to what is affirmatively claimed, I have no intention to put forward another mechanical theory which, in one form or another, states again that by at income distribution is determined by natural, or technical or even accidental, circumstances, which in any case are such that they make any action taken by either part, in order to modify it, futile. ... I do not see any difficulty in the determination of the rate of profit through a controlled or conventional interest rate, provided that the rate of profit will not be assumed to be determined by external unchangeable circumstances. (Sraffa Papers, D 3/12/111, letter of Piero Sraffa to Pierangelo Garegnani; translated by Panico 2001, p. 302)

These remarks are of interest, from the point of view developed in this paper, since they confirm that, in defending the idea that the rate of profit is determined by the rate of interest, Sraffa in fact refused an *alternative* theory based on "natural, or technical, or even accidental, circumstances". He clearly preferred an explanation located outside Garegnani's "core" namely within "society" as such. This confirms that even in the 1960 book, Sraffa did not consider the economic formation of prices as a closed system but as an open system embedded in "society". This is one of the reasons why he never accepted *a pure economic* determination of wages (based on marginal productivity, for instance) or of the rate of profit (based on an economic mechanical equalisation process between this rate and the rate of interest). We can thus understand why Sraffa wrote:

> The *"closed system"* is in communication with the world. When we have defined our *"economic field"*, there are still outside causes which operate in it; & its effects go beyond the boundary. This must happen in any concrete case.

> Consider, e.g. the so-called "natural causes" of rent. The surplus may be the effect of the outside causes; & the effects of the distribution of the surplus may lie outside. (Sraffa, D 3/12/7 161 5)

These previous remarks are obviously in line with the point of view we defended in this contribution. They are not sufficient, however, to furnish us with a ready-made and comprehensive answer to how best to analyse and model these "outside causes", and thus to a full explanation of business cycles and economic policy, derived from an exhaustive representation of the institutional and organisational settings of modern societies. What they do, though, is to help pave the way for economists interested in an "open economics" (e.g. Arena *et al.* 2009) that is not self-contained and that incorporates the contributions of other social sciences in a way that recognises that history matters and that excludes what Sraffa called "external unchangeable circumstances".

Acknowledgements

I would like to thank two anonymous referees and all participants at the International Conference: Crises, Business Cycles Theories, and Economic Policy, Les Treilles from 12 to 17 September 2011, and, in particular, P. Bridel, M. Dalpont, M. Gallegati, H. Hagemann, and A. Leijonhufvud for their comments, critiques, and suggestions. Remaining errors or mistakes are only mine. I am also grateful to the PROCOPE French-German programme for its support.

References

Arena, R., 1992. Libre-concurrence et concurrence entravée: trois exemples historiques. *Cahiers d'Economie Politique*, (20−21): 77−92.

Arena, R., 1998. The nation as an organized system of production: Smith, Marshall and the Classics. *In*: M. Bellet and C. L'Harmet, eds. *Industry, space and competition*. Cheltenham: Edward Elgar, 51−69.

Arena, R., 2002. Monetary policy and business cycles: Hayek as an opponent of the quantity theory tradition. *In*: J. Birner, P. Garrouste, and T. Aimar, eds. *F. A. Hayek as a political economist*. London: Routledge, 64−78.

Arena, R., 2008. On the relation between economics and sociology: Marshall and Schumpeter. *In:* I. Shionoya and T. Nishizawa, eds. *Marshall and Schumpeter on evolution − economic sociology of capitalist development*. Cheltenham: Edward Elgar, 65−92.

Arena, R., 2010. Corporate limited liability and Cambridge economics in the inter-war period: Robertson, Keynes and Sraffa. *Cambridge Journal of Economics*, 34 (5): 869−83.

Arena, R., 2014. Sraffa's and Wittgenstein's reciprocal influences: forms of life and snapshots. *In:* E.S. Levrero, A. Palumbo, and A. Stirati, eds. *Sraffa and the reconstruction of economic theory: Volume Two*. London: Palgrave, Macmillan. Forthcoming.

Arena, R., Dow, S., and Klaes, M., eds., 2009. *Open economics; economics in relation to other disciplines*. London: Routledge, 84−105.

Benetti, C., Bidard, C., and Klimovsky, E., 2007. Classical dynamics of disequilibrium. *Cambridge journal of economics*, 31 (1): 41−54.

Bidard, C., 2004. *Prices, reproduction and scarcity*. Cambridge: Cambridge University Press.

Blankenburg, S., Arena, R., and Wilkinson, F., 2012. Piero Sraffa and the 'true object of economics': the role of unpublished manuscripts. *Cambridge journal of economics*, 36 (6): 1267−90.

Chiodi, G., 1993. Un'interpretazione delle quantità date di merci negli schemi teorici di Sraffa. *Il Pensiero Economico Italiano*, (2): 199−206.

Chiodi G. and Ditta L., 2008. Introduction. *In*: G. Chiodi and L. Ditta, eds. *Sraffa or an alternative economics*. New York: Palgrave Macmillan, 1−22.

Cozzi, T. and Marchionatti, R., eds., 2001. *Piero Sraffa's political economy, a centenary estimate*. London: Routledge.

De Cecco, M., 1993. Piero Sraffa's 'Monetary inflation in Italy during and after the war': an introduction. *Cambridge journal of economics*, 17 (1): 1−5.

De Cecco, M., 2008. Sraffa's lectures on continental banking. *In*: H. Kurz, L. Pasinetti, and N. Salvadori, eds. *Piero Sraffa: the man and the scholar – exploring his unpublished papers*. London: Routledge, 185–94.

De Vivo, G., 2001. Some notes on the Sraffa's papers. *In*: T. Cozzi and R. Marchionatti, eds. *Piero Sraffa's political economy, a centenary estimate*. London: Routledge, 157–64.

Garegnani, P., 1981. Valore e distribuzione in Marx e negli economisti classici. *In*: R. Panizza and S. Vicarelli, eds. *Valori e prezzi nella teoria di Marx*. Torino: Einaudi, 32–53.

Garegnani, P. 1998. Sui manoscritti di Piero Sraffa. *Rivista Italiana Degli Economisti*, 3 (1): 151–6.

Garegnani, P., 2005. On a turning point in Sraffa's theoretical and interpretative position in the late 1920s. *European journal of history of economic thought*, 12 (3): 453–92.

Hahn, F., 1982. The Neo-Ricardians. *Cambridge journal of economics*, 6 (4): 353–74.

Keynes, J.M., 1936. *The general theory of employment, interest and money*. London: Macmillan.

Kurz, H., 2000. The Hayek–Keynes–Sraffa controversy reconsidered. *In*: H. Kurz, ed. *Critical essays on Piero Sraffa's legacy in economics*. Cambridge: Cambridge University Press, 257–303.

Kurz, H., Pasinetti, L., and Salvadori, N., eds., 2008. *Piero Sraffa: the man and the scholar, exploring his unpublished papers*. London: Routledge.

Kurz, H., and Salvadori, N., 2008. Representing the production and circulation of commodities in material terms: on Sraffa's objectivism. *In*: H. Kurz, L. Pasinetti, and N. Salvadori, eds. *Piero Sraffa: the man and scholar. Exploring his unpublished papers*. London: Routledge, 249–78.

Naldi, N., 2007. "6 November 1924: Piero Sraffa and Keynes' new theory and social policy. *Rivista di Storia Economica*, 23 (2): 121–57.

Newman, P., 1962. Review of production of commodities by means of commodities. *Schweizerische Zeitschrift für Volkswirtschaft und Statistik*, XCVIII: 58–75.

Panico, C., 2001. Monetary analysis in Sraffa's writings. *In*: T. Cozzi and R. Marchionatti, eds. *Piero Sraffa's political economy: a centenary estimate*. London: Routledge, 285–310.

Pasinetti, L., 2001. Continuity and change in Sraffa's thought: an archival excursus. *In*: T. Cozzi and R. Marchionatti, eds. *Piero Sraffa's political economy, a centenary estimate*. London: Routledge, 139–56.

Ranchetti, F., 2001. On the relationship between Sraffa and Keynes. *In*: T. Cozzi and R. Marchionatti, eds. *Piero Sraffa's political economy, a centenary estimate*. London: Routledge, 311–32.

Robinson, J., 1965. Piero Sraffa and the rate of exploitation. *New left review*, (31) May–June: 28–34.

Roncaglia, A., 1978. *Sraffa and the theory of prices*. New York: John Wiley and Sons.

Roncaglia, A., 2001. Production of commodities by means of commodities between criticism and reconstruction: the given quantities assumption. *In*: T. Cozzi and R. Marchionatti, eds. *Piero Sraffa's political economy, a centenary estimate*. London: Routledge, 207–23.

Salanti, A. and Signorino, R., 2001. From the 1925-6 articles to the 1960 book: some notes on Sraffa's not so implicit methodology. *In*: T. Cozzi and R. Marchionatti, eds. *Piero Sraffa's political economy, a centenary estimate*. London: Routledge, 165–86.

Sraffa, P., 1920. *L'inflazione monetaria in Italia durante e dopo la guerra*. Milano: Scuola Tipografica Salesiana. English translation by: Harcourt, W. and Sardoni, C., 1993. Monetary inflation in Italy during and after the war. *Cambridge journal of economics*, 17: 7–26.

Sraffa, P., 1922a. The bank crisis in Italy. *Economic journal*, 32: 178–97.

Sraffa, P., 1922b. Italian banking to-day. the Manchester Guardian Commercial. *Reconstruction in Europe*, Supplement 7 (December): 675–6.

Sraffa, P., 1925. Sulle relazioni tra costo e quantità prodotta". *Annali di economia, II.*, A. : *In*: L.L. Pasinetti, ed. *Italian economic papers.* Vol. II. 277-328. English translation by Eatwell, J. and Roncaglia, A. *In:* L.L. Pasinetti, ed., *Italian economic papers,* Vol. 3. Bologna: Il Mulino and Oxford: Oxford University Press, 323–63.

Sraffa, P., 1926. The laws of returns under competitive conditions. *Economic journal,* (36): 249–251.

Sraffa, P., 1927. Politica monetaria. Due lettere sull'articolodi Angelo Tasca 'La revalutazione della lira e la crisi dell'economia italiana'. *Lo Stato Operaio* I (9–10): 1089–95.

Sraffa P., 1929–1930. *Lectures on continental banking.* In Sraffa papers. Cambridge: Wren Library, Trinity College.

Sraffa, P., 1932. 'Dr. Hayek on money and capital' and 'A rejoinder'. *Economic journal,* (42) (March): 42–53 and 249–251.

Sraffa, P., 1941–1943. *Lectures on industry. In: Sraffa papers.* Cambridge: Wren Library, Trinity College.

Sraffa, 1960. *Production of commodities by means of commodities.* Cambridge: Cambridge University Press.

Sraffa, P., *Sraffa papers.* Cambridge: Wren Library, Trinity College.

Tasca A., 1927. La rivalutazione della lira e la crisi dell'economia. In: P. Sraffa, Politica monetaria. Due lettere sull' articolo di Angelo Tasca 'La rivalutazione della lira e la crisi dell'economia italiana'. *Lo Stato Operaio* I (9–10): 1089–95.

Walsh, V. and Gram, H., 1980. *Classical and neoclassical theories of general equilibrium: historical and mathematical structure.* New York: Oxford University Press.

Zappia, C., 1999. L'influenza di Sraffa sull'evoluzione della teoria di Hayek. *Rivista Italiana degli Economisti, SIE - Societa' Italiana degli Economisti (I)*, 4 (3): 303–34.

Abstract

This paper is based on an investigation of the Sraffa Archives and tries to characterise Piero Sraffa's approach to business cycles and economic policy. It includes two parts. The first part of the paper shows the importance of economic institutions and social conventions in Sraffa's contribution to economics and their relation with social conflicts. The second part of the paper shows how this importance permits to understand better business cycles and economic policy but also indirectly contributes to a re-interpretation of Sraffa's contribution to economics.

Mr Keynes, the Classics and the new Keynesians: A suggested formalisation

Rodolphe Dos Santos Ferreira

1. Introduction

The title is a tribute to Hicks (1937) and to Leijonhufvud (1967). "In order to elucidate the relation between Mr. Keynes and the 'Classics'," Hicks "invented a little apparatus" (Hicks 1937, p. 138), which became, under the name of the *IS–LM model*, an almost inescapable way of gaining access to Keynes. Yet, "this standard model appears [...] a singularly inadequate vehicle for the interpretation of Keynes's ideas" (Leijonhufvud 1967, p. 401). In its light, "the model which Keynes called his 'general theory' is but a special case of the classical theory, obtained by imposing certain restrictive assumptions on the latter" (*ibid.*). In the words of Hicks himself, "the General Theory of Employment is the Economics of Depression" (Hicks 1937, p. 138), rather than a generalisation of classical economics as claimed by Keynes.

Leijonhufvud did unfortunately not propose an alternative model which would be better suited for the interpretation of Keynes's ideas. The aim of this paper is to try to fill this gap. Modelling the *General Theory* is not just a translation exercise. It is a way of positioning Keynes *vis-à-vis* the Classics, old and new. How legitimate is the epithet "general" identifying Keynes's theory? What in this theory is pure rephrasing of classical concepts, axioms and propositions, and what are the brand-new elements? And are such elements, if any, just newly exploited specifications of classical relations, or rather extensions and variations of classical concepts and propositions? Moreover, modelling the *General Theory* is a way of evaluating the structuring of the book. Should we take for granted Leijonhufvud's assessment that, apart from Keynes's model being "not logically watertight," "the *General Theory* was in several respects, as has frequently been said, 'a badly written book'" (Leijonhufvud 1968, p. 10)?

Keynes himself eventually gave up building a formal model of his "general theory," not even in the rudimentary form of the "fundamental equations" of the *Treatise on Money* (Keynes 1930, book III) or, in the same vein, of the four equations used in his lecture of 4 December 1933 (see Rymes 1989, p. 125) or else of the similar equations introduced in his mid-1934 drafts of the *General Theory* (Keynes 1973, Vol. XIII, pp. 439–442, 480–484). We still find some scattered equations along different chapters of the published version, but not enough to support a complete model, however simple. Yet, in many crucial passages, Keynes is sufficiently precise to unambiguously suggest a formal rendering of his verbal discourse. So, we should not be surprised to find, immediately after the publication of the *General Theory*, several attempts performed in that direction, of which Hicks (1937) is the best known. I am referring to Champernowne (1936), Reddaway (1936), Harrod (1937), Meade (1937), Lange (1938) and, in the following decade, Modigliani (1944), Klein (1947a, 1947b) and Patinkin (1948, 1949).[1]

These models, which have contributed to shape Keynesian thinking during the second third of the last century as a component of a "neoclassical synthesis," exhibit some common features which make them unfit for a thorough comprehension of Keynes. First, they are highly aggregated, being consequently unable to take explicitly into account some significant instances of heterogeneity and, above all, of interactivity among agents and industries. Second, they involve perfectly competitive output markets, an assumption which obscures the reading of book I of the *General Theory*. Third, most of them simply ignore the labour market, which is incompatible with the analysis of unemployment, or else treat this market as perfectly competitive, which blurs the distinction between "voluntary" and "involuntary" unemployment. Fourth, they all refer to some common conceptual framework, of which the classical and the Keynesian models are just two different avatars, distinguished only by the specifications of the main functional relationships.

---

1 Dimand (2007) emphasises the continuity between Keynes's Cambridge lectures of the Michaelmas term of 1933, the two articles of Champernowne and Reddaway, who both attended those lectures, and possibly the article of Hicks himself, who was a joint editor of the *Review of Economic Studies* where Champernowne's paper was published. The four-equation system of the lecture of 4 December 1933 exactly corresponds to what Hicks calls Keynes's *special theory*, "*not the General Theory*" (Hicks 1937, p. 152), except that Keynes makes explicit the parameterisation of the consumption, investment and money demand functions by the "state of the news" (later "state of long-term expectations").

Leijonhufvud (1968) initiated a reappraisal of this theoretical edifice, claiming that Keynes "departed from the postulates of Classical doctrine on only one point," his model being "characterised by the absence of a 'Walrasian auctioneer' assumed to furnish, without charge and without delay, all the information needed to obtain the perfect coordination of the activities (both spot and future) of all traders" (Leijonhufvud 1968, pp. 47–48; see also Leijonhufvud 1988). With Leijonhufvud, the coordination of agents' actions and plans becomes the central theme of the Keynes vs. the Classics debate. In the classical perspective, perfect (costless, instantaneous and complete) coordination is enough to ensure the implementation of an efficient full employment equilibrium, to which the economy would promptly converge should one realistically allow for some friction. By contrast, the main message of the *General Theory* concerns the possibility for the economy of being stuck in a "bad" underemployment equilibrium, resulting from systemic *coordination failures*. This expression may mean that coordination is incomplete, not fully extending in particular to agents' plans for the future so as to ensure their mutual consistency and realisability (cf. Leijonhufvud 1981, pp. 139–140), or else that coordination is inefficient, selecting a Pareto inferior equilibrium in a context of equilibrium multiplicity (cf. Cooper and John 1988). We shall find instances of both kinds of coordination failures in my rendering of the *General Theory*.

Coordination failures constitute one of the major themes of the new Keynesian literature, born in the 1980s (cf. Mankiw and Romer 1991). Other characteristic themes of this literature are output, labour and financial market imperfections, in particular those associated with imperfect competition or resulting from costly and staggered price and wage adjustments, leading to nominal rigidities. However, if imperfect wage flexibility – partly assigned by Keynes, as we shall see, to some form of coordination failure in the labour market – is indeed an important feature of his analysis, price stickiness is in fact completely absent from the *General Theory*. Now, even if my understanding of Keynes's work is certainly in agreement with a significant part, but by no means all, of the new Keynesian corpus, the systematic confrontation of the two approaches is out of my purpose, which remains focused on the opposition between Keynes and the classics. Let me just add at this point that, for reasons that will be developed in the next section, the kind of modelling I am suggesting is of the Hicksian temporary equilibrium variety, with possible unfulfilment of the expectations of future prices and quantities. By contrast, we are quite generally in presence of Hicksian equilibria over time in new Keynesian modelling, which has eventually incorporated the rational expectations framework. As a matter of fact, even among the early contributions to the new Keynesian theme of coordination failures, we already find a simple Keynes-type micro-founded model exhibiting a continuum of rational expectations underemployment equilibria (Bryant 1983).

From the early new Keynesian literature, I essentially want to retain the model of monopolistic competition in output markets that had been introduced in another context by Spence (1976) and Dixit and Stiglitz (1977), and that was adapted to international trade by Krugman (1979) and extended to macroeconomics by Rotemberg (1982), Weitzman (1985), Svensson (1986) and Blanchard and Kiyotaki (1987). Although not designed to formalise Keynes's analysis, contrary to its predecessors of the 1930s and 1940s, this model is a very convenient way of doing so. Indeed, it first offers a disaggregated approach to output markets, allowing to take into account in a simple way the important distinction between chosen variations in individual prices and quantities and resulting variations in price and quantity indices for the whole economy. Second, these indices are here well-defined, offering an advantageous alternative to Keynes's practice of deflating nominal aggregates by the wage unit, which hinders comparisons with modern macroeconomic analysis. Third, the model makes demand for output depend not only upon the prices, as in the Walrasian model, but also upon the level of expenditure, which clarifies the reading of book I (chapter 3 in particular, but also chapter 5) of the *General Theory*.[2] Last but not least, the model exactly fits the assumption of a *given degree of competition* which is explicitly formulated in the beginning of chapter 18.[3]

In spite of a persistent and largely widespread belief about Keynes's approach to output markets in the *General Theory*, perfect competition is there nothing but a possible limit case, when the degree of competition reaches its maximum. It is true that output market power does not play in Keynes's analysis the same prominent role as in new Keynesian macroeconomics.[4] The argument developed in the *General Theory* would not be significantly different under the assumption of perfectly competitive

---

2 Numbered chapters and books will always refer in the following to chapters and books of the *General Theory*, unless otherwise specified.

3 The assumption of a *given degree of competition* appears only in the published version of the *General Theory* and was still absent from its first proof, circulated in 1935 (cf. Keynes 1973, vol. XIV, p. 502 *in fine*). Also, even if imperfect competition is already mentioned in that proof as a possible qualification to the first fundamental postulate of classical economics, the postulate has been rephrased accordingly in the final text so as to cover imperfect competition: "the wage of an employed person is equal *in value to the product* which would be lost if employment were to be reduced by one unit" becomes "... equal *to the value* which would be lost..." (cf. Keynes 1973, XIV, p. 352; my emphasis).

4 See Silvestre (1993) and Dixon and Rankin (1994) for surveys of the place occupied by imperfect competition in the early new Keynesian macroeconomics.

markets. It is only after the so-called "Dunlop–Tarshis observation" of the relative movements of real and money wages that Keynes (1939) considered the necessity of pushing imperfect competition in output markets to the fore, in particular by going beyond the simplifying assumption of a *given* degree of competition, independent of the output level[5]:

> There remains the question whether the mistake lies in the approximate identification of marginal cost with price, or rather in the assumption that for output as a whole they bear a more or less proportionate relationship to one another irrespective of the intensity of output. For it may be the case that the practical workings of the laws of imperfect competition in the modern quasi-competitive system are such that, when output increases and money wages rise, prices rise less than in proportion to the increase in marginal money cost. (Keynes 1939, p. 46)

Proceeding from output to labour markets, we find another important component of many new Keynesian models which I shall also adopt because it seems appropriate to render Keynes's analysis in chapters 2 and 19, namely the intervention of wage setting or wage bargaining unions. Keynes allusively considers the wage setting process in chapter 2, and then treats money wages as fixed until chapter 19, where the analysis of the effects of money wage adjustments becomes partly dynamic. I will, however, refrain from going beyond comparative statics in the present analysis, referring to its dynamic counterpart in Dos Santos Ferreira and Michel (2013). The discussion of the Phillips curve, which appears in fact not to be an ingredient of Keynes's analysis, will accordingly be left to that companion paper.

The article is organised as follows. Section 2 is devoted to some methodological questions concerning the role of expectations and aggregation, which can be seen as an echo to book II of the *General Theory*. Section 3 presents the model of classical economics as viewed by Keynes. It roughly corresponds to book I. Section 4 closes the model in what is suggested to be Keynes's way, developed in books III and IV, plus chapter 19. It emphasises coordination failures working through both the financial and the labour markets. Section 5 concludes.

2. Modelling the *General Theory*

The main purpose of the suggested new Keynesian formalisation of the *General Theory* is not to obtain a literal translation of Keynes's verbal argument, but just to design a convenient instrument to interpret and assess

---

5 See d'Aspremont *et al.* (2011) on the role played by imperfect competition in the business cycle theory developed in the late Thirties, in particular in relation to the "Dunlop–Tarshis observation" and to Keynes's (1939) response.

Keynes's theoretical contribution. However, this instrument cannot be credible if it does not more or less fit Keynes's methodology. So, I shall start by discussing how my formalisation is related to the methodological choices of book II concerning the treatment of expectations and the aggregation issues.

2.1 Expectations

Keynes distinguishes two types of expectations to which he successively devotes chapters 5 and 12 of the *General Theory*. "The first type is concerned with the price which a manufacturer can expect to get for his 'finished' output at the time when he commits himself to starting the process which will produce it; output being 'finished' (from the point of view of the manufacturer) when it is ready to be used or to be sold to a second party. The second type is concerned with what the entrepreneur can hope to earn in the shape of future returns if he purchases (or, perhaps, manufactures) 'finished' output as an addition to his capital equipment. We may call the former *short-term expectation* and the latter *long-term expectation*" (Keynes 1936, pp. 46–47).

Even if he may explicitly consider an arbitrary number of future dates (for instance in chapter 11, when defining the marginal efficiency of capital), Keynes basically refers to two periods, which we may call the *present* and the *future*. The present is a short enough period to justify taking in particular as given "the existing skill and quantity of available labour, the existing quality and quantity of available equipment, the existing technique, the degree of competition, the tastes and habits of the consumer, the disutility of different intensities of labour and of the activities of supervision and organisation" (Keynes 1936, p. 245). As to the future, it might in principle involve an arbitrarily long time horizon. I shall, however, opt for consistency and treat the two periods as of equal length. Moreover, although I will not engage in dynamics, I shall assume at the price of realism an overlapping generations structure with two classes of consumers – *workers* and *entrepreneurs* – who live for two periods, being active when young and inactive when old. We thus obtain quite naturally the three categories of consumers appearing in the *General Theory*, since both workers and entrepreneurs become *rentiers* when retired.

Keynes's entrepreneurs form, as producers, short-term expectations about the present and, as investors, long-term expectations about the future. The two types of expectations are treated quite differently:

> Express reference to current long-term expectations can seldom be avoided. But it will often be safe to omit express reference to short-term expectation, in view of the

fact that in practice the process of revision of short-term expectation is a gradual and continuous one, carried on largely in the light of realised results; so that expected and realised results run into and overlap one another in their influence. For, although output and employment are determined by the producer's short-term expectations and not by past results, the most recent results usually play a predominant part in determining what these expectations are. (Keynes 1936, pp. 50–51)

That short-term expectations are revised in light of realised results seems to point to adaptive expectations.[6] The present period is, however, viewed as long enough for producers to completely adjust their expectations to the output market equilibrium prices:

I began [...] by regarding [the] difference [between expected and actual income, due to a mistake in the short-period expectation,] as important. But eventually I felt it to be of secondary importance, emphasis on it obscuring the real argument. For the theory of effective demand is substantially the same if we assume that short-period expectations are always fulfilled. [...] I now feel that if I were writing the book again I should begin by setting forth my theory on the assumption that short-period expectations were always fulfilled; and then have a subsequent chapter showing what difference it makes when short-period expectations are disappointed. (Keynes 1937 Lecture Notes in Keynes 1973, XIV, p. 181)

By contrast, "it is of the nature of long-term expectations that they cannot be checked at short intervals in the light of realised results. Moreover, [...] they are liable to sudden revision. Thus the factor of current long-term expectations cannot be even approximately eliminated or replaced by realised results" (Keynes 1936, p. 51). In Marshallian terms, the situations considered by Keynes may be approached as *short-period equilibria*, with fulfilled short-term expectations, but generally not as *long-period equilibria*. In Hicksian terms, they are *temporary equilibria*, not *equilibria over time*. Or, using modern terminology, the idea of a rational expectations equilibrium is unreservedly adopted by Keynes as concerns the short term, not as concerns the long term, a major difference between Keynes and the new Keynesians, who eventually integrated the full rational expectations hypothesis as one of the unquestionable traits of their models.

2.2 Aggregation

Aggregation enters the stage as a road to surpass partial equilibrium analysis of a particular industry, which appears inappropriate to found a general

---

6 Errors of short-term expectations and their correction process play a significant role in the short-period dynamics sketched in the *Treatise on Money* (see Dos Santos Ferreira and Michel, 2013, for a suggested formalisation).

theory of employment. Keynes discards as a false division the separation of the theories of value and money, and writes: "The right dichotomy is, I suggest, between the Theory of the Individual Industry or Firm and of the rewards and the distribution between different uses of a *given* quantity of resources on the one hand, and the Theory of Output and Employment *as a whole* on the other hand" (Keynes 1936, p. 293; Keynes's emphasis). The very opposition between the theory of the individual industry or firm, on one hand, and the theory of output and employment as a whole, on the other, suggests merging together the first two of the three layers of the firm-industry-economy, at least for the sake of simplicity. This is precisely what Keynes often does (for instance in chapter 20), and what I will do, in accordance with most new Keynesian models.[7]

Except if one is ready to embark on a fully detailed general equilibrium model, the theory of output as a whole requires some procedure of *aggregation over goods*, allowing to measure "quantities" of output for the whole economy. Chapter 4 of the *General Theory* is devoted to this question. Keynes opts for aggregation in money value, purely nominal variations being erased through deflation of money aggregates by the money wage. The separation between nominal and real output variations is, however, blurred under this procedure by changes in the real wage. By contrast, this separation is neat in the Keynesian one-commodity models of the neoclassical synthesis, but at the price of an excessive level of aggregation. By allowing for the use of well-defined price and quantity indices, the new Keynesian model offers, as we are going to see, an acceptable compromise.

Additional difficulties stem from aggregation over producers if one wants to avoid double counting. Keynes tackles this question in chapter 6, where he introduces a concept of user cost, covering both intermediate consumption and depreciation, to be deducted from each producer's proceeds before aggregation, which is thus performed in value added and on a net basis. The new Keynesian model gets rid of this requirement by directly assuming vertically integrated industries (with capital formation but no intermediate consumption)[8] and by introducing a constant rate of

---

7 In some sense, the very concept of monopolistic competition implies the assimilation of firm and industry. Of course, treating all industries more or less symmetrically, again in accordance with most new Keynesian models, remains, however, a heroic assumption.

8 In new Keynesian models, the monopolistic sector is sometimes assumed to supply elementary intermediate goods to a competitive final sector, not directly to the consumers. Hence, the elementary goods are then the arguments of a sub-production function instead of being the arguments of a subutility function. The two approaches are essentially equivalent. In both cases, there is no intermediate consumption in the monopolistic industries.

capital depreciation, which I will take as 100% for simplicity (an innocuous assumption, given the static nature of the short-period model I am suggesting). Assuming identical technologies for all the producers and identical homothetic preferences over consumption goods for all consumers completes the conditions for easy *aggregation over agents*.

As a matter of fact, technologies and preferences are assumed to be congruous in the sense that the model has a single composite consumption and investment good, common to all consumers and investors. This may appear as a retreat from the two-sectoral approach of some of the already mentioned early modelling essays (Hicks 1937; Meade 1937), where consumption and investment goods are different goods, but does not contradict Keynes's ultimate position. In a 1934 draft of the *General Theory*, we find a chapter titled "Consumption goods and investment goods" where this division is based on the importance of the interest charges in their respective production costs – clearly "a matter of degree" as Keynes readily admits (Keynes 1973, XIII, pp. 428–430). This projected chapter becomes a section of chapter 5 in the three first proofs of the book, where the division is now between consumption and capital goods, and results from the distinction between short- and long-term expectations as determinants of their respective production (Keynes 1973, XIV, pp. 396–397). This section and the very division into two kinds of goods completely disappears in the final text. More significantly still for the present discussion, the first proof formally presents expenditures in consumption goods D_1 and capital goods D_2 as depending upon the employment levels in two different classes of industries with specific production functions: $D_1 = f_1(N_1)$ and $D_2 = f_2(N_2)$ – a division which disappears from the second proof on (see Keynes 1973, XIV, p. 373–374). These observations suggest that, during the writing of the *General Theory*, Keynes ceased at some stage to see the two-sectoral modelling of production as relevant for his purpose.

To conclude this section, let us look formally at the new Keynesian model of monopolistic competition. A "quantity" Y of the composite good enters as an argument of the utility and production functions in the form of an aggregate of quantities y_j of each elementary good $j \in [0, 1]$: $Y = \left(\int_0^1 \eta_j^{1-\delta} y_j^\delta \, dj \right)^{1/\delta}$, with a parameter $\delta \in (0, 1)$ and positive weights $\eta_j^{1-\delta}$ such that $\int_0^1 \eta_j \, dj = 1.$[9] It is straightforward to verify that choosing the

---

9 For simplicity of notation at later stages, while not for realism, I am taking the continuous version of the model, where the set of elementary goods is a continuum represented by the unit interval. For clarity of later discussion, it is also convenient to provisionally allow for asymmetry of the elementary goods (otherwise, $\eta_j = 1$ for any j).

quantities y_j so as to maximise the aggregate Y under the budget constraint $\int_0^1 p_j y_j \, dj \leq X$ (with p_j denoting the price of good j and X the expenditure on the composite good) leads to the demand function for the jth good $D_j(p_j) = (p_j/P)^{-1/(1-\delta)} \eta_j X/P$. In this expression, δ can be viewed as the *degree of competition*,[10] taken as given by Keynes (1936, p. 245), and P as the price of the composite good, a weighted power mean of the prices p_j of the elementary goods: $P = \left(\int_0^1 \eta_j p_j^{-\delta/(1-\delta)} \, dj \right)^{-(1-\delta)/\delta}$. We thus obtain well-defined price and quantity indices P and Y, exactly decomposing the aggregate money value: $X = \int_0^1 p_j y_j \, dj = PY$.

3. Classical economics as viewed by Keynes

In the third sentence of chapter 1 of the *General Theory*, Keynes announces that he "shall argue that the postulates of the classical theory are applicable to a special case only and not to the general case, the situation which it assumes being a limiting point of the possible positions of equilibrium" (Keynes 1936, p. 3). The statement is precise, and although it is generally understood that Keynes purports to generalise the classical theory to situations of less than full employment, not enough attention has often been paid to the formal meaning of this sentence. One possible reason for this neglect is that many readers of the *General Theory* tend either to bypass chapter 2, devoted to the "Postulates of the Classical Economics" and focused on the labour market, or at least to be satisfied with a cursory reading of it.[11] I shall on the contrary devote to this chapter a significant part of this section. I will conclude with Keynes's critique of Say's law in chapter 3, involving a discussion of the role of the rate of interest which is developed in chapter 14. These developments extend to the output and financial markets his appraisal of classical economics, started in relation to the labour market.

---

10 From the expression of $D_j(p_j)$ we see that the Marshallian elasticity of the demand for the jth good is $1/(1-\delta)$, which is also the (constant) elasticity of substitution between elementary goods. Under monopolistic competition among producers of elementary goods, its reciprocal $1 - \delta$ is Lerner's index of the degree of monopoly, and δ (the corresponding complement to 1) the degree of competition.

11 Hoover (1995) is a valuable exception in providing a careful reading of chapter 2. The author suggests an efficiency wage model rationalising Keynes's relative wage hypothesis, whereas I pursue the same objective on the basis of a wage bargaining model. We thus refer to two different brands of new Keynesian modelling of the labour market.

3.1 The first fundamental postulate: demand for labour and price setting

The first of the two "fundamental postulates of the classical theory of employment" states, in Keynes's words, that "*the wage is equal to the marginal product of labour*" (Keynes 1936, p. 5). We are all familiar with such formulation of the first-order condition for profit maximisation. It is, however, useful to spend some time on this postulate, in particular because Keynes reminds us that "the equality may be disturbed, in accordance with certain principles, if competition and markets are imperfect" (*ibid.*).

Acting as a producer, each entrepreneur $j \in [0,1]$ maximises his profit $p_j y_j - w_j n_j$, where p_j, y_j and n_j are their decision variables, namely price, output and employment, respectively, and where w_j is the money wage, which is taken as given at this stage. Profit maximisation is performed under two constraints, requiring the output to be both feasible and vendible: $y_j \leq F_j(n_j) \equiv A\bar{k}_j^{1-\alpha} n_j^{\alpha}$ (with $A > 0$, $0 < \alpha < 1$ and capital $\bar{k}_j > 0$, given in the short period) and, according to the expression of the demand function established in Section 2.2, $y_j \leq D_j(p_j) = (p_j/P)^{-1/(1-\delta)} \eta_j X/P$. Each producer j is assumed to know the demand function D_j, and to make consistent *short-term expectations* of the mean price $P = \left(\int_0^1 \eta_j p_j^{-\delta/(1-\delta)} dj \right)^{-(1-\delta)/\delta}$, of the aggregate expenditure X and of the exogenous component η_j of his market share.

The first-order condition for profit maximisation can be expressed as the equality of marginal cost and marginal revenue:

$$\frac{w_j}{F_j'(n_j)} = \delta p_j, \text{ with } p_j = D_j^{-1} \circ F_j(n_j). \tag{1}$$

This condition states that the price p_j is optimally set by applying to marginal cost a markup factor equal to the reciprocal $1/\delta$ of the degree of competition. It equivalently states that "the wage of an employed person is equal to the value which would be lost if employment were to be reduced by one unit" (Keynes 1936, p. 5): $w_j = \delta p_j F_j'(n_j)$. Referring to the real wage $\omega_j \equiv w_j/P$ and to the real output $Y \equiv X/P$, and using the expression for the demand function D_j for good j, we can rewrite this first-order condition as the first fundamental postulate in the following terms:

$$\omega_j = \delta F_j'(n_j)(\frac{\eta_j Y}{F_j(n_j)})^{1-\delta} \equiv \Omega^{\mathrm{I}}\left(\underset{-}{n_j}, \underset{+}{\eta_j Y} \right), \tag{2}$$

with Ω^{I} decreasing in employment n_j and increasing in the level $\eta_j Y$ of demand for the jth good. The function $\Omega^{\mathrm{I}}(\cdot, \eta_j Y)$ is the inverse labour demand function.

Notice that, instead of proceeding from the first-order condition (1) to the inverse labour demand function, we may proceed from the same condition as a price-setting equation to the *aggregate supply function* of chapter 3, namely "the aggregate supply price of the output from employing N men" (Keynes 1936, p. 25):

$$\frac{p_j}{P} F_j(n_j) = \frac{1}{\delta\alpha} \omega_j n_j, \tag{3}$$

here expressed in real terms, that is, deflated by the price index P. [12] On the (expected) demand side, we correspondingly obtain what Keynes calls the *aggregate demand function*, that is, "the proceeds which entrepreneurs expect to receive from the employment of N men" (Keynes 1936, p. 25):

$$\frac{D_j^{-1} \circ F_j(n_j)}{P} F_j(n_j) = (\eta_j Y)^{1-\delta} F_j(n_j)^{\delta}. \tag{4}$$

In Keynes's terminology, the value of this function at the point of intersection with the aggregate supply function is the *effective demand* (Keynes 1936, p.25). Notice that a "representative firm" j^* setting the mean price $p_{j^*} = P$ would choose employment $\widehat{n}_{j^*}$ so as to serve a demand $\eta_{j^*} Y$ by supplying the corresponding output $F_{j^*}(\widehat{n}_{j^*}) = \eta_{j^*} Y$. Thus, the value $\eta_{j^*} Y$ unambiguously appears as the effective demand addressed to the representative firm j^*. By extension, I shall refer in the following to $\eta_j Y$ as the effective demand for (any) good j and to Y as the effective demand, simply.

Now, observe that the aggregate demand function as defined by (4) coincides with the production function when the competition is perfect (when $\delta = 1$), so that what Keynes calls "effective demand" depends then on the demand proper only through the mean price which is implicit in $\omega_j = w_j/P$ and which determines the slope of the aggregate supply function. Otherwise, when the competition is imperfect (when $\delta < 1$), the aggregate demand function is equal to the geometric mean of the production function and of the effective demand for the producer's good. Keynes's emphasis on the role played in producers' employment decisions

---

12 The aggregate supply function is linear with respect to employment n_j, as shown in Keynes (1936, pp. 55–56, n. 2). This footnote, which is somewhat problematic as regards the slope which Keynes attributes to the aggregate supply line, has been discussed at length, together with its context, in Dos Santos Ferreira and Michel (1991).

by the "expectations as to the sale-proceeds" of the corresponding output (Keynes 1936, p. 47) comes only then into its own.

In order to prepare the discussion of the second fundamental postulate in the next subsection, and in particular to explain the meaning of "throwing over the second postulate" while "maintaining the first" (cf. Keynes 1936, pp. 16–17), as well as the semantics involved in the opposition "voluntary" vs. "involuntary" unemployment, two further remarks may be useful at this stage. First, notice that the first fundamental postulate, as formulated by Keynes (*"the wage is equal to the marginal product of labour"*), is in fact more than the statement of the condition for profit maximisation. It requires this condition to be actually satisfied in equilibrium (the wage *is* equal to the marginal product of labour (MPL), not the wage *should be* equal to the MPL for profit to be maximised). In other words, profit maximisation is an equilibrium condition: in equilibrium the producer is on his labour demand curve, as defined by the first-order condition.

Second, consider firm j's aggregate supply price $p_j F(n_j)$, equal by Equation (3) to its competitive value $w_j n_j / \alpha$ augmented by the application of the markup factor $1/\delta$. Imperfect competition pivots the aggregate supply curve upwards or, equivalently, to the left: in some sense, in order to ensure the conditions for a higher price, the firm is voluntarily rationing its own sales and correspondingly curtailing in a proportion δ the employment it creates.

3.2 The second fundamental postulate: labour supply and wage setting

The second fundamental postulate states that *"the utility of the wage when a given volume of labour is employed is equal to the marginal disutility of that amount of employment"* (Keynes 1936, p. 5). In order to keep computations simple, let me assume that a worker chooses present and future consumption C and $\widehat{C}$, respectively, of the composite good, and further decides on his labour market participation $l \in \{0,1\}$, in order to maximise the utility function $\Gamma C^\gamma \widehat{C}^{1-\gamma} - vl$ (with $0 < \gamma < 1$, $\Gamma = \gamma^{-\gamma}(1-\gamma)^{-(1-\gamma)}$ and $v > 0$). Utility maximisation is performed under the present and future budget constraints: $PC + PS \leq wl$ and $\widehat{P}\widehat{C} \leq (1+i)PS$, where S is real saving, w the money wage, $\widehat{P}$ the expected future price of the composite good and i the nominal rate of interest. As is well known, optimal consumption is given, in the case of the Cobb–Douglas function $C^\gamma \widehat{C}^{1-\gamma}$, by $C = \gamma wl/P$ and $\widehat{C} = (1-\gamma)wl(1+i)/\widehat{P}$, so that γ is what Keynes calls the *marginal propensity to consume* (Keynes 1936, chapter 10), here taken as constant because of the Cobb–Douglas specification. For ease of notation, I shall refer to the real wage $\omega \equiv w/P$ and to the expected real rate of interest $\hat{r}$, such that $1 + \hat{r} \equiv (1+i)P/\hat{P}$. By substituting the expressions for optimal present and future consumption in the utility function, we obtain, for $l = 1$, $u(\omega) \equiv (1+\hat{r})^{1-\gamma}\omega$ as the (indirect) utility of the real wage. Hence, the worker participates in the labour market only if $u(\omega) \geq v$, that is, if the real wage is at least equal to its reservation value:

$$\omega \geq \frac{v}{(1+\hat{r})^{1-\gamma}} \equiv \underline{\omega}(\hat{r}). \tag{5}$$

Now, assume that there is a continuum $[0,1]$ of workers potentially employable by each firm, identical except for their labour disutility, which is continuously distributed over $[0,\infty)$ with the same distribution function V for all firms. Thus, there is a set of workers of size $V(v)$ whose labour disutility is at most equal to $v = u(\omega)$: the utility $u(\omega)$ of the real wage is equal to the marginal disutility v of the amount $V(v)$ of employment, as in Keynes's formulation of the second fundamental postulate. Each firm j faces consequently the *labour supply function*

$$\Lambda(\omega) \equiv V \circ u(\omega) = V((1+\hat{r})^{1-\gamma}\omega). \tag{6}$$

According to Keynes, "the traditional theory maintains [...] *that the wage bargains between the entrepreneurs and the workers determine the real wage*, so that, assuming free competition amongst employers and no restrictive combination amongst workers, the latter can, if they wish, bring their real wages into conformity with the marginal disutility of the amount of employment offered by the employers at that wage" (Keynes 1936, p. 11). In other words, the real wage is supposed to adjust to its market balancing value, such that labour demand n_j equals labour supply $\Lambda(\omega_j)$ or, referring to the inverse demand for labour given by (2), $\omega_j = \Omega^l(V \circ u(\omega_j), \eta_j Y)$.

The second postulate is, however, "subject to the qualification that the equality for each individual unit of labour may be disturbed by combination between employable units analogous to the imperfections of competition which qualify the first postulate" (Keynes 1936, pp. 5–6). We must accordingly introduce collective bargaining between a *union* and the firm, "labour [... being] in a position to decide the real wage for which it works, though not the quantity of employment forthcoming at this wage" (Keynes 1936, p. 11). In other words, bargaining concerns the sole wage, while the firm keeps its "right to manage" regarding employment. It has become usual to refer to the so-called generalised Nash solution to the bargaining problem, maximising a weighted geometric mean of the firm's and the union's objectives (or rather of the excesses of these objectives over the respective fallbacks), with the weights reflecting the relative bargaining powers of the two parties. For a large enough bargaining power of the firm, the Nash solution coincides with the competitive equilibrium value of the real wage. In order to emphasise "the qualification that the equality for each individual unit of labour may be disturbed by combination between employable units," and also for the sake of simplicity, I shall assume the opposite limit case of a monopoly union.[13]

Assume for instance a utilitarian union with utility $U(\omega_j)$ equal to the sum of workers' surpluses $u(\omega_j) - v$, to be maximised under the constraint $n_j \leq N_j(\omega_j, \eta_j Y)$, where $N_j(\cdot, \eta_j Y)$ is the labour demand function, that is, the inverse of $\Omega^1(\cdot, \eta_j Y)$ as defined by (2). If they are efficiently rationed, the workers are employed in increasing order of their labour disutilities: the lower the disutility, the higher the eagerness for a job and the higher the probability of finding one. By weighting the surplus of the worker with disutility v by the corresponding density $V'(v)$, and integrating over the space of labour disutilities from 0 to the marginal disutility $\bar{v}(\omega_j) \equiv V^{-1} \circ N_j(\omega_j, \eta_j Y)$ of the employment available at ω_j, we obtain

$$U(\omega_j) = \int_0^{\bar{v}(\omega_j)} (u(\omega_j) - v) V'(v) dv \qquad (7)$$
$$= u(\omega_j) N_j(\omega_j, \eta_j Y) - \int_0^{\bar{v}(\omega_j)} v V'(v) dv.$$

By a straightforward computation, we find that the first-order condition for the maximisation of $U(\omega_j)$ is

$$u(\omega_j) = \frac{\bar{v}(\omega_j)}{\delta \alpha} = \frac{V^{-1} \circ N_j(\omega_j, \eta_j Y)}{\delta \alpha}. \qquad (8)$$

The utility $u(\omega_j)$ of the wage when the volume of labour $N_j(\omega_j, \eta_j Y)$ is employed is equal not to the marginal disutility $\bar{v}(\omega_j)$ of that amount of employment, but to that disutility multiplied by the markup factor $1/\delta \alpha$ (a higher degree of monopoly of the firm in the output market induces a higher degree of monopoly of the union in the labour market). This first-order condition determines the real wage ω_j, given the expected effective demand $\eta_j Y$ for good j. However, we may equivalently refer to the employment–real wage space (n_j, ω_j) and take the real wage as determined by the intersection of the curves representing the two fundamental postulates,

---

13 The monopoly union model was introduced in 1944 by Dunlop, a student of Keynes.

$\omega_j = \Omega^{\mathrm{I}}(n_j, \eta_j Y)$ and

$$\omega_j = \frac{1}{\delta\alpha} \frac{V^{-1}(n_j)}{(1+\widehat{r})^{1-\gamma}} \equiv \Omega^{\mathrm{II}}_{+}(n_j, \widehat{r}), \qquad (9)$$

with Ω^{II} increasing in employment n_j and decreasing in the expected real rate of interest $\widehat{r}$. Recall that the function $\Omega^{\mathrm{I}}(\cdot, \eta_j Y)$ is just the inverse labour demand function. Similarly, $\Omega^{\mathrm{II}}(\cdot, \widehat{r})$ is the inverse labour supply function, augmented according to the markup factor $1/\delta\alpha$.

As the firm exercising its output market power voluntarily rations its own sales, the union exercising its monopoly power voluntarily rations potential employment, in order to keep the real wage above its competitive value (the value that balances labour demand and labour supply). Also, as emphasised with respect to the first fundamental postulate, the second postulate states more than just the first-order condition (8): it states that this condition is actually satisfied in equilibrium; in other words, in equilibrium, the union is in fact on the augmented inverse labour supply curve (9). Hence, Keynes's rejection of the second fundamental postulate should by no means be interpreted as a denial of standard economic behaviour by workers and unions. It just means that, contrary to the classical viewpoint, the maximisation of either workers' or unions' objectives should not be taken as an equilibrium condition; in other words, that equilibrium is compatible with workers and unions being *off their supply curves*.

3.3 How full is full employment?

In order to approach unemployment as an overall phenomenon, not limited to the micro labour market j, we must resort to general equilibrium analysis. A rough but simple way of going directly to the essentials of the question is to assume complete symmetry across output and labour markets (implying $\overline{k}_j = \overline{k}$ and $\eta_j = 1$ for any j). The first fundamental postulate can then be reformulated for any market (without having to refer to index j) in terms of the equation $\omega = \Omega^{\mathrm{I}}(n, F(n))$, incorporating the equality $Y = F(n)$ deduced from the binding constraints on the individual producer. We thus obtain a simple relation involving only employment and the real wage. Keynes points out a different situation as regards the second postulate: "[Classical economists] do not seem to have realised that, unless the supply of labour is a function of real wages alone, their supply curve for labour will shift bodily with every movement of prices" (Keynes 1936, pp. 8–9). The real interest rate, an argument of the inverse labour supply function and of its augmented version Ω^{II}, is indeed influenced by price movements either directly or indirectly (through the money rate of interest).

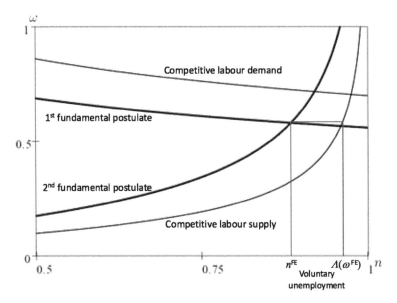

Figure 1. Full employment equilibrium.

Rather than a single curve, as in the case of the first postulate, we thus obtain in the employment–real wage space a family of curves parameterised by $\hat{r}$, all of them potential representatives of the second postulate.

Let us provisionally neglect the influence of P on $\hat{r}$, by taking the real rate of interest as exogenous. If the two fundamental postulates are simultaneously satisfied, that is, if $\omega = \Omega^{I}(n, F(n)) = \Omega^{II}(n, \hat{r})$, we unambiguously obtain an equilibrium pair (n^{FE}, ω^{FE}), corresponding to a "state of affairs we shall describe as 'full' employment, both 'frictional' and 'voluntary' unemployment being consistent with 'full' employment thus defined" (Keynes 1936, pp. 15–16). Figure 1 represents in the space (n, ω) the competitive aggregate labour demand and supply curves (the thin decreasing and increasing curves, respectively), as well as the corresponding curves modified by imperfect competition, which can be identified with the first and second fundamental postulates $\Omega^{I}(\cdot, F(\cdot))$ and $\Omega^{II}(\cdot, \hat{r})$ (the thick decreasing and increasing curves, respectively).[14] Full employment equilibrium is determined by the intersection at the point (n^{FE}, ω^{FE}) of the two thick curves, when both fundamental postulates of classical economics are satisfied. The volume of voluntary unemployment corresponds

---

14 Figure 1 was computed with the following parameter values: $A\bar{k}^{1-\alpha} = 1, \alpha = 0.7,$ $\delta = 0.8, \gamma = 0.75, \hat{r} = 0.075$. Labour disutility was assumed to be lognormally distributed, with mean 0.1 and variance 1.

to the distance between the two increasing curves at the equilibrium real wage, that is, to $\Lambda(\omega^{FE}) - n^{FE}$.

Putting aside the somewhat trivial category of frictional unemployment, which does not involve delicate interpretation issues, it should be stressed that the second "postulate is also compatible with 'voluntary' unemployment due to the refusal or inability of a unit of labour, as a result of legislation or social practices or of combination for collective bargaining or of slow response to change or of mere human obstinacy, to accept a reward corresponding to the value of the product attributable to its marginal productivity" (Keynes 1936, p. 6).[15] The category *voluntary unemployment* covers thus more than the simple "combination for collective bargaining," and is in fact still more comprehensive than stated here: this "apparent unemployment" [*sic*] is not only "the effect of a trade union 'closed shop' on the employment of free labour", but also "the result [...] of monopolistic practices on the part of employers" [*sic*], as we read in the second proof of the *General Theory* (Keynes 1973, XIV, pp. 363–364). From the point of view of the individual worker, the term "voluntary" seems of course inappropriate when there is "inability", not "refusal", of a unit of labour to accept the right reward, the one that corresponds to the value of its marginal productivity and that also exceeds its reservation value. However, Keynes refers explicitly to the "whole body of labour" and implicitly to all participants in the labour market, including employers and the legislator. As far as the workers are concerned, the so-called voluntary unemployment is, *ex ante*, a deliberate consequence of strategic behaviour, as much so as the deliberate restrained supply by the monopolistic producer, although no one would willingly accept *ex post* to draw an unlucky number when looking for a job.[16] I will not

---

15 Notice that voluntary unemployment may be due to the refusal of a unit of labour to accept a reward corresponding to its marginal productivity, but only *as a result of* legislation, combination, and so forth. Otherwise, as a result of utility maximisation, the refusal will simply lead to chosen *leisure*. This distinction was overlooked by Richard Kahn, when he attributed to Pigou, writing in 1914, the first use of the term "involuntary unemployment", whereas Pigou was in fact referring to involuntary *idleness*, that is, to unemployment proper as opposed to leisure (see Kahn 1976, p. 19).

16 "Thus there is an involuntary element in all unemployment, in the sense that no one chooses bad luck over good; there is also a voluntary element in all unemployment, in the sense that however miserable one's current work options, one can always choose to accept them" (Lucas 1981, p. 242). See also the discussion of Lucas' position in De Vroey (2004, chapter 14). This is correct, but Lucas and to some extent De Vroey missed the point, since they focussed exclusively on the individual worker's choice when they assessed Keynes's distinction between voluntary and involuntary unemployment, thus ignoring the combination and coordination issues that called for the distinction.

insist on semantics, but it is essential to understand, when coming to political issues, that Keynes's "full" employment does by no means exclude a high and possibly highly variable observed rate of unemployment. Keynes's rate of voluntary unemployment essentially corresponds to Friedman's "natural rate of unemployment", which supposes that imbedded in the general equilibrium equations are "the actual structural characteristics of the labor and commodity markets, including market imperfections, [...]" (Friedman 1968, p. 8).

3.4 Say's law

As Keynes puts it in the beginning of chapter 3 of the *General Theory*, "the substance of the General Theory of Employment" is that "the volume of employment is given by the point of intersection between the aggregate demand function and the aggregate supply function; for it is at this point that the entrepreneurs' expectation of profits will be maximised" (Keynes 1936, p. 25). So, if we continue to refer to a symmetric economy, short-term expectations of effective demand Y select, quite independently of the second fundamental postulate, one particular point in the graph of the function $\Omega^{I}(\cdot, Y)$ which represents the first postulate, namely the point corresponding to $n = F^{-1}(Y)$.

The significant question concerns, however, the adjustments that might be induced by the violation of the second postulate, either the upward adjustment of producers' short-term expectations or the downward adjustment of unions' wage targets. Let me consider the former alternative, and reserve to the next section the discussion of the latter. If producers' short-term expectations lead to a situation of less than full employment, will more optimistic expectations be systematically validated? Yes, if we admit that "Supply creates its own Demand", which amounts to accept the supposedly self-fulfilling nature of short-term expectations: "The classical theory assumes, in other words, that the aggregate demand price (or proceeds) always accommodates itself to the aggregate supply price" (Keynes 1936, p. 26), so that Y is always eventually adjusted to its full employment value $F(n^{FE})$.

How does this adjustment work? If the utility procured by present and future consumption is equal to $\Gamma C^{\gamma}\widehat{C}^{1-\gamma}$ (with $0 < \gamma < 1$) for both workers and entrepreneurs, real income Y generates consumption $C = \gamma Y$ of the composite good and saving $S = (1 - \gamma)Y$, which must be equal to investment, assumed to materialise as a purchase of the composite good. How is that investment induced? The young entrepreneur j, acting as an investor, chooses future capital k_j so as to maximise, under the technological and sales constraints, the expected real future profit $\widehat{\Pi}_j(k_j)$ of the firm, net of the interest on borrowed capital plus the corresponding principal to be reimbursed $(1+\widehat{r})k_j$. By (2), (3) and the specification of the production function $\widehat{F}(k_j, \widehat{n}_j) = Ak_j^{1-\alpha}\widehat{n}_j^{\alpha}$ (with a hat to qualify any expected variable, here $\widehat{n}$), this expected net real profit is

$$\widehat{\Pi}_j(k_j) - (1+\widehat{r})k_j = (1-\delta\alpha)\left(\left(\frac{\delta\alpha}{\widehat{\omega}_j}\right)^{\delta\alpha}(Ak_j^{1-\alpha})^{\delta}(\widehat{n}_j\widehat{Y})^{1-\delta}\right)^{\frac{1}{1-\delta\alpha}} - (1+\widehat{r})k_j. \quad (10)$$

I am assuming complete depreciation of capital. The corresponding first-order condition for maximisation of $\widehat{\Pi}_j(k_j) - (1+\widehat{r})k_j$ is

$$\underbrace{\delta(1-\alpha)\left(\left(\frac{\delta\alpha}{\widehat{\omega}_j}\right)^{\delta\alpha}(Ak_j^{1-\alpha})^{\delta}(\widehat{n}_j\widehat{Y})^{1-\delta}\right)^{\frac{1}{1-\delta\alpha}}\frac{1}{k_j}}_{\widehat{\Pi}_j'(k_j)} - 1 = \widehat{r}, \quad (11)$$

which is nothing but the equality of the *marginal efficiency of capital* $\widehat{\Pi}_j'(k_j) - 1$ and the rate of interest $\widehat{r}$, formulated in chapter 11 of the *General Theory*. This equality can be reformulated so as to express investment directly:

$$k_j = \left(\delta A^{\delta}\left(\frac{1-\alpha}{1+\widehat{r}}\right)^{1-\delta\alpha}\left(\frac{\alpha}{\widehat{\omega}_j}\right)^{\delta\alpha}\right)^{\frac{1}{1-\delta}}\widehat{n}_j\widehat{Y} \equiv I(\underset{-}{\widehat{r}}, \widehat{\omega}_j)\widehat{n}_j\widehat{Y}, \quad (12)$$

as an increasing linear function of expected future effective demand $\widehat{n}_j\widehat{Y}$ for good j, and a decreasing function of both the expected real rate of interest $\widehat{r}$ and the expected future real wage $\widehat{\omega}_j$.

The preceding analysis of the *propensity to consume* and of the *inducement to invest* is common to Keynes and the Classics. Keynes adopts in particular an essentially classical approach to investment, Fisherian to be precise. The equilibrium analysis of output markets also ends up for Keynes and the Classics with the same equality of saving and investment. In our framework, if we take again the simplifying assumption of full symmetry across firms or industries, and if we provisionally ignore transfers from entrepreneurs to rentiers, which would reduce their available income, we obtain the equality $(1-\gamma)Y = I(\widehat{r}, \widehat{\omega})\widehat{Y}$. Keynes separates from the Classics only with regard to the way this equality is brought about. According to Keynes, there is a unique equilibrium value of the effective demand Y, given long-term expectations $\widehat{Y}$, $\widehat{w}$ and $\widehat{P}$ (hence $\widehat{\omega} = \widehat{w}/\widehat{P}$), given the money wage w and given the nominal interest rate i, as determined by the state of liquidity preference and the quantity of money in wage units.[17] By contrast, in the classical tradition, any feasible level of output will be validated by an appropriate adjustment of the rate of interest, which appears as the price equilibrating the primary market for securities, issued by the investors and purchased by the savers: "this tradition has regarded the rate of interest as the factor which brings the demand for investment and the willingness to save into equilibrium with one another" (Keynes 1936, p. 175). Hence, "effective demand, instead of having a unique equilibrium value, is an infinite range of values all equally admissible; and the amount of employment is indeterminate except in so far as the marginal disutility of labour sets an upper limit. [...] Thus Say's law, that the aggregate demand price of output as a whole is equal to its aggregate supply price for all volumes of output, is equivalent to the proposition that there is no obstacle to full employment" (Keynes 1936, p. 26).

4. Generalising the theory of employment

In Keynes's view of classical theory, Say's law states that *any* pair (n, ω) of employment and real wage levels satisfying the first fundamental postulate is sustainable in terms of demand, thanks to appropriate adjustments of the interest rate. More precisely, such adjustments allow demand expectations triggering any feasible level of output to be systematically fulfilled: "the amount of employment is indeterminate except in so far as the marginal disutility of labour sets an upper limit." In this context, it will always be possible for the economy to experience "an expansion of employment up to the point at which the supply of output as a whole ceases to be elastic" (Keynes 1936, p. 26). In other words, the economy will eventually set at the full employment equilibrium, determined by combining the first and the second fundamental postulates.

By contrast, Keynes wants to show that there is a *unique* pair (n, ω) that satisfies both the first fundamental postulate and what he calls the *principle of effective demand* (Section 4.1), meaning that only in that situation is there enough demand, ultimately induced by producers' expectations, for these expectations to be verified. This makes him move from demand as expected by producers (in chapter 3) to demand as decided by consumers and investors (sketched in chapter 3 and developed in chapters 8–12 of the *General Theory*). An underemployment equilibrium is then quite generally obtained. In Section 4.2, it will, however, appear that the reasons for

---

17 The real rate of interest $\hat{r}$ and in fact the nominal rate of interest i itself depend on the price level P, which is, however, perfectly correlated with output Y, given the money wage w, through the first fundamental postulate: $w/P = \Omega^1(F^{-1}(Y), Y)$.

the failure of Say's law as regards the appropriateness of interest rate adjustments had yet to be examined, as part of a novel theory of the working of capital markets (developed in chapters 13–17 of the *General Theory*). The last important point requiring explanation (provided in Section 4.3) is of course the inability of wage reductions to restore full employment (a point discussed principally in chapter 19 of the *General Theory*).

4.1. The link between labour and output markets: the principle of effective demand

Opposing to Say's law his principle of effective demand, Keynes rejects the second fundamental postulate, thus admitting the possibility of underemployment equilibria:

> [T]he volume of employment is not determined by the marginal disutility of labour measured in terms of real wages, except in so far as the supply of labour available at a given real wage sets a *maximum* level to employment. The propensity to consume and the rate of new investment determine between them the volume of employment, and the volume of employment is uniquely related to a given level of real wages — not the other way round. If the propensity to consume and the rate of new investment result in a deficient effective demand, the actual level of employment will fall short of the supply of labour potentially available at the existing real wage, and the equilibrium real wage will be *greater* than the marginal disutility of the equilibrium level of employment. (Keynes 1936, p. 30).

Let me express formally these ideas within my suggested model. In my discussion of Say's law, I have considered two categories of consumers: active workers and active entrepreneurs, the latter with the dual role of producers and investors. Both were assumed to devote to consumption a proportion γ of their respective incomes. However, consumers of both classes become old and retired, and a third category of consumers must be considered: old rentiers, spending in consumption the whole of their wealth, inclusive of their interest income. The output market equilibrium condition must be adjusted accordingly, while keeping the assumption of full symmetry across firms or industries, to simplify the analysis. Young entrepreneurs are born endowed with inherited physical capital $\bar{k}$, to which corresponds a financial liability denominated in money units $\overline{Pk}$, $\overline{P}$ being the price of the composite good in the previous period.[18] Thus, the

---

18 In the simple overlapping generations framework I have adopted, entrepreneurs are active during one period only, becoming retired rentiers in the next. Also, in Keynes's short-period approach, investment realised in the present affects production capacity only in the future. Consequently, investment $\bar{k}$, decided and effected in the past period by now retired entrepreneurs, is taken over in the present by young entrepreneurs. These entrepreneurs must also bear the charge of the debt $\overline{Pk}$, incurred by their predecessors to finance that investment.

retired consumers' real wealth is equal to the real revenue of this financial capital (principal and interest at the given past rate $\bar{\imath}$) $(1+\bar{\imath})\overline{P}\,\bar{k}/P \equiv (1+r)\bar{k}$, plus their real money holdings, equal to the given quantity of money $\overline{M}$ deflated by P. Also, the aggregate real income of active consumers is equal to the sum Y of real wages and profits, net of the real charges of their debt $(1+r)\bar{k}$. Adding the different components of aggregate demand, namely induced consumption by the young, autonomous consumption by the old, and investment, we obtain in real terms

$$Y = \gamma(Y - (1+r)\bar{k}) + (1+r)\bar{k} + \overline{M}/P + I(\hat{r},\hat{\omega})\widehat{Y}$$
$$= (1+r)\bar{k} + \frac{1}{1-\gamma}\left(\frac{\overline{M}}{P} + I(\hat{r},\hat{\omega})\widehat{Y}\right), \tag{13}$$

where we find the standard *Keynesian multiplier* $1/(1-\gamma)$ applied to the sum of real money holdings and investment.

In nominal terms, using the definitions of the present and future real interest factors $1 + r \equiv (1+\bar{\imath})\overline{P}/P$ and $1 + \hat{r} \equiv (1+i)P/\widehat{P}$, we have

$$PY = (1+\bar{\imath})\overline{P}\,\bar{k} + \frac{1}{1-\gamma}\left(\overline{M} + PI\left(\frac{(1+i)P}{\widehat{P}} - 1, \frac{\hat{w}}{\widehat{P}}\right)\widehat{Y}\right), \tag{14}$$

where the nominal output PY appears as a decreasing function of the nominal rate of interest i, corresponding to the *IS curve* introduced in Hicks (1937, p. 153). Notice, however, that the nominal output is also a decreasing function (by (12)) of the endogenous price index P,[19] so that we obtain in fact in the space (PY, i) a family of *IS* curves, parameterised by P. We can alternatively use the equality $Y = F(n)$ and transform Equation (14) into a function representing the *principle of effective demand*:

$$n = F^{-1}\left(\frac{(1+\bar{\imath})\overline{P}\,\bar{k}}{P} + \frac{1}{1-\gamma}\left(\frac{\overline{M}}{P} + I\left(\frac{(1+i)P}{\widehat{P}} - 1, \frac{\hat{w}}{\widehat{P}}\right)\widehat{Y}\right)\right) \tag{15}$$
$$\equiv N^{\text{ED}}(\underset{-}{P}, \underset{-}{i}, \underset{-}{\hat{w}}, \underset{+}{\widehat{P}}, \underset{+}{\widehat{Y}}).$$

---

19 This is because the negative effect of a price increase on the volume of investment through the marginal efficiency of capital dominates the direct positive effect on its value (see (12)).

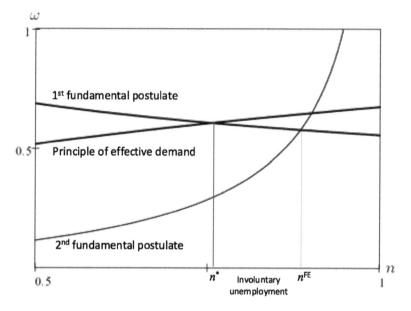

Figure 2. Underemployment equilibrium.

Employment is thus decreasing in the price index (by the Pigou effect and the effect through the marginal efficiency of capital), the nominal interest rate and the expected future money wage, and increasing in the expected future price and quantity indices. If we introduce the "temporary assumption that money-wages are constant" (Keynes 1936, p. 29), equal to w, so that $P = w/\omega$, we obtain in the space (n, ω) a family of increasing curves parameterised by the money wage w, the rate of interest i and the state of long-term expectations $(\widehat{w}, \widehat{P}, \widehat{Y})$.

The graph of the function $\omega \mapsto N^{\mathrm{ED}}(w/\omega, i, \widehat{w}, \widehat{P}, \widehat{Y})$ is represented by the increasing thick curve in Figure 2, where the two other curves correspond to the two fundamental postulates and are taken up from Figure 1.[20] If we follow Keynes's argument, employment is not jointly determined by

---

20 This is not perfectly exact. The expected real rate of interest $\widehat{r}$ was provisionally taken as fixed in Figure 1, so that the second fundamental postulate corresponded to the set of points (n, ω) such that $\omega = \Omega^{\mathrm{II}}(n, \widehat{r})$. Now, I am taking as fixed the nominal rate of interest i, so that $\widehat{r}$ is dependent on ω: the second fundamental postulate corresponds now to the set of points (n, ω) such that $\omega = \Omega^{\mathrm{II}}(n, (1 + i)w/(\omega\widehat{P}) - 1)$. However, by construction, the two expressions of Ω^{II} define curves that have the same intersection with the curve defined by Ω^{I}, at the point $(n^{\mathrm{FE}}, \omega^{\mathrm{FE}})$.

the two fundamental postulates, but by the principle of effective demand together with the first postulate, as long as the intersection of the corresponding curves lies on the left of the curve representing the second postulate. The difference between the equilibrium level of employment n^* and its full employment value n^{FE} corresponds to what Keynes calls *involuntary unemployment*.

We must, however, recall that the curve representing the principle of effective demand is just one of a family of curves parameterised by the money wage, the nominal rate of interest (itself dependent upon the money wage, as we shall see) and the state of long-term expectations. By letting anyone of the two former variables decrease, we make the representative curve shift to the right, resulting in higher and higher equilibrium levels of employment. Hence, the distinction between the consequences of adopting the principle of effective demand instead of Say's law is yet to be clarified as regards the adjustments of the rate of interest. Also, as a decrease in the money wage seems to be employment improving, we must take into account Hawtrey's objection when referring to "involuntary" unemployment: "if unemployment is to be regarded as 'involuntary', it must be such that a reduction of wages would not remedy it" (letter to Keynes, dated 29.04.1936, in Keynes 1973, XIV, p. 30). I shall address these two points in the following two subsections.

4.2. Coordination failures through financial markets

Why does the interest rate fail to respond adequately to an imbalance of saving and investment, leaving that task to the level of employment and thus invalidating Say's law? To answer to this question, we must consider how financial markets coordinate firms' and consumers' decisions.

The first significant point about financial markets is that most of them do not even exist, as illustrated by Keynes's parable of the postponed dinner, at the beginning of chapter 16 of the *General Theory*. As Keynes puts it, "if saving consisted not merely in abstaining from present consumption but in placing simultaneously a specific order for future consumption, [...] the expectation from some future yield from investment would be improved, and the resources released from preparing for present consumption could be turned over to preparing for the future consumption" (Keynes 1936, pp. 210–211). This is, however, not generally true when markets are incomplete: futures markets, where such specific orders would be made explicit, do actually not exist for many goods and dates (or events), so that future price and output levels, $\widehat{P}$ and $\widehat{Y}$, cannot be directly inferred from observed market signals.[21] They can only be *expected* to prevail later in the relevant *spot* markets. As pure long-term expectations, they do not play the required role of coordinating signals and, because of their inherent volatility, they may even place investment decisions under the influence of *animal spirits*, as suggested by Keynes in chapter 12. Also, they may be too responsive to currently observed price and demand levels, P and Y, thus neutralising the necessary adjustments or, worse, making them destabilising. Such is the case of elastic expectations, formally introduced by Hicks (1939, pp. 205, 255) but already contemplated by Keynes in chapter 19 of the *General Theory*, as we shall see in the next subsection. A decrease in the money wage w and the resulting decrease in the price level P, instead of triggering a favourable decrease in the expected real interest rate $\hat{r}$, as it would under a *given* nominal interest rate i and *given* expected price level $\hat{P}$, may then be followed by a reverse effect on $\hat{r}$, if $\hat{P}$ declines more than P.

Let us, however, examine how the nominal interest rate itself responds to decreasing prices. A first obstacle in the way of full employment is that, since this rate remunerates holders of assets that are denominated in money, and since the cost of holding money is negligible, the nominal rate of interest is never negative, contrary to the marginal efficiency of capital, which may well be negative at full employment equilibrium. The adjustment of the rate of interest can consequently fall short of full employment because of its zero lower bound. A second, more significant, obstacle lies in the fact that transactions in the financial markets involve not only savers, buying securities in order to transfer part of their current income to the future, and investors, issuing securities in order to finance their investments, but mostly holders of previously issued securities wanting to modify their portfolios. In other words, financial markets are principally secondary markets. As a consequence, the prospective yield of a security may be mainly determined not by the interest or the dividends it is going to pay, but by its expected future market value at the (uncertain) time of its liquidation.

---

21 Market incompleteness is associated in contemporary general equilibrium theory with long-period equilibria (Hicksian equilibria over time): agents are assumed to correctly anticipate future prices and all future (spot) markets are assumed to clear. In such context, the consequence of market incompleteness is essentially to impose restrictions upon wealth transfers among states. I am, however, referring to the context of short-period equilibrium (Hicksian temporary equilibrium), where nothing is assumed about long-term expectations fulfilment or about future spot markets clearance. In this context, an important consequence of market incompleteness is the absence of market signals coordinating agents' expectations and plans for the future.

In order to model this idea, I assume that savings can be held either in money or in bonds. A bond represents one unit of money available the next period and purchased at price $q \in (0,1)$, hence bearing interest at the nominal rate $i = 1/q - 1$. When choosing the portfolio, the representative young consumer is assumed to face a liquidity constraint with two components. First, he has to keep his money balance at a proportion not smaller than μ of his savings PS, because of the *transactions* and *precautionary motives* for liquidity preference, introduced in Keynes (1936, p. 170). Second, with probability ρ, he may have to renounce to deferred payments at some time in the future, being then forced to liquidate his bonds before maturity. If, on the contrary, with probability $1 - \rho$, payments can at that time be surely deferred until the end of the next period, then he will be able to convert his money balance in interest-bearing bonds. Thus, if the expected future price of a bond sold before maturity is $\widehat{q} \in (0,1)$, then the young consumer secures at the end of the next period, by choosing to hold a cash balance $m \in [\mu PS, PS]$, an expected value of his wealth equal to

$$\rho\left(m + \frac{PS - m}{q}\widehat{q}\right) + (1 - \rho)\left(m\widehat{q} + \frac{PS - m}{q}\right)$$

$$= \left(\rho + \frac{1 - \rho}{\widehat{q}}\right)\left(\left(1 - \frac{\widehat{q}}{q}\right)m + \frac{\widehat{q}}{q}PS\right). \qquad (16)$$

Clearly, he chooses $m = \mu PS$ if $\widehat{q} > q$ (if he is a *bull*) and $m = PS$ if $\widehat{q} < q$ (if he is a *bear*). A *bull* holds money just because of the transactions and precautionary motives for liquidity preference; a *bear* has in addition a *speculative motive* to hold money (Keynes 1936, p. 170).

Suppose now that the expected future price of bonds is distributed in the consumers' population according to the distribution function Q: $Q(q)$ is the proportion of consumers expecting the future price of bonds to be smaller than q (the proportion of *bears* when the price of bonds is q). The aggregate demand M for money is then

$$M = Q(q)PS + (1 - Q(q))\mu PS$$

$$= (\mu + (1 - \mu)Q(q))(1 - \gamma)(PY - (1 + \overline{\imath})\overline{P}\,\overline{k}), \qquad (17)$$

where the proportions μ and $(1 - \mu)Q(q)$ of young consumers' aggregate savings $PS = (1 - \gamma)(PY - (1 + \overline{\imath})\overline{P}\,\overline{k})$ correspond to the transactions/precautionary and speculative components of money demand, respectively (the complementary proportion of savings, $(1 - \mu)(1 - Q(q))$, being held in bonds by the *bulls*). Thus, if we take as given the quantity of money $\overline{M}$, then the equilibrium price of bonds (the one entailing $M = \overline{M}$) is a non-increasing function of the nominal output PY:

$$q = Q^{-1}\left(\frac{\overline{M}}{(1 - \mu)(1 - \gamma)(PY - (1 + \overline{\imath})\overline{P}\,\overline{k})} - \frac{\mu}{1 - \mu}\right). \qquad (18)$$

By Equation (18), the nominal rate of interest $i = 1/q - 1$ is a non-decreasing function $L(\cdot, \overline{M})$ of the nominal output PY, the graph of which is nothing but the *LM curve* (*LL* as introduced in Hicks 1937, p. 153).

The *LM* curve is usually presented as nearly horizontal for low levels of the nominal output and the rate of interest, since "there is some minimum below which the rate of interest is unlikely to go" (Hicks 1937, p. 154). Hence, when the economy is severely depressed, the rate of interest is supposed to become irresponsive to an expansionary monetary policy, giving rise to the so-called *liquidity trap*. This is a reason for Hicks to claim that "the General Theory of Employment is the Economics of Depression" (Hicks 1937, p. 155). This occurrence, plainly defined nowadays as a situation in which the short-term nominal interest rate is zero or close to zero, has been again evoked in the late 1990s in relation to the Japanese slump (Krugman 1998). It is true that Keynes mentions the possibility "that, after the rate of interest has fallen to a certain level, liquidity-preference may become virtually absolute in the sense that almost everyone prefers cash to holding a debt which yields so low a rate of interest" (Keynes 1936, p. 207). However, he also emphasises that "the rate of interest is a highly conventional [...] phenomenon. For its actual value is largely governed by the prevailing view as to what its value is expected to be. *Any* level of interest which is accepted with sufficient conviction as *likely* to be durable *will* be durable" (Keynes 1936, p. 203; Keynes's emphasis).

How can we translate this idea in the model we have suggested? The distribution function Q may be discontinuous at some point $\widehat{q}$ (be it large or small) if the future price of bonds is unanimously expected to be $\widehat{q}$ among a non-negligible subset of market participants, who are *bulls* for $q < \widehat{q}$ and become *bears* as soon as $q > \widehat{q}$. Correspondingly, the graph of Q^{-1} in (18) then exhibits a horizontal portion, indicating that the price of bonds (or the rate of interest) ceases locally to respond to variations of either PY or $\overline{M}$. Of course, when the expected future bond prices are very concentrated, although not on a single point, the graph of Q^{-1} is flat, if not horizontal, over some interval(s). Figure 3 represents, together with two decreasing *IS* curves associated with two different values of P (the thick curve with the higher P), two increasing *LM* curves, computed for the same parameter values, except that the thick curve results from highly

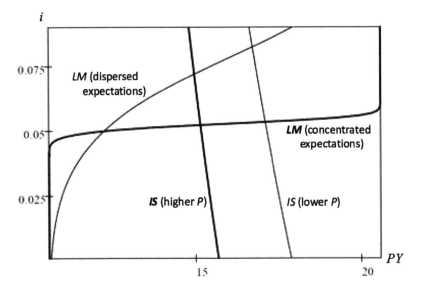

Figure 3. The *IS–LM* diagram.

concentrated expectations and the thin curve from more dispersed expectations, around the same future interest rate of 5%.[22] Thus, quite independently of the phase of the business cycle, whether a depression or not, the classical equilibrating adjustment of the rate of interest which is required by Say's law can be blocked or become ineffective under converging expectations of future interest rates. Admittedly, converging expectations may be more likely in specific phases of the business cycle. In particular, the *special* form of the *LM* curve which Hicks attributes to Keynes, with its flat portion when *PY* and *i* are both small, corresponds to one possible situation in which the concentration of expectations becomes quite likely, since the occurrence of a current interest rate approaching its zero lower bound leaves no place for bulls. The recent macroeconomic analysis, since Krugman's revival of the liquidity trap, has rightly put more emphasis on the role of expectations of future interest rates than the old Keynesian literature tended to do in this context (see Eggertsson 2008). However, the issue of their distribution over heterogeneous agents went on to be

---

22 The parameter values are those that have been used in Figures 1 and 2 (with, in addition, $\mu = 0.2$). Expectations $\hat{q}$ of the future price of bonds are assumed to be lognormally distributed, with mean $1/1.05$, and, for the thick *LM* curve, standard deviation equal to 0.001, while for the thin one, equal to 0.015.

neglected in spite of the fact that, even with an interest rate far away from its lower bound, the occurrence of a highly concentrated distribution is not an implausible event. "The energies and skill of the professional investor and speculator are mainly occupied [...] with foreseeing changes in the conventional basis of valuation a short time ahead of the general public" (Keynes 1936, p. 154). As illustrated by the analogy of the *beauty contest*, professional investors devote their "intelligences to anticipating what average opinion expects the average opinion to be" (Keynes 1936, p. 156). The coordination of expectations among market operators becomes largely the aim of the game, independently of any reference to fundamentals, a kind of coordination that, by its very effectiveness, partly accounts for the possibility of a systemic coordination failure originating in the financial markets.

The model is now complete. Using, under symmetry across firms, the first fundamental postulate (2) and the principle of effective demand (15), together with the *LM* equation $i = L(PY, \overline{M})$ and the equalities $P = w/\omega$ and $Y = F(n)$, we obtain

$$\omega = \Omega^{\mathrm{I}}(n, F(n)), \tag{19}$$

$$n = N^{\mathrm{ED}}(w/\omega, L((w/\omega)F(n), \overline{M}), \widehat{w}, \widehat{P}, \widehat{Y}), \tag{20}$$

a system of two equations determining the equilibrium values (n^*, ω^*) of the employment and the real wage, given the money wage w, the money supply $\overline{M}$ and the state of long-term expectations $(\widehat{w}, \widehat{P}, \widehat{Y})$ relative to the labour and output markets,[23] plus the distribution Q of expectations concerning the financial market (which are implicit in L).[24] Under involuntary unemployment $(n^* < n^{\mathrm{FE}}$, with n^{FE} determined by the first and

---

23 By varying the state of long-term expectations, we obtain a continuum of possible equilibria. This is a first step allowing to identify in the *General Theory* the possibility of "a continuum of steady-state unemployment rates" (Farmer 2012, p. 3). The second step in the way of a continuum of *steady-state* equilibria is, however, missing: nothing is said about *self-fulfilment* of the long-term expectations.

24 "Thus we can sometimes regard our ultimate independent variables as consisting of (1) the three fundamental psychological factors, namely, the psychological propensity to consume [γ, implicit in N^{ED}], the psychological attitude to liquidity [L] and the psychological expectation of future yield from capital-assets [resulting from $(\widehat{w}, \widehat{P}, \widehat{Y})$], (2) the wage-unit [$w$] as determined by the bargains reached between employers and employed, and (3) the quantity of money [$\overline{M}$] as determined by the action of the central bank; so that, if we take as given the factors specified above, these variables determine the national income (or dividend) [$Y = F(n)$] and the quantity of employment [n]" (Keynes 1936, pp. 246–247).

second fundamental postulates[25]), we may expect a downward adjustment of the money wage w, heretofore provisionally taken as fixed (as in the *General Theory*, until chapter 19). Such an adjustment would in principle increase n^* and lower n^{FE} (so diminishing involuntary unemployment), in particular through a decline in the money rate of interest. This decline, as just shown, can, however, be blocked by convergent expectations of the price of bonds. As to the decline in the real rate of interest due to a decrease in the price level P, we have seen that, under elastic expectations, it may be neutralised or even reversed by a corresponding decrease in the expected price level $\hat{P}$.[26]

We have finally to consider the real balance effect of a generalised price decline, supposed to increase consumption and investment. Keynes considered the possibly favourable effect of an increase in the quantity of money expressed in wage units, through a declining money interest rate (the so-called *Keynes effect*, working through L), but ignored the resulting direct increase in consumers' wealth (the *Pigou effect*). The Pigou effect is, however, not the end of the story: "the method of increasing the quantity of money in terms of wage-units by decreasing the wage-unit increases proportionately the burden of debt" (Keynes 1936, p. 268), with a "depressing influence on entrepreneurs,"since "the embarrassment of those entrepreneurs who are heavily indebted may soon reach the point of insolvency [if the fall of wages and prices goes far]" (*ibid.*, p. 264). The point of insolvency is indeed reached as soon as the entrepreneurs' real income $F(n) - \omega n$ becomes smaller than the real charges of their debt $(1 + \bar{\imath})\overline{Pk}/P$, so that the overall wealth effect of wage deflation cannot be assessed on the sole basis of an increase in $\overline{M}/P$.

4.3. Coordination failures originating in the labour market

Financial markets are not alone responsible for the emergence of coordination problems resulting in the failure of Say's law and the consequent possibility of underemployment equilibria. In Keynes's analysis of chapters 2 and 19 of the *General Theory*, the working of the labour market, making it impossible to promptly achieve the appropriate money wage adjustments, is also a source of such problems. At this point, it might seem that we are after all reaching the neoclassical indictment that Keynes's theory

---

25 Since the function Ω^{II}, representing the second fundamental postulate, has the real rate of interest $\hat{r}$ as its second argument, we must again resort to the LM equation plus the equalities $P = w/\omega$ and $Y = F(n)$ to determine n^{FE}.

26 The adverse effect of elastic expectations of the future price level $\hat{P}$ will be mitigated if the expectations of the future money wage $\hat{w}$ are themselves elastic.

ultimately differs from classical theory by the sole assumption of money wage rigidity. The usual meaning given to this assumption, making it result from labour market imperfections, is, however, inadequate. Just as the "rigidity" of the money rate of interest which may neutralise its coordinating role is due, not to any financial market imperfection, but to the concentration of expectations on a too high future interest rate, money wage "rigidity" may naturally result from decentralised bargaining in an otherwise perfect market.

Let us consider the reasons for this money wage rigidity. It has been assumed in Section 3 that wage bargains take place at the firm/industry level. However, the labour market is not supposed to be segmented: workers can circulate, although imperfectly, from one micro-market to another, so that violations of money wage uniformity can only be transitory. This implies that in a transparent and fluid labour market the solution to the bargaining problem analysed in Section 3.2 would in fact be constrained to satisfy $w_j = \max_{j'}\{w_{j'}\} \equiv w$.[27] Setting $w_j < w$ would represent for union j as well as for firm j the threat of making the workers move to other micro labour markets.[28] This simple fact is the clue to the downward rigidity of the money wage, coupled with the perfect flexibility of the real wage: as "the effect of combination on the part of a group of workers is to protect their relative real wage," "every trade union will put up some resistance to a cut in money-wages, however small," whereas "no trade union would dream of striking on every occasion of a rise in the cost of living" (Keynes 1936, pp. 14–15).

This characteristic of wage behaviour is the direct consequence of decentralised bargaining in a perfect market for homogeneous labour, and does not have to be explained, as usually done, in terms of money illusion, observance of relative wage norms, preference externalities, or whatever. As Keynes observes, "except in a socialised community where wage policy is settled by decree, there is no means of securing uniform wage reductions for every class of labour" (Keynes 1936, p. 267). This has as a natural consequence the possibility of a coordination failure: employers and unions can be stuck in corner solutions to their bargaining problems,

---

27 This constraint is seen to be consistent with the modelling of the output market, once it is recalled that we assume differentiated output but homogeneous labour. Indeed, if we remove product differentiation, accounting for some monopoly power in the output market, that is, if we take $\delta = 1$, the violation of the constraint $p_j = \min_{j'}\{p_{j'}\} \equiv P$ implies *zero demand* for the output of firm j.

28 One might object that unemployed workers would want to apply for a job in firm j, even if $w_j < w$. Costs of turnover incurred by firm j may, however, more than compensate the gain obtained through the reduction of w_j.

without being able to independently decrease real wages to their target values. Such a coordination failure in the labour market may thus be made responsible for the violation of the second fundamental postulate, that is, for the existence of equilibria with less than full employment. We may be tempted to speak in this case of "involuntary" unemployment. Think, however, of Hawtrey's objection as quoted above: "if unemployment is to be regarded as 'involuntary', it must be such that a reduction of wages would not remedy it."

Hawtrey's objection had in fact already been anticipated by Keynes, when he wrote: "there may exist no expedient by which labour as a whole can reduce its *real* wage to a given figure by making revised *money* bargains with the entrepreneurs" (Keynes 1936, p. 13). The question here is not that of finding the real wage corresponding to full employment, but that of implementing that real wage through an appropriate stimulation of the effective demand. As Keynes writes,

> When we enter on a period of weakening effective demand, a sudden large reduction of money-wages to a level so low that no one believes in its indefinite continuance would be the event most favourable to a strengthening of effective demand. But this could only be accomplished by administrative decree and is scarcely practical politics under a system of free wage-bargaining. On the other hand, it would be much better that wages should be rigidly fixed and deemed incapable of material changes, than that depressions should be accompanied by a gradual downward tendency of money-wages, a further moderate wage reduction being expected to signalise each increase of, say, 1 per cent. in the amount of unemployment. For example, the effect of an expectation that wages are going to sag by, say, 2 per cent. in the coming year will be roughly equivalent to the effect of a rise of 2 per cent. in the amount of interest payable for the same period. (Keynes 1936, p. 265)

When employers and unions all agree that the real wage is too high, tentative money wage reductions in some sector, made possible by the "imperfect mobility of labour" (Keynes 1936, p. 14), may be the signal triggering the required adjustment in the whole economy. Because of insufficient coordination across micro labour markets, this adjustment tends, however, to be slow and lasting, creating a deflationary bias in the expectations of the future price level, hence increasing the real rate of interest and depressing effective demand.

Since Keynes's objective is to generalise the theory of employment, we should finally not forget that "the same observations apply *mutatis mutandis* to the case of a boom" (Keynes 1936, p. 265). However, if money wage reductions can be blocked, or slowed down, by decentralised bargaining, the same argument does not apply in the opposite sense. A money wage increase may originate in a single industry j where full employment prevails, as a consequence of an increase in the effective demand for its output $\eta_j Y$, resulting either from an idiosyncratic positive shock on η_j or from an aggregate shock on Y generated, for instance, by an expansionary monetary or fiscal policy. If the labour market is sufficiently integrated, the constraint $w_{j'} \geq w_j$ impending on any other industry j' will then determine the propagation of the wage increase to the whole economy, even in general conditions of less than full employment.[29] *A fortiori*, government efforts to reduce *voluntary* unemployment, however high, by an expansionary macroeconomic policy will necessarily have inflationary consequences without a significant improvement of the employment situation. This illustrates the importance, from the viewpoint of economic policy, of Keynes's distinction between voluntary and involuntary unemployment.[30] It further shows that, contrary to a persistent belief, Keynes's analysis can be easily applied to what had been called stagflation in the mid-1960s.

5. Concluding remarks

In order to reconsider the relation between Keynes and the Classics, in particular by assessing the relative generality of their respective theories, I suggested a *new Keynesian* model of the *General Theory*. As with Hicks's *IS–LM* model, we may reduce it to a simple diagram. However, instead of focusing on the financial market, with the nominal income and the money rate of interest involved, my diagram focuses on the labour market and involves employment and the real wage. Three curves represent significant relationships between these two variables, corresponding to what Keynes calls the two fundamental postulates of classical economics and the principle of effective demand. This representation enlightens the comprehension of book I of the *General Theory*, and in particular of the supposedly obscure chapter 2, which is completely neglected in the *IS–LM* representation. Above all, it illustrates the generalisation of classical theory,

---

29 "That the wage-unit may tend to rise before full employment has been reached, requires little comment or explanation. Since each group of workers will gain, *cet. par.*, by a rise in its own wages, there is naturally for all groups a pressure in this direction, which entrepreneurs will be more ready to meet when they are doing better business. For this reason a proportion of any increase in effective demand is likely to be absorbed in satisfying the upward tendency of the wage-unit" (Keynes 1936, p. 301). Downward nominal wage rigidity and stochastic shocks in the demand for the output of individual firms are the main features embedded in the macroeconomic model of Akerlof, Dickens and Perry (1996), which is similar, as regards the output and labour markets, to the model presented in this paper.
30 Rivot (2011) studies the relationship between this distinction and Keynes's economic policy positions as sustained in his political writings.

according to which the three curves always intersect at the same point, and allows for a clear-cut distinction between voluntary and involuntary unemployment.

The *IS–LM* relationships are also implicit in the suggested model, as determinants of the principle of effective demand. In my interpretation, they are, however, very much dependent upon the state of expectations, a point which has been largely recognised with respect to the *position* of the curves, supposed to shift in response to shocks in expectations. A crucial point in Keynes's argument, since it concerns one of the main sources of failure of Say's law, namely the irresponsiveness of the money interest rate, is, however, that the *distribution* of expectations of future interest rates *shapes* the *LM* curve, making it flatter and flatter as dispersion decreases to zero. We thus have another rationale for the *liquidity trap*, which appears as a result of unanimous expectations, not necessarily close to the (zero) lower bound of possible interest rates.

A last concluding remark should be added. Keynes's underemployment equilibria do not result as often pretended from wage rigidity, even if they suppose an imperfect downward flexibility of money wages. This is explicitly related to the impossibility for firms and unions to simultaneously *coordinate* at the economy level on the real wage required for full employment equilibrium. As a consequence, money wage bargains at the firm or industry level must take into account the protection of *relative* wages. Keynes's relative wage hypothesis is not the result of irrational behaviour or of non-standard workers' preferences. It may be easily rationalised by a competitiveness constraint: unions and firms occupy opposite positions in the bargaining process going on in each micro-market, but they compete for labour, side by side, against the rest of the labour market.

Acknowledgements

I wish to thank Robert Dimand, Frédéric Dufourt, Jean-Luc Gaffard and two anonymous referees for numerous valuable remarks and suggestions on a first version of this article. My intellectual debt to Axel Leijonhufvud, incurred through reading and talking, is still larger than what might be inferred from this article. I owe to my late friend Philippe Michel the project of a step-by-step formalisation of the *General Theory*, and to my late friend Louis-André Gérard-Varet my entrance into new Keyncsian modelling, pursued for years with him and Claude d'Aspremont. The recurrent discussions with Michel De Vroey, stemming from an old and persistent disagreement about Keynes's theoretical contribution, helped to keep me alert on this matter.

References

Akerlof, G.A., Dickens, W.T., and Perry, G.L. (1996). The macroeconomics of low inflation. *Brookings Papers on Economic Activity*, 1996(1): 1–76.

d'Aspremont, C., Dos Santos Ferreira, R., and Gérard-Varet, L.-A. (2011). Imperfect competition and the trade cycle: Aborted guidelines from the late 1930s. *History of Political Economy*, 43: 513–36.

Blanchard, O. and Kiyotaki, N. (1987). Monopolistic competition and the effects of aggregate demand. *American Economic Review*, 77: 647–66.

Bryant, J. (1983). A simple rational expectations Keynes-type model. *Quarterly Journal of Economics*, 98: 525–8.

Champernowne, D.G. (1936). Unemployment, basic and monetary: The classical analysis and the Keynesian. *Review of Economic Studies*, 3: 201–16.

Cooper, R. and John, A. (1988). Coordinating coordination failures in Keynesian models. *Quarterly Journal of Economics*, 103: 441–63.

De Vroey, M. (2004). *Involuntary Unemployment: The Elusive Quest for a Theory*. London: Routledge.

Dimand, R. (2007). Keynes, IS-LM, and the Marshallian tradition. *History of Political Economy*, 39: 81–95.

Dixit, A. and Stiglitz, J. (1977). Monopolistic competition and optimum product diversity. *American Economic Review*, 67: 297–308.

Dixon, H. and Rankin, N. (1994). Imperfect competition and macroeconomics: A survey. *Oxford Economic Papers*, 46: 171–199.

Dos Santos Ferreira, R. and Michel, P. (1991). Keynes' aggregate supply function and the principle of effective demand. *Recherches Economiques de Louvain*, 57: 159–87.

Dos Santos Ferreira, R. and Michel, P. (2013). Keynes' wage-price dynamics. *Metroeconomica*, 64: 44–72.

Dunlop, J.T. (1944). *Wage Determination Under Trade Unions*. New York: Macmillan.

Eggertsson, G.B. (2008). Liquidity Trap. In S.N. Durlauf and L.E. Blume (Eds.), *The New Palgrave Dictionary of Economics*, 2nd ed. Basingstoke: Palgrave Macmillan.

Farmer, R.E.A. (2012). The evolution of endogenous business cycles. NBER Working Paper 18284. Forthcoming in *Macroeconomic Dynamics* (2014).

Friedman, M. (1968). The role of monetary policy. *American Economic Review*, 58: 1–17.

Harrod, R.F. (1937). Mr. Keynes and traditional theory. *Econometrica*, 5: 74–86.

Hicks, J.R. (1937). Mr. Keynes and the "Classics"; A suggested interpretation. *Econometrica*, 5: 147–59.

Hicks, J.R. (1939). *Value and Capital: An Inquiry into Some Fundamental Principles of Economic Theory*. Oxford: Clarendon Press.

Hoover, K.D. (1995). Relative wages, rationality, and involuntary unemployment in Keynes's labor market. *History of Political Economy*, 27: 653–85.

Kahn, R. (1976). Unemployment as Seen by the Keynesians. In D.N. Worswick (Ed.), *The Concept and Measurement of Involuntary Unemployment* (pp. 19–25). London: Allen & Unwin.

Keynes, J.M. ([1930] 1971). *A Treatise on Money*. Vols V and VI of *The Collected Writings of John Maynard Keynes*. London: Macmillan and St. Martin's Press.

Keynes, J.M. (1936). *The General Theory of Employment, Interest and Money*. London: Macmillan.

Keynes, J.M. (1939). Relative movements of real wages and output. *Economic Journal*, 49: 34–51.

Keynes, J.M. (1973). *The General Theory and After* (edited by D. Moggridge). Vols XIII and XIV of *The Collected Writings of John Maynard Keynes*. London: Macmillan and St. Martin's Press.

Klein, L.R. (1947a). Theories of effective demand and employment. *Journal of Political Economy*, 55: 108–31.

Klein, L.R. (1947b). *The Keynesian Revolution*. New York: Macmillan.

Krugman, P.R. (1979). Increasing returns, monopolistic competition, and international trade. *Journal of International Economics*, 9: 469–79.

Krugman, P.R. (1998). It's baaack: Japan's slump and the return of the liquidity trap. *Brookings Papers on Economic Activity*, 29: 137–206.

Lange, O. (1938). The rate of interest and the optimum propensity to consume. *Economica*, 5: 12–32.

Leijonhufvud, A. (1967). Keynes and the Keynesians: A suggested interpretation. *American Economic Review*, 57 (Papers and Proceedings): 401–10.

Leijonhufvud, A. (1968). *On Keynesian Economics and the Economics of Keynes: A Study in Monetary Theory*. New York: Oxford University Press.

Leijonhufvud, A. (1981). The Wicksell Connection: Variations on a Theme. In A. Leijonhufvud (Ed.), *Information and Coordination, Essays in Macroeconomic Theory* (pp. 131–202). New York: Oxford University Press.

Leijonhufvud, A. (1988). Did Keynes mean anything? Rejoinder to Yeager. *Cato Journal*, 8: 209–17.

Lucas, R.E. Jr. (1981). *Studies in Business Cycle Theory*. Cambridge, MA: The MIT Press.

Mankiw, N.G. and Romer, D. (Eds.) (1991). *New Keynesian Economics*. Vol. 1: *Imperfect Competition and Sticky Prices*. Vol. 2: *Coordination Failures and Real Rigidities*. Cambridge, MA: MIT Press.

Meade, J.E. (1937). A simplified model of Mr. Keynes' system. *Review of Economic Studies*, 4: 98–107.

Patinkin, D. (1948). Price flexibility and full employment. *American Economic Review*, 38: 543–64.

Patinkin, D. (1949). Involuntary unemployment and the Keynesian supply function. *Economic Journal*, 59: 360–83.

Reddaway, W.B. (1936). The general theory of employment, interest and money. *Economic Record*, 12: 28–36.

Rivot, S. (2011). Special remedies for special causes: Involuntary unemployment in Keynes' political writings. *Cambridge Journal of Economics*, 35: 785–803.

Rotemberg, J.J. (1982). Monopolistic price adjustment and aggregate output. *Review of Economic Studies*, 49: 517–31.

Rymes, T.K. (1989). *Keynes's Lectures, 1932-35: Notes of a Representative Student*. London: Macmillan.

Silvestre, J. (1993). The market-power foundations of macroeconomic policy. *Journal of Economic Literature*, 31: 105–41.

Spence, M. (1976). Product selection, fixed costs, and monopolistic competition. *Review of Economic Studies*, 43: 217–35.

Svensson, L.E.O. (1986). Sticky goods prices, flexible asset prices, monopolistic competition, and monetary policy. *Review of Economic Studies*, 53: 385–405.

Weitzman, M.L. (1985). The simple macroeconomics of profit sharing. *American Economic Review*, 75: 937–53.

Abstract

The paper suggests a *new Keynesian* model of the *General Theory*. A reduced form entails a diagram with three curves relating employment and the real wage, which represent the two fundamental classical postulates and the principle of effective demand. This diagram illustrates better than *IS–LM* the generality of Keynes's theory, clarifying the distinction between voluntary and involuntary unemployment. Other significant features are the role of the distribution of expected interest rates among heterogeneous agents, whether dispersed or concentrated, in shaping the *LM* curve, as well as the role of wage competitiveness constraints as a foundation of Keynes's relative wage hypothesis.

Three macroeconomic syntheses of vintage 1937: Hicks, Haberler, and Lundberg

Hans-Michael Trautwein

1. Introduction

Macroeconomics is probably the most quarrelsome subdiscipline of the dismal science. Its history is full of fundamental controversies about the character and causes of cyclical fluctuations, the relations between cycles and growth, the neutrality of money, and other issues of contention. At the bottom of these controversies are different views about the mechanisms that coordinate decentralised decisions about consumption and production over time, and about the importance of the flexibility of prices and wages. Since the mid-twentieth century the disputing factions have mostly been characterised as neoclassical (or New Classical) on the one hand, and Keynesian (with varying prefixes) on the other. Depending on which side is taken, the conclusions about the role of the state and the design and effectiveness of fiscal and monetary policies differ substantially, even though some of the positions have shifted over time.

Because of the quarrels, however, macroeconomics also shows recurrent tendencies towards synthetic theorising. In order to find ground for consensus much effort is invested in the search for a unified analytical framework, a general theory in which different outcomes of the interaction of private-sector agents and policy-makers in a market system can be derived from variations of the same base model. There are long phases that can be characterised by the emergence and dominance of such consensus views. The most prominent examples are the *Neoclassical Synthesis*, the ruling paradigm from the late 1940s until the 1970s, and the *New Neoclassical Synthesis*, which gained currency in the late 1990s and continues to hold sway. It has developed from New Keynesian attempts to integrate deviations of actual from potential output into the frameworks of real business cycle theory. The latter was originally an outgrowth from New Classical economics, which (following up on monetarism) had crushed the consensus on the old synthesis. The main advantage of the new over the old synthesis is seen in its microeconomic foundations in terms of dynamic stochastic general equilibrium (DSGE) modelling. Apart from starting with explicit specifications of preferences and technology, the DSGE models differ from the old synthesis by proceeding from the assumptions of rational expectations and continuous market clearing. The theoretical foundations and policy conclusions of the New Neoclassical Synthesis are most prominently spelt out in Woodford's (2003) *Interest & Prices*. There is no similarly representative book in the old Neoclassical Synthesis, which aimed at integrating Keynesian underemployment into neoclassical frameworks of general equilibrium analysis. The notion of such a synthesis was made popular by Samuelson in the 1951 and 1955 editions of his *Economics* textbook, but in passing rather than in systematic exposition (Pearce and Hoover 1995). Even though key contributions, such as those of Modigliani (1944) or Tobin (1956, 1958), can be easily identified, the contours of the old synthesis have hardly ever been clear. It has been described as a "historical compromise" (Snowdon and Vane 2005, p. 109), a textbook consensus rather than rigorous theory, and its "intellectual mushiness" was deplored (most articulately by Leijonhufvud 1968 and 1981, p. 179), even before it was dethroned. However, the origins of the Neoclassical Synthesis have never been in dispute. They are traced back to the invention of the IS-LM model in Hicks' (1937a) *Mr. Keynes and the "Classics"*.

Much has been written about the IS-LM model, its history, flaws, and strange persistence (De Vroey and Hoover 2004); Hicks himself was very critical of it later in life (Hicks 1980, Klamer 1989). This paper takes a look at the origins of IS-LM from a different angle, from a perspective that at first might look like a matter of sheer coincidence: Hicks' attempt at finding a synthetic framework for macroeconomic analysis was not the only exercise of its kind at the time. Two other works with similar ambitions were published in the same year. One is Haberler's *Prosperity and Depression*, the other is Lundberg's *Studies in the Theory of Economic Expansion*. While Hicks constructed his synthesis in order to "isolate Mr. Keynes' innovations, and so to discover what are the real issues in dispute" (1937a, p. 148), Haberler set himself the task of "analysing existing theories of the business cycle and deriving there from a synthetic account of the nature and possible causes of economic fluctuations" (1937, p. 1). Lundberg, in turn, was concerned "with the possibility of formulating a dynamic theory or the analysis of the total development in a closed economy", from which model sequences could be "selected with a view to elucidating the concepts and methods adopted in current theories, as well as scrutinising their conclusions regarding the 'crisis' of the development" (1937, 1 and V).

As will be shown in this paper, these three syntheses of vintage 1937 differ in their scope, form, and contents. They have nevertheless much in common, and they played complementary roles in the further development of macroeconomics. All of them can be read as reactions to the challenge posed by Keynes' *General Theory of Employment, Interest and Money* (1936).[1] The syntheses of Hicks and Haberler were complementary in the sense that IS-LM became the canonical textbook model in macroeconomics, while Haberler's *Prosperity and Depression* figured as the canonical text in courses on business cycle theory. Some of Lundberg's analytical tools, such as the multiplier-accelerator model, the Lundberg-lag, and the concept of inflation gaps were used to underpin further work in the mainstream of Neoclassical Keynesianism.

What makes a comparison of the three syntheses of 1937 vintage particularly interesting is their apparent contrast with the old and new Neoclassical Syntheses concerning the causes that let market systems fail to preserve, or return to, the optimal steady state. The Neoclassical Syntheses stress nominal rigidities as the general cause. In the New Neoclassical Synthesis, frictions in the adjustment of prices to shocks are explicit in the DSGE core model in which intertemporal optimisation interacts with price-setting in monopolistic competition and the interest-rate targeting of the central bank (Woodford 2003, Part I). Market structures were less explicit in the old synthesis, but after Modigliani (1944) macroeconomics had largely settled on the consensus that liquidity traps and investment traps have no solid theoretical foundations, leaving nominal wage rigidities as the sole explanation of underemployment. The "historical compromise" was to argue à la Samuelson that neoclassical theory is correct, in principle, about the stability of full-employment equilibrium, but that real balance effects are too slow to ignore the capacities of Keynesian stabilisation policies to achieve Pareto superior results.

While frictions in goods and labour markets are considered to be indispensable for integrating Keynesian ideas into the two Neoclassical

---

[1] In the case of Haberler it might be argued that this is true only for the revised and enlarged edition of 1939 of *Prosperity and Depression*, where much space was dedicated to the discussion of Keynes' *General Theory* – in contrast with the 1937 edition, where it played a minor role. However, Haberler had published a detailed critique of Keynes' multiplier concept in 1936, and the group of experts whom Haberler had invited in Summer 1936 to comment on his "synthetic exposition" prior to its publication, had debated the integration of Keynes' *General Theory*; cf. Haberler (1936), Boianovsky and Trautwein (2006b) and Section 3 below.

Syntheses that have dominated the field since the mid-twentieth century, the quarrels that induced the synthesising activities of 1937 vintage were played out in a different arena. Most of them took place on the premises of incomplete information and imperfect intertemporal coordination. In his *General Theory*, Keynes (1936, Chapter 19) argued that a downward flexibility of money wages might aggravate the effective demand failures that lead to persistent underemployment; nominal wage rigidity would help to stabilise the price level *and* employment rather than cause unemployment. Keynes stressed investment uncertainty as the basic cause of macroeconomic instability and severed the links between investment and saving with his liquidity preference theory of interest. Most of his contemporaries, and most prominently those with a "Wicksell connection" (Leijonhufvud 1981), focused on investment–saving (IS) imbalances that were caused either by failures of the interest-rate mechanism to achieve intertemporal coordination or by real rigidities in the propagation of impulses from changes in technology, preferences, or other "external factors". It should be noted that in Wicksellian approaches too, wage and price flexibility was seen as a critical factor that contributed to IS imbalances.[2] There was a great variety of views, but it was definitely not in the arena of wage and price stickiness where synthesisers in the 1930s would look for common ground. They set their focus on incomplete information about the equilibrium rate of interest and the feasibility of long-term investment. Consequentially, IS imbalances were a general theme in the syntheses of Hicks, Haberler, and Lundberg under review here.

The question is then why and how that shift of focus from imperfect intertemporal coordination to imperfect wage or price flexibility took place. A push factor has been identified in Keynes' "bootstrap theory" of interest which cuts off the links to IS imbalances by making saving a purely passive variable and investment dependent upon a vaguely defined speculative demand for money (Leijonhufvud 1981). A pull factor could be seen in the transition from Marshallian, Wicksellian, and Fisherian modes of

---

[2] This was particularly obvious in Lindahl (1930) and Hayek (1931); cf. Hagemann and Trautwein (1998) and Boianovsky and Trautwein (2006a). In contrast with the New Neoclassical Synthesis, which proceeds from the assumption of rational expectations, Wicksell and his followers in the Stockholm School regarded the formation of forward-looking expectations as endogenous to cumulative changes in the price level. In their view, forward-looking expectations (for which Lundberg [1930] 1994, p. 34 actually used the term "rational expectations") resulted from coordination failures of the intertemporal price-mechanism and had the potential to aggravate the latter; see also Tamborini et al. (in press).

thinking to Walrasian modes, in which deviations from Pareto-optimal general equilibrium are conceivable only in terms of frictions, of which nominal rigidities appear to be easiest to handle (e.g. Blanchard 2000).[3] A thorough assessment of the push and pull factors requires a longitudinal study that is beyond the scope of this paper. It is confined to a cross-sectional study with the vantage point of 1937, exploring what Hicks, Haberler, and Lundberg at that time may or may not have contributed to the shift of focus.[4]

A related question is what may have been lost out of sight by that shift of focus. This too is an issue much big for this paper. Here it will be dealt with in regard to the three syntheses only.[5] The remainder of the paper is structured as follows: Sections 2, 3 and 4 outline the relevant contexts and contents of the three syntheses, starting with Hicks and ending with Lundberg (on a scale of increasing complexity). Section 5 compares the approaches of Hicks, Haberler, and Lundberg in terms of their content, methods, and impact. Section 6 concludes with an assessment of the perspectives that the three syntheses offered in contrast to subsequent developments in macroeconomics.

2. Hicks on *Mr. Keynes and the "Classics"*

2.1. Context

When the *General Theory* was published in January 1936, its author Keynes was also the editor of the *Economic Journal.* Half a century later, John Hicks (1904–1989) remembered in an interview:

---

[3] De Vroey (2004) places the New Neoclassical Synthesis in the Marshallian camp, while he has the underlying RBC framework in the Walrasian camp; the reason for this split is "imperfect competition". It should be noted, though, that monopolistic competition is introduced in the standard models of the new synthesis as a purely formal tool for including nominal rigidities. Unlike the literature in the spirit of Marshall, it is not embedded in explicit analysis of market structures and trade technology.

[4] Therefore, the later works of the three writers are not (or not systematically) considered here. This is particularly relevant in the case of Hicks, whose recourse to comparative statics in *Mr.Keynes and the Classics* appears to stand in stark contrast with his emphasis on the use of dynamic methods in *Value and Capital* (1939) and many later writings. In the present paper, Hicks' reflections on macroeconomic dynamics are considered only to the extent that they were relevant for the making of IS-LM.

[5] For discussions of what was lost with the old Neoclassical Synthesis see, e.g. Leijonhufvud (1981) and Backhouse and Laidler (2004). For detailed checks of what is lost with the New Neoclassical Synthesis see, e.g., Tamborini et al. (in press) and Trautwein and Zouache (2009).

I was to my great surprise invited to review the book for the *Economic Journal*. That was one of the greatest honors I have received.

Greater than the Nobel Prize?

Yes, I think so. I once had a talk with Austin Robinson [the assistant editor in 1936]... He said that they picked me because they thought I was not a member of their gang but could be relied upon to take the book seriously. (Hicks in Klamer 1989, p. 176)

In his review Hicks (1936) was rather critical of Keynes' "conservative method" (that of Marshall), but praised Keynes' ingenious application of that method to the explanation of unemployment. The review was published in June 1936 and about the same time Hicks began to scrutinise the *General Theory* again, now preparing a presentation for the Oxford meeting of the Econometric Society in September 1936. This came to be the paper on *Mr. Keynes and the "Classics"*, published in *Econometrica* in April 1937.

Hicks' interpretation of the *General Theory* was not the only one circulating at the time. Champernowne and Reddaway had written articles about it, and Harrod and Meade presented papers at the same Oxford session. All of them described Keynes' theory in systems of simultaneous equations and Hicks had seen these papers in advance. This may have influenced his choice of equations and notation (Young 1987). There is no doubt, however, that Hicks was particularly well qualified for assessing the innovations in the *General Theory* by contrasting it with the "orthodoxy" that Keynes described as "Classical economics". Hicks had acquainted himself with the major approaches to neoclassical economics to a much greater degree than most other British economists at the time (Hicks 1977). As a student in Oxford and lecturer at the London School of Economics (LSE) he had studied and taught general equilibrium theory on the base of Walras, Pareto, and Wicksell. At the LSE he was exposed to the Austrian views of Hayek and Robbins. He had published about Edgeworth and Marshall at an early stage and had taken a position as a lecturer in Cambridge, where the neoclassical tradition was Marshallian. At the time of writing *Mr. Keynes and the "Classics"*, Hicks was working on his *Value and Capital* (1939), a book that in its static parts (I and II) is based on Pareto and Marshall,[6]

---

[6] As one referee has pointed out, Part I of *Value and Capital* was published in French language around that time; see Hicks (1937b).

while the dynamic parts (III and IV) are strongly inspired by the Wicksellian approaches of Lindahl and Myrdal (Hicks 1991).[7]

2.2. Content

Whatever the Walrasian and Austrian influences on other writings of Hicks, the *"Classics"* in Hicks' 1937 paper are all Marshallian in the first three sections, while the synthesis takes a Wicksellian turn in the last section. In the first section Hicks (1937a, pp. 147–8) points out that the *"Classics"*, from which Keynes thought to have made a breakaway with his *General Theory*, are a strawman of Keynes' making – a caricature whose features do not correspond to the theories of Pigou (Keynes' adversary in the *General Theory*) or any "ordinary classical economist". In order "to isolate Mr. Keynes' innovations", Hicks deems it "worthwhile to try to construct a typical 'classical' theory, built on an earlier and cruder model than Professor Pigou's". In modern textbook notation (not identical with Hicks' lettering), the "crude model" of Section I is given by the following system of simultaneous equations:

$$M = kY \tag{1.1}$$

$$I = I(i) \tag{1.2}$$

$$I = S(i, Y), \tag{1.3}$$

where Equation (1.1) is the quantity-theoretical Cambridge equation, related to nominal income, Y. Equation (1.2) is "what becomes the marginal efficiency of capital schedule in Mr. Keynes' work", with investment, I, in monetary values. Equation (1.3) is the condition for capital market equilibrium, with S for nominal saving. Due to the cash-balance effect, this model implies that an increase in the money supply tends to raise employment, as long as money wages remain constant. A rise in money wages will, *ceteris paribus*, "necessarily diminish employment". Hicks (1937a, p. 150)

---

[7] Leijonhufvud (1994, p. 145) aptly characterizes Hicks' inclination to synthesize as follows: "Far from indoctrinated in a particular analytical tradition, he had the inestimable benefit of not having been trained in economics at all... When it came to learning economic theory, he set about it as a task of creating a personal synthesis, making up his own mind through wide and eclectic reading about what were the best elements, how they might be improved, and how fit together. The personal synthesis of economic theory that he was building had far more of Lausanne, Chicago, Vienna and Stockholm than of Cambridge in it."

points out that it follows from this theory, which he locates somewhere between Ricardo and the early Marshall, "that you may be able to increase employment by direct inflation; but whether or not you decide to favour that policy still depends upon your judgment about the probable reaction on wages, and... about the international standard".

In Section II Hicks makes critical qualifications of the crude classical model, with reference to works of Marshall, Pigou, and Lavington in the early 1920s. He posits that the money supply (M) is not exogenous, that the cash-holding coefficient (k) is not constant, but related to the state of confidence which is determined by other variables in the system, and that holding money is a sacrifice of interest for convenience and security. "The demand for money depends upon the rate of interest! The stage is set for Mr. Keynes" (p. 151). The equations change to

$$M = L(i) \tag{2.1}$$

$$I = I(i) \tag{1.2}$$

$$I = S(Y), \tag{2.3}$$

where money demand (in Equation (2.1)) is now a function of liquidity preference, and saving (in Equation (2.3)) is determined by income only.

> Although it means that the third equation becomes the multiplier equation, ... this second amendment is a mere simplification, and ultimately insignificant. It is the liquidity preference doctrine which is vital. For it is now the rate of interest, not income, which is determined by the quantity of money. (p. 152)

As Keynes includes the transactions motive to the demand for money, the system changes to

$$M = L(Y, i) \tag{3.1}$$

$$I = I(i) \tag{1.2}$$

$$I = S(Y), \tag{2.3}$$

and Keynes' *General Theory* "becomes hard to distinguish from ... Marshallian orthodoxy" (p. 153).

At this point Hicks (1937a, p. 153) introduces the famous IS-LM diagram (in his notation: IS-LL) to demonstrate that Keynes' first innovation is a theory that recognises a higher degree of interdependence in the determination of income and interest. The second innovation is the liquidity trap, discussed in Section III. With the aid of another diagram, Hicks shows that Keynes' LM curve has a strong curvature, with a horizontal part to the left that indicates a lower bound for the (real) interest rate at a significant range of low levels of income:

> [I]t is this doldrum to the left of the diagram which upsets the classical theory. If IS lies to the right, then we can indeed increase employment by increasing the quantity of money; but if IS lies to the left, we cannot do so; merely monetary means will not force down the interest rate any further. So the General Theory of Employment is the Economics of Depression. (p. 155)

So far, Hicks' IS-LM synthesis is well known. Section IV is less known, even though Hicks here goes beyond Keynes by sketching what he calls a "Generalized General Theory" (156). This is achieved by giving the "little apparatus ... a little run on its own". The system changes to

$$M = L(Y, i) \tag{3.1}$$
$$I = C(Y, i) \tag{4.2}$$
$$I = S(Y, i), \tag{4.3}$$

where an accelerator effect is integrated in Equation (4.2), and the IS equation in Equation (4.3) is no longer an *ex post* identity, but displays a loanable-funds equilibrium where the slopes of the investment and saving schedules (*C* and *S*) are related to the rate of interest, while income-related multiplier effects shift the schedules (p. 157; see Figure 1).

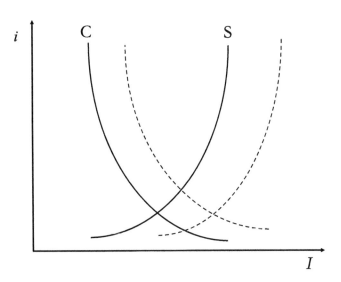

Figure 1 Hicks' generalised IS relation

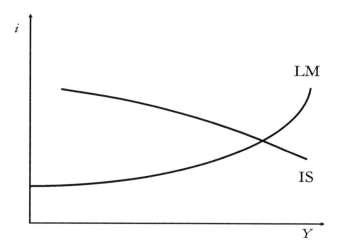

Figure 2 Hicks' Wicksellian IS-LM model

"When generalized in this way, Mr. Keynes' theory begins to look very like Wicksell's" (p. 158), especially if the money supply is elastic in the sense that bank lending increases the volume of money rather than letting the money rate of interest rise. This is also demonstrated by a second IS-LM diagram (p. 157; see Figure 2) where the two curves are flatter than in the first, such that IS intersects with LM much farther to the right.

It should be noted that Hicks' famous IS-LM paper ends with a number of caveats. It is evident that he, in 1937, did not at all expect the intermediate version Equations ((3.1), (1.2), and (2.3)) of his "little apparatus" to become the workhorse model of future macroeconomics. He considered this "skeleton apparatus ... a terribly rough and ready sort of affair".

> In particular, the concept of 'Income' is worked monstrously hard; most of our curves are not really determinate unless something is said about the distribution of Income as well as its magnitude. Indeed, what they express is something like a relation between the price-system and the system of interest rates; and you cannot get that into a curve. Further, all sorts of questions about depreciation have been neglected; and all sorts of questions about the timing of the processes under consideration. The *General Theory of Employment* is a useful book; but it is neither the beginning nor the end of Dynamic Economics. (pp. 158–9)

While Hicks' synthesis worked on the comparative statics of Keynes' and the *"Classics"*, the syntheses of Haberler and Lundberg were more concerned with macroeconomic dynamics.

3. Haberler on *Prosperity and Depression*

3.1. Context

Similar to Hicks, Gottfried Haberler (1900–1995) had a solid background of experiences with different academic environments and approaches to economic theorising.[8] Between 1919 and 1927, he had studied at the University of Vienna and achieved lecturer status with a habilitation thesis on index numbers and aggregation problems. Between 1927 and 1932, he spent several years as Rockefeller fellow and visiting professor at Harvard University. During his time in Vienna, Haberler was a member of Mises' famous private seminar and a close colleague of Hayek, but came to side with the falsificationism of the philosophers Kaufmann and Popper as opposed to the *apriorism* of Mises and Hayek (Boianovsky 2000). His empirical orientation was reinforced by work and studies at Harvard and at the Economic Intelligence Service of the League of Nations in Geneva.

In March 1934, roughly four years after the outbreak of the Great Depression, Haberler started to work at the League on an inquiry into the causes of the recurrence of periods of economic depression. The study, which three years later came out as the League of Nations report on *Prosperity and Depression,* was financed by a grant from the Rockefeller Foundation with the objective of constructing a testable consensus theory. Its first part was a "Systematic Analysis of the Theories of the Business Cycle", based on a survey for which Haberler corresponded with about 60 economists, among them nearly all prominent names in business cycle research at the time. In a letter to Haberler on 31 October 1934 Keynes criticised Haberler's plan of distilling a synthesis from a wide variety of views on the depression:

> My essential point is that the method you have adopted forces you to a high degree of superficiality ... I cannot believe that the solution can be reached by bringing together ... excerpts from the views of a large number of writers, each differing from the other more or less in fundamentals. The answer must lie somewhere much deeper down, yet your method tempts you to skating rather than digging.
>
> (Keynes, quoted after Boianovsky and Trautwein 2006b, p. 50)

By Spring 1936 Haberler had nevertheless managed to draft the second part, a "Synthetic Exposition Relating to the Nature and Causes of Business Cycles". He circulated the draft and discussed it intensively in a

---

[8] This section draws on the detailed account of the genesis of Haberler's *Prosperity and Depression* in Boianovsky and Trautwein (2006b).

conference with a "committee of experts", among them J.M. Clark, A. Hansen, Morgenstern, Ohlin, Rist, Robbins, Robertson, and Tinbergen.[9] After completing the manuscript of the report in September 1936, Haberler left for Harvard, where he came to stay until the end of his academic career in 1971.

3.2. Content

Haberler's survey in the first part of *Prosperity and Depression* (1937) classified the theories of the business cycle in six groups as follows:

(i)   The purely monetary theory (Hawtrey)
(ii) Overinvestment theories
   (A) Monetary (Hayek, Mises, Robbins, and other "Neo-Wicksellians").
   (B) Non-monetary (Wicksell, Cassel, Spiethoff, Robertson, partly also Pigou, and Schumpeter).
   (C) The Acceleration Principle (Aftalion, Clark, Mitchell, and Harrod).
(iii) Changes in costs, horizontal maladjustments, and overindebtedness (Beveridge, Fisher, Mitchell, and Pigou)
(iv) Under-consumption theories (Hobson and Lederer)
(v)   "Psychological theories" (Keynes, Lavington, and Pigou)
(vi) Harvest theories (Jevons and Moore)

In the first edition of *Prosperity and Depression* the emphasis was on the assessment of overinvestment theories, which occupied nearly half the space of the survey (76 out of 153 pages). Keynes' *General Theory* was systematically reviewed only in the second edition (1939, Chapter 8), but then in a separate chapter of 86 pages. Many of the key points of that review had nevertheless been discussed already at the above-mentioned 1936 conference (Boianovsky and Trautwein 2006b). However, Haberler's "Synthetic Exposition" in the 1937 edition was in most parts a synthesis of overinvestment theories, and it remained that even in subsequent editions, despite some qualifications with regard to Keynesian ideas.

The "Synthetic Exposition" starts with a chapter on the definition and measurement of the business cycle (1937, Chapter 9), where Haberler stresses four stylised facts whose explanation should define the common ground for a consensus view. The first of these "basic facts" is the

---

[9] For a summary and discussion of the verbatim records of that conference, which took place from 29 June to 2 July 1936, see Boianovsky and Trautwein (2006b, pp. 62–73).

subdivision of the business cycle into the four phases: *upswing – downturn – downswing – upturn*. With reference to their usage in the literature, Haberler also takes recourse to two other sets of synonyms for these phases: *expansion – upper turning point – contraction – lower turning point*, and *prosperity – crisis – depression – revival*.

The second fact is that "each cycle is an historical individual", but "a general theory is possible" ([1937] 1964, p. 275). This general theory is to be based on "two regular features of the cycle", the two remaining stylised facts. One is the "parallelism of production and monetary demand" in the sense of procyclical movements of the price level. The other is constituted by "specially wide fluctuations in producers' goods", i.e. an accelerator effect of a change in the production of consumer goods on investment (pp. 277–82).

In the following chapter, Haberler discusses "The Process of Expansion and Contraction". Upswings and downswings are described as cumulative, self-reinforcing processes: "If there is anything like common ground in modern business cycle theory, we are likely to find it here" (p. 283). Haberler argues that processes of economic expansion normally start from positions with unemployed resources and underutilised capacity, rejecting Hayek's categorical imperative that every analysis of business cycles must start from full-employment equilibrium (p. 284, footnote 1). The parallel expansion and contraction of production and demand is explained in terms of loanable-funds theory. In the first edition, this is elaborated in verbal terms (pp. 289–339); in the second edition (1939), the argument is supported by the introduction of a diagram developed by Abba Lerner. The diagram looks similar to Hicks' "generalized IS relation" (see Figure 1), but adds hoarding and bank lending (hence also monetary policy) to the explanation of shifts in the investment and saving schedules ([1939] 1964, pp. 183–191). The surrounding discussion is based on the famous "Stockholm School" critique of Keynes' *General Theory* in Ohlin (1937). Even though it supports Haberler's own synthesis, it is not embedded in the corresponding Chapter 10, but included in the survey department of *Prosperity and Depression*, as part of the newly added Chapter 8 on "Recent Discussions on the Trade Cycle".

For the explanation of the cumulative character of the expansions and contractions, Haberler (1937) does not employ the Keynesian concept of the multiplier. In a critical review of the *General Theory* (originally submitted to the *Economic Journal*, where Keynes was the editor, but then published in the Austrian *Zeitschrift für Nationalökonomie*), Haberler (1936) had sharply criticised Keynes' concept of the multiplier. In Chapter 8 of

Prosperity and Depression, Haberler ([1939] 1964, p. 193, n. 2) likewise argues that Keynes' multiplier is based on a tautological definition of saving:

> It is misleading to say that income must change, in order to ensure the equality of S and I. Whatever the level of income may be, S and I must be equal, because they are made so by definition. The change of level of income comes in as a condition only because Mr. Keynes takes the 'multiplier' – 'the marginal propensity to consume'... – as a constant quantity... If we assume (expect) something about the magnitude of the multiplier, we implicitly assume (expect) something about the change in income subsequent to a change... in investment. Income must change... because we have assumed it by assuming the multiplier.

As Haberler ([1939] 1964, pp. 249–50) points out one of the underlying problems with Keynes' theory is its "essentially static" character. A "multiplier relationship" would actually be acceptable to Haberler as an element of business cycle theory, but only if it is "formulated dynamically, by allowing a time-lag between investment and the resulting increase in consumption demand".

Instead of looking for such a multiplier relationship, Haberler stresses in his synthesis the importance of "the acceleration principle", according to which "investment is explained by a previous change in the demand for the product" ([1937] 1964, p. 250), as the explanation for the cumulative character of upswings and downswings. To increase output, it is necessary to make "heavy investments ... in fixed capital, the fruits of which investments mature only in the more or less distant future" ([1937] 1964, p. 95). The volume of investment is determined by "changes in demand for the finished product ... What matters is, strictly speaking, anticipated demand ... But actual demand is certainly one of the most powerful factors in shaping the expectations of business-men as to future demand" (p. 306).

While Chapter 10 deals with expansion and contraction, Chapter 11 contains synthetic propositions about the turning points, i.e. crisis and revival. A dividing line between business cycle theories is often drawn with regard to the endogeneity or exogeneity of the causes behind the disruptions of an upswing. Haberler does not consider the influence of exogenous and endogenous forces as mutually exclusive. He emphasises the interaction of "organic counterforces" and "accidental disturbances" (pp. 346–7). A crisis can thus be explained by maladjustments in the expansion process that lead to inelasticities in the supply of means of production or in the money supply. These bottlenecks create first inflation and then make the system increasingly vulnerable to deflationary shocks (pp. 355–77). A revival, in turn, can be explained by the emergence of idle capacities in the course of the depression. The concomitant increase in the elasticities of the goods and loan supplies makes the system more sensitive to stimulating influences, including those of stabilisation policies that aim at reducing unemployment by way of public works (pp. 377–405). Haberler ([1937] 1964, p. 378) points out that there is consensus on a fundamental asymmetry in the effectiveness of monetary policy:

> An expansion can always be stopped and a contraction process started by a restriction of credit by the banks. A contraction, however, cannot always be ended promptly merely by making credit cheap and plentiful... [T]he demand for investible funds may be at so low an ebb that there is no rate (short of a negative figure) which will lead to a revival of investment.

It is in this context that Haberler discusses a real balance effect later to be known as Pigou effect.[10] Discussing whether there are "natural forces" of readjustment to full-employment equilibrium, Haberler turns to "one very important type of adjustment which under a competitive price system would appear to be the natural cure for unemployment – namely, the reduction of money wages" (p. 395). Haberler argues that a positive net effect of wage reductions on employment is less likely to be achieved through the factor cost channel, since wage cuts tend to lower consumer demand and the price level. It would rather be induced by the concomitant increases in the real value of money hoards and the systemic level of liquidity (pp. 403–4).[11] He concedes that a wage cut therapy of unemployment may be considered as a "logical conclusion", but warns that even the indirect channel of dishoarding is uncertain and that wage cuts may therefore not be politically advisable.

In the final section of Chapter 11, Haberler makes an interesting distinction between small open economies and economies that are sufficiently big to have "a free hand" as to their monetary policies. Small open economies tend to come under greater pressure to cut wages, but might have to devalue their currencies in order to avoid an intensification of the contraction. Big economies could eliminate the contractive effects of wage cuts by combining "a policy of wage reduction with expansionary measures such as public works financed by inflationary methods. The effect will be to forestall any decrease in total wage disbursements, and consequently in the

---

[10] This is another example of Stigler's law of eponymy, according to which no scientific discovery is named after its original discoverer. Pigou's (1943) critique of Keynes' proposition about the stability of underemployment came out six years after Haberler's *Prosperity and Depression*.

[11] He actually adds that "[i]n Keynesian terminology, less money is needed to satisfy the transactions motive and more becomes available for 'speculative holding'" (p. 403, n. 2).

demand for consumers' goods, which might otherwise result from the wage reduction" (p. 405). With these passages Haberler makes clear that the consensus view at the time of Keynes' *General Theory* was not as negative towards fiscal demand management and accommodating monetary policies as propagators and adversaries of the "Keynesian revolution" would make later generations believe (cf. Laidler 1999).

4. Lundberg's *Studies in the Theory of Economic Expansion*

4.1. Context

If Hicks and Haberler can be regarded as open minds with an unusually broad background in economics, the same holds true for Erik Lundberg (1907–1987). Cassel, Lindahl, and Myrdal were his teachers at Stockholm University. Even though Lundberg is frequently considered as a (younger) member of the Stockholm School, he was an independent thinker. In his master thesis on the concept of economic equilibrium, which was published as an article in *Ekonomisk Tidskrift* (the predecessor of the *Scandinavian Journal of Economics*), Lundberg ([1930] 1994, pp. 32–36) criticised his masters Lindahl and Myrdal for using methods of including expectations into the determination of general equilibrium that are unsuitable for dynamic analysis. In this context he was one of the first to use the notion of "rational expectations" (Trautwein in press). Like Haberler, Lundberg received a Rockefeller fellowship for studies in the United States and stayed there for two years from 1931 to 1933. Unlike Haberler, he did not stay at Harvard only, but visited a large number of departments and research institutes, among them the Universities of Chicago and Minnesota, Columbia University, the National Bureau of Economic Research, the Brookings Institution, and the Federal Reserve Bank of New York (Lundberg 1994). He met most of the prominent American economists and profited from exchanges on empirical research with Mitchell, Hansen and Kuznets. After his return from the United States, Lundberg gained practical experience in the positions of a secretary at *Riksbanken,* the Swedish central bank, and adviser to the central bank of Iceland.

When Keynes lectured at the Political Economy Club in Stockholm in October 1936, the event that gave rise to the "Stockholm School" article of Ohlin (1937), Lundberg was one of the most outspoken critics of Keynes. His main point of criticism was Keynes' use of the comparative static method for the analysis for genuinely dynamic phenomena. In many aspects, however, Lundberg was a great admirer of Keynes (and remained so throughout his life). This is also evident from his doctoral dissertation, *Studies in the Theory of Economic Expansion,* which he defended in January 1937, shortly before he became the head of *Konjunkturinstitutet,* the newly founded Business Cycle Research Institute of Sweden.

4.2. Content

In the foreword to his *Studies,* Lundberg (1937) writes that the objective of his thesis is "to investigate the conditions of a determinate sequence in time of economic changes", applying "the methods developed by Wicksell and his followers to the system of explanation formulated by Keynes". More specifically, Lundberg studies a process of macroeconomic expansion, induced by an increase in effective demand, in which cumulative effects of growth may disrupt the dynamic equilibrium. For this, he employs his own method of disequilibrium analysis to demonstrate how investment–saving imbalances generate instability of the full-employment equilibrium. He develops a variety of model sequences that capture the theories of Keynes, Hayek, and others as extensions from an identical analytical base. Lundberg makes "no claim thereby to having made a complete, or even an 'unbiased' selection amongst the numerous theories of money and business cycles". His interest is rather to use different theories as "illustrations of the need of greater precision in the concepts" and to achieve "a more adequate selection of variables and relations". This is the synthetic aspect of Lundberg's sequence analysis.

In Chapters I–IV of the *Studies,* Lundberg reviews the concepts of monetary equilibrium and disequilibrium sequences in the works of Wicksell, Robertson, Hayek, Keynes, and others. He raises three main objections to Keynes' *General Theory* (Lundberg 1937, pp. 32–45). The first is that Keynes, by adhering to comparative statics, does not show "how and why" the system would move to an underemployment equilibrium. The second point is that, by assuming a constant income multiplier of (autonomous) investment, Keynes dodges the issue of explaining the observable cyclical changes in the relative output of consumer goods and investment goods: "[T]he required theory must explain both the size of investments *and* the consumption expenditures as independent variables; the latter cannot be derived from the former, as in Keynes' system" (pp. 37–38). Lundberg's third objection relates to the fact that the number of equations in Keynes' system is one less than the unknowns. Referring to Keynes' three "psychological reaction functions" – the income-related consumption function, liquidity preference and the marginal efficiency of capital – Lundberg (1937, pp. 33–34) points out that the "ultimate assumption always is that the total quantity of money is given". He finds this closure of the model inadequate, in particular with regard to the objective of demonstrating that the system can land in a liquidity trap that causes underemployment. Lundberg shows that in this case the interest rate must be exogenous, independent of the total stock of money. It is only in this case that Keynes' system yields a determinate equilibrium:

> The most serious criticism of the equilibrium system is not directed against its indefiniteness in the general case, however, but against the choice of simultaneously variable factors... During an "adaptation" process of an arbitrary type, where income, savings, etc. undergo certain changes, the curve for the marginal efficiency of capital must also be assumed to shift and, consequently, the investment volume as well. The quantity of capital and money as well as the interest rate cannot be considered as given data any longer. (pp. 43–44)

The successive determination of these variables needs to be captured by sequence analysis. In Chapters V–VIII of the *Studies*, Lundberg develops the conceptual tools for such a method, the "fundamental dynamic relations":

> First of all, regard is paid to the fact that production takes time... The costs of producing consumption goods sold during a certain period will have been paid during preceding periods. [These] costs paid out as income... are not necessarily used for the purchase of those same goods. (p. 52)

The first step is thus to analyse the purchasing power of firms (in terms of the ratio of sales over costs) as an outcome of the variable relationship between *production periods* and *expenditure periods*. The next step is the determination of the time it takes for output to react to unexpected increases in aggregate demand; this lag defines the (variable) *unit period*, which has found its way into standard multiplier analysis as "Lundberg lag" (but there inadequately kept constant). Changes in the time intervals of production, expenditure, and unit periods create unexpected gains and losses for firms, which tend to bring investment and saving out of balance. Such changes and their consequences are discussed with the aid of sophisticated calculations and diagrams (especially in Chapters IV and VII), and with respect to the velocity of circulation of money (Chapter V), the nature of saving (Chapter VI), and the determinants of investment (Chapter VIII).

The core part of Lundberg's *Studies* is Chapter IX on "The Construction of Model Sequences". Its point of departure is defined in the opening sentences of section 2:

> The subject of our analysis is an economic system during a period of expansion ... Production, consumption, income, savings, and investments are all increasing at

certain rates, and we ask whether this growth can continue in some sort of dynamic equilibrium, or whether discrepancies must automatically come into being within the system itself, which have the tendency to interrupt the process. The conditions for continued growth may not be reconcilable to the cumulative effects of the expansion during previous periods... Cassel's simple assumption of a [uniformly progressive economy] is hence viewed as a problem to be investigated. (p. 183)

Lundberg formalises Cassel's conditions for steady-state growth in two separate footnotes[12] which anticipate the core of the Harrod and Domar growth models (Berg 1991, pp. 220–22). In the main text he formulates the conditions as follows:

> The amount of new investments must be sufficiently large to balance the amount of savings forthcoming at that level of employment and income, which ensures full utilization of the new capital at remunerative... prices. To preserve this full utilization of capital, the new investments in each period must amount to a fixed proportion of the capital at the beginning of the period. (p. 185)

These conditions provide the benchmarks for the analysis of effects of the expansion that tend to disrupt the dynamic equilibrium. Possible causes are "undersaving" à la Hayek, "underinvestment" (static Keynes), "overcapacity" (Keynes dynamised), or "underconsumption" in the spirit of Lederer (1931).[13] Lundberg embeds the consistency check of these theories in a series of model sequences that are ordered by the increasing complexity of the reaction patterns, following from a step-by-step endogenisation of investment and interest rates. In some cases he employs systems of first- and second-order difference equations, but does not always solve them, and he uses numerical examples in a way similar to modern simulation techniques (Berg 1991, Baumol 1991).

Lundberg (1937, Chapter IX) describes five types of model sequences, classifying them by the impulses that increase the growth rate of aggregate output:

---

[12] "Indicating total income with E, savings with S, investments with I, and total capital with K, the assumed conditions can be expressed as follows: $S = \Lambda E(t)$; $I = S$; $K_t = K_0 + \int I(t)\,dt$; $K = \mu E$, where Λ is the proportion of income saved, μ is the fixed relation between capital and income, and t is the time. From these equations we get the condition $\mu \cdot E(t) = K_0 + \Lambda \int E(t)\,dt$ and, after derivation, $\mu \cdot E(t) = \Lambda E(t)$ [because] $E(t) = c \cdot e^{(\Lambda/\mu)\,t}$" (Lundberg 1937, p. 185, n. 1). Footnote 1 on p. 240 further clarifies the relationship between new investments and the initial capital stock.

[13] The title of Lederer (1938) might suggest that it is the English translation of the 1931 monograph; however, as one of the referees has correctly pointed out, it is quite a different book, in which the Marxian argument of underconsumption is much less prominent.

(I) Expansion of the production of consumption goods at a constant volume of investments
(II) Expansion determined by investments in working capital
(III) Expansion determined by investments in fixed capital
(IV) The influence of a variable rate of interest
(V) Expansion determined by a "rationalisation process"

Each of these types of sequences can be subdivided into numerous scenarios by varying basic assumptions. The number of sequences could thus be doubled to 10 by assuming, (a) an elastic supply of goods (inventories) at constant prices and (b) an inelastic supply (no inventories) at flexible prices. This exercise is carried out explicitly only for the sequences of type I, where I(a) yields the equivalent of the standard Keynesian investment multiplier, tending towards a stable equilibrium (p. 188–96), whereas I(b) opens a Wicksellian inflation gap, with an indefinite process of changes in the price level (p. 196–7). In sequences of type II, investments in inventories are brought into the picture. The sequence shows an inventory cycle, and "here we have traced the first example of a formalised combined multiplier-accelerator principle" (Berg 1991, p. 212). In the sequences of type III, the "principle" is applied to fixed capital, exemplified by residential houses (pp. 204–16). In his explanation of housing booms and busts, Lundberg points out that the stability properties of the system depend on the mathematical properties of the solution of the difference equation for changes in producers' receipts: "Certain areas can be found, where the conditions give rise to exponential movements and others, where cyclical oscillations occur" (p. 215, n. 1). In sequences of type IV, the focus is set on the influence of variations in nominal interest rates, both exogenously and endogenously determined. Lundberg develops Wicksellian scenarios of cumulative changes in prices and costs, generated by gaps between "real interest rates" (expected rates of return on capital) and "nominal rates" (banks' lending rates), which may be reversed in the course of an expansion. The sequences include a Hayekian scenario of an investment boom and reversal towards a more direct production of consumption goods, where savings play an active role (216–34). In the last section of Chapter IX (pp. 235–42), Lundberg explores sequences of type V, in which entrepreneurs use their profits for reinvestments in new machinery. The rationalisation process makes the increases in total wages fall behind the growth of total output. The ensuing surplus profits are reinvested again, but – as demand for consumption goods is redirected towards capital goods – the crucial question is now the size of the "necessary increase of investments in industry to preserve full use of capacity" (p. 239).[14]

In the final chapter, Lundberg sums up and argues on a synthetic note that the wide range of model sequences which can be constructed from fairly general concepts "may be conceived to elucidate the possible applicability of such opposite theories as those presented by Keynes and Hayek upon *different types of business cycles,* existing in reality" (p. 255 – italics in the original). He admits that much more empirical work and correspondingly detailed specifications would be required to test "such abstract theories". Lundberg ends his *Studies* with the suggestion that "the practice obtained in the setting up of various model sequences for a total economic system may offer a more diversified training in economic thinking than that in the equally abstract method of handling demand and supply curves" (p. 256).

5. Divided paths over common ground

The three works by Hicks, Haberler, and Lundberg discussed in the previous sections were all published between January and April 1937. This simultaneity may look rather accidental, but there was more simultaneity prior to publication. Between June and August 1936, Hicks started to work on *Mr. Keynes and the "Classics"*, just when Haberler completed his work on *Prosperity and Depression* with the conference of experts and revisions of the manuscript. Towards the end of September Hicks presented his paper at the Econometric Society meeting at Oxford, which Keynes did not attend, because he was on his way to Stockholm, where Lundberg came to be one of his main critics in the discussion at the Political Economy Club. Every member of our trio perceived Keynes' *General Theory* as a challenge and reacted to it by attempting to integrate Keynes' ideas into larger frameworks – even though in Haberler's case this became more obvious only with the new Chapter 8 in the 1939 edition of *Prosperity and Depression*. In personal aspects, too, it is easy to see that Hicks, Haberler, and Lundberg had much in common. They were roughly of the same age, cosmopolitan, well trained and open minded with regard to different traditions of economic thinking. Leijonhufvud's characterisation of Hicks' eclectic approach of creating "a personal synthesis" (quoted in footnote 7 above) fits Haberler and Lundberg, too.

However, if one compares the syntheses of Hicks, Haberler and Lundberg, it is the differences between them that stand out at first sight.

---

[14] It is in this context that Lundberg develops an early form of the Domar condition for steady-state growth (p. 240, n.1).

Looking at the different paths taken by the three authors helps neverthe-less to see where they have gone over common ground and where they have reached similar conclusions about the compatibility of macroeco-nomic theories. In the following, the differences between the three synthe-ses will be discussed systematically concerning their formats and objectives, their methods and mechanisms and the reactions to and by Keynes. Based on these comparisons it will be shown what the three syntheses had in com-mon and what distinguishes them from the Neoclassical Syntheses, old and new.

5.1. Divided paths

It is evident that the *formats* of the three works under review are extremely different. Hicks' *Mr. Keynes and the "Classics"* was a conference talk, turned into a short journal article. Haberler's *Prosperity and Depression* was a mis-sion report, and Lundberg's *Studies* a doctoral dissertation. As such, the three works differed also in their gestation periods. Hicks' article was pro-duced within a few weeks in Summer 1936. By contrast, the works of Hab-erler and Lundberg were conceived quite independently of Keynes' *General Theory*. Haberler had started his inquiry in 1934, while Lundberg had begun with the preparations for his *Studies* as early as 1930.

Format follows function, and the *objectives* of the syntheses clearly dif-fered. Hicks' article was constructed as a pedagogic device, aimed at *isolat-ing* the innovations of Keynes. Haberler's report was presented as an endeavour to produce a *consensus* on hypotheses for empirical testing, embedded in a project aimed at supporting the international coordination of stabilisation policies (Boianovsky and Trautwein 2006b). Lundberg's objective was to provide a novel framework for stability analysis, which would *combine* Keynes' ideas (as well as those of others) with Wicksellian and Casselian approaches to dynamics, while discarding Keynes' method of comparative statics.

In connection with the differing objectives of the syntheses we also see strong differences in the *styles of argumentation*. Hicks' style is "casually for-mal" and reductionist, working with general functions in simultaneous equations and with graphs that illustrate the main points in a heuristic fashion. Haberler's style is altogether literary, comparing concepts, clari-fying notions, and developing hypotheses in a discourse based on several rounds of feedbacks from the peers. Lundberg's style is formal, by the standards of the day, and kaleidoscopic in the sense of demonstrating the multiplicity of plausible scenarios in which economic growth goes off the rails. Lundberg assembles his own toolkit, making use of calculus, geometry, and algebra, illustrating the instability of a "simple economic system" with complex graphs, and constructing model sequences in terms of difference equations and simulations.

The *objects* of the syntheses, i.e. their underlying theses and antitheses, are more similar, but not fully congruent. They overlap only to the extent that Wicksell is seen as a contributor of key concepts for synthetic theory building. Keynes plays the antithetical part in Hicks' synthesis, and an agenda-setting role in Lundberg's analysis, but a rather marginal role in Haberler's synthetic exposition. Hicks studies the points where Keynes departs from the Marshallian tradition and where his "general theory" could be transformed into a "generalized general theory" in Wicksellian fashion. Lundberg constructs a Wicksellian general theory in much greater detail and refers to a literature on dynamics far beyond the Marshallian world of supply and demand schedules. He compares his sequence analysis to the approaches of Hansen, Lederer, Frisch, Tinbergen, and Kalecki, arguing that they either lack stringency or oversimplify, as they ignore the investment–saving imbalances at the core of the theories that Lundberg wants to nest in his framework (Lundberg 1937, pp. 249–53). Haberler brings together an even wider variety of pre-Keynesian business cycle theories, ranging from Hawtrey and Aftalion to Spiethoff and Schumpeter.

Concerning the *scope* in terms of explaining different states and changes in a macroeconomic system, Haberler's synthesis has the full business cycle in view. Hicks compares the states of full employment and depression, where the former is understood as a stable equilibrium, not as the upper turning point or some "normal position" in the cycle. Lundberg, on the other hand, uses a steady-state growth definition as the norm (hypothetical reference) from which the system can deviate in downturns and cyclical oscillations. Keynesian underemployment equilibrium is possible and demonstrated for the simplest sequence, but in the tables of the numerical examples for most of the sequences Lundberg terminates the calculation of the values for the variables after a few periods in disequilibrium.

The differences in scope correspond to differences in the methods of thinking about *equilibrium and changes* in the system. Hicks conceptualises macroeconomic equilibrium in his IS-LM model as the point in which the "partial equilibrium" loci of the goods markets and the money market intersect; this serves to show Keynes' point of a general interdependence of aggregate income and the rate of interest. Lundberg uses Cassel's definition of steady-state growth equilibrium as a notional reference path for the construction of disequilibrium sequences. Haberler is generally critical towards the use of the notion of equilibrium benchmarks in the context of business cycle analysis (e.g., [1937] 1964, p. 284, n.1; p. 390, n.2; p. 391). Haberler and Lundberg argue in terms of dynamics, but Haberler confines himself to making verbal conjectures about dynamic methods, while

Lundberg attempts to capture the dynamics of expansion and downturns in mathematical terms. With regard to statics and dynamics, Hicks is a special case: He uses Keynes' method of comparative statics, not only for the sake of comparability, but also because he thinks that the "*General Theory* is a brilliant squeezing of dynamic economics into static habits of thought" (Hicks 1977, p. 148; cf. Hicks 1936). This at least is Hicks' recollection of his own state of mind in 1937, expressed at a later stage in life when he had become very critical about IS-LM, *inter alia* because of incongruencies in the length of the periods implied in the model (cf. Hicks 1980, Leijonhufvud 1994). As mentioned in Section 2.2., Hicks' IS-LM paper itself ends on the critical note that Keynes' *General Theory* "is neither the beginning nor the end of Dynamic Economics" (1937a: 159). Moreover, Hicks traces the heuristic origin of the IS-LM diagram not to Keynes (1936), but back to his own attempt to construct a dynamic model of the interaction between (real) factor prices in *Wages and Interest: the Dynamic Problem* (Hicks 1935). As Hicks (1980, pp. 141–2) writes in retrospect,

> ... the idea of the IS-LM diagram came to me as a result of the work I had been doing on three-way exchange, conceived in a Walrasian manner. I had already found a way of representing three-way exchange on a two-dimensional diagram (to appear in due course in chapter 5 of *Value and Capital*). As it appears there, it is a piece of statics; but it was essential to my approach (as already appears in 'Wages and Interest: the Dynamic Problem') that static analysis of this sort could be carried over to 'dynamics' by redefinition of terms. So it was natural for me to think that a similar device could be used for the Keynes theory.

5.2. The Keynesian challenge

There are noteworthy differences in the reactions of Hicks, Haberler and Lundberg to Keynes and in the reactions by Keynes to their works. It has been pointed out that Keynes plays the antithetical part in Hicks' synthesis, an agenda-setting role in Lundberg's *Studies*, and a marginal role in Haberler's consensus view. This can be described more precisely in terms of what innovation they saw in Keynes' *General Theory*, what they criticised about it, and what they built into their syntheses. In Hicks' view, Keynes' central innovation was to demonstrate the interdependence of the monetary and real spheres, which in a depression may manifest itself in a liquidity trap and underemployment equilibrium. Even so, Hicks criticises Keynes for exaggerating the differences between himself and the other Marshallians, and for not going the full way towards a general theory of employment, interest, and money. The Keynesian flavour of Hicks' synthetical IS-LM model is nevertheless obvious: It is all about effective demand, the marginal efficiency of capital is the underlying concept of the investment function, the liquidity trap is built into the LM curve, and it is emphasised that the IS curve could be stuck to the left of the income level required for full employment.

Keynes did not react in public to Hicks' *Econometrica* article, but in a letter to Hicks (dated 31 March 1937) he famously wrote – to the regret of many a Post Keynesian – that he had "really... next to nothing to say by way of criticism" (Keynes 1973, p. 79). In the same letter, however, Keynes pointed out that Hicks' "crude model" (Equations 1.1–1.3) is "scarcely fair to the classical view", as "[a] strictly brought-up classical economist would not admit that ... the increase in the quantity of money is capable of increasing employment". He conceded that "[t]he story that you give is a very good account of the beliefs which, let us say, you and I used to hold", but considered this thinking "an inconsistent hotchpotch". Therefore, while Hicks accused of Keynes of selecting the wrong representative for the *"Classics"* (Pigou), Keynes retorted that Hicks' strawman was the earlier Keynes and company. Even so, Keynes (1979, p. 80–81) insisted on two differences between himself and what he considered as "the classicals": The first is the classical understanding of the rate of interest as an essentially non-monetary variable. The second is his concept of marginal efficiency of capital which differs from classical notions of marginal productivity and the acceleration principle as it emphasises expected rather than current income.[15]

Haberler (1939, Chapter 8) argues that the innovations of Keynes are largely matters of terminology. Describing Keynes' concepts of aggregate saving and the multiplier as tautological, he reduces the controversy between Keynes and "classical" writers about involuntary unemployment to differences in wording (1939, Chapter 8, section 5). Haberler argues that free competition among workers would lead to a downward flexibility of money wages, so that observable unemployment could not be described as an *equilibrium* (p. 238). He concedes that Keynes (1936, Chapter 19) is right to point out that reductions in money wages do not necessarily lead to proportional changes in real wages. However, they tend to raise the level

---

[15] In both regards Keynes does not differ, though, from the Wicksellian approaches of Lindahl (1930) and Myrdal (1931), which were well known to Hicks (who had reviewed Myrdal; cf. Hicks 1934), and also to Keynes (who at the time of writing his letter to Hicks was engaged in the debate with Ohlin about the Stockholm School's approach to the theory of interest; cf. Ohlin 1937, Keynes 1937a). As one referee has pointed out, Keynes' letter to Hicks is not consistent with the *General Theory*, where Keynes (1936, p. 178) declares: "Nor is there material difference... between my schedule of the marginal efficiency of capital or investment demand-schedule and the demand curve for capital contemplated by some of the classical writers."

of liquidity in the economy. This brings Haberler to the conclusion that classical theory is right, in principle, about the self-stabilisation of full employment under free competition, but that state intervention might be required in reality: "Thanks largely to Mr. Keynes, there is to-day almost general agreement that Government spending, barring psychological repercussions and assuming an elastic liquidity-preference schedule, will stimulate employment" (p. 236). This combination of neoclassical principles and Keynesian practice comes close to the compromise perspective of the Neoclassical Synthesis taken by Samuelson, who had been a student of Haberler at Harvard.

Keynes reviewed the second edition of *Prosperity & Depression* anonymously in the *Economic Journal*, noting that "Prof. Haberler accepts the broad line of Mr Keynes' theory as valid, but finds nothing significantly new in it" (1979, p. 275). In a 1939 letter to Austin Robinson, Keynes (1979, p. 274) remarked that Haberler "has come the whole way round and swallows [*The General Theory*] bait, hook and line. But his digestion tells him that it is all very familiar diet... and that [earlier theories] can be shown to be compatible with my theory, – with all of which I cordially agree!"

Lundberg is evidently more impressed by Keynes, even though he admires the *Treatise on Money* (1930) more than the *General Theory* (1936). What he appreciates about the latter is Keynes' emphasis on the instability of full-employment equilibrium. However, he deems Keynes "static method" inappropriate for that purpose, and criticises him for taking recourse to an exogenously determined quantity of money. For Lundberg's sequence analysis, Keynes' *General Theory* does not serve as an encompassing framework, but several of its core ideas are captured in model sequences I(a), II and III.

To my knowledge, Keynes never reacted directly to Lundberg's attempts to translate his ideas into sequence analysis. Keynes' inclusion of a "finance motive" into the demand for money (1937a, 1937b), primarily in reaction to Ohlin (1937), may be interpreted as an indirect response, as the relevant arguments about flow demands for money were shared in the Stockholm School. It is noteworthy that Lundberg developed a notion of inflationary gaps between aggregate demand and supply (in model sequence I(b)) three years before Keynes (1940) published his *How to Pay for the War*, which is often seen as the origin of inflation gap analysis. However, there is no evidence that Keynes was inspired by Lundberg's *Studies*.

5.3. Common ground

Despite all their differences in format, method, and scope, the three macroeconomic syntheses of vintage 1937 have some common ground in their views of what constitutes the core of a general theory of business cycles and underemployment. This common ground can be described in terms of imperfect intertemporal coordination: Failures of the interest-rate mechanism to coordinate aggregate investment and saving lead to cumulative income adjustments. In contrast with Keynes, all three authors stress that saving is not a passive variable which automatically adjusts to investment *ex post*. Saving is defined as an independent variable, determined separately from investment, and the saving schedule is described as a function both of income and of the interest rate in loanable-funds frameworks. However, contrary to what Keynes (1937a, 1937b) insinuates about loanable-funds approaches, the three synthesisers consider the rate of interest as a monetary variable. The references show that, composing their syntheses, Hicks, Haberler, and Lundberg have the German version of Myrdal (1931) under the belt, and they argue in line with Lindahl's and Myrdal's critiques of Wicksell's concept of the "natural rate of interest". Their loanable-funds approaches include bank lending and (dis)hoarding of money stocks in the determination of interest rates. All three of them treat Keynes' liquidity-preference theory as, in principle, compatible with loanable-funds theory. Hicks (1937a, p. 155), Haberler (1939, pp. 218–9), and Lundberg (1937, pp. 40–42) consider Keynes' concept of the liquidity trap to be a special case.[16]

In the views of the three authors, it is important to treat saving as an independent variable, since deviations of the system from full-employment equilibrium are essentially explained by imbalances of investment and saving. All of them stress the volatility of expectations about future yields of capital (e.g., Hicks 1937a, pp. 156–8, Haberler 1937, p. 306 and pp. 342–4, Lundberg 1937, pp. 175–80). Since any new piece of information can change agents' expectations, the causes of IS imbalances are manifold. Hicks, Haberler, and Lundberg do not conceptualise them in purely Wicksellian terms, i.e. they do not reduce them to discrepancies between "the" money rate of interest and the equilibrium rate (the expected rate of return on capital that brings investment in line with planned saving). Nor do they consider the Keynesian multiplier as a sufficient description of the interaction of aggregate investment and income. They all employ the "acceleration principle" as a key mechanism. Hicks (in his "generalized general theory") and Lundberg (in sequences II–V) combine the accelerator with the Keynesian multiplier. Similarly, Haberler ([1937] 1964, p. 344) stresses that cumulative processes develop "through the operation of the acceleration principle and the dependence of consumers' purchasing power on gross investment", adding in a footnote that "the multiplier is more or less explicitly implied in any description of the 'Wicksellian process'".

---

[16] Hicks (1937a, p. 158) contrasts Keynes' "Slump Economics" with Wicksell's cumulative inflation, which he considers to be another special case.

Finally it should be noted that the three authors give their analytical frameworks a high degree of openness. Hicks (1937a, p. 158) points out that his "slight extension of Mr. Keynes' similar skeleton [apparatus] remains a terribly rough and ready sort of affair". He argues that IS-LM cannot capture the relation between the price system and the system of interest rates, nor other important aspects such as depreciation and the timing of the processes. Lundberg goes much farther in stringently analysing aspects of timing, but admits that the "possibilities of testing such abstract theories as those implied in the model sequences are ... very limited" (1937, p. 256). He provides a general framework for sequence analysis, which permits to examine a large variety of scenarios, but he does not claim to have a general theory. In a similar fashion, Haberler (1937, p. 2) stresses that his "synthetic exposition" is "not a closed and rigid system, but a flexible and open one: there are many points where no definite solution can be proposed, but where the existence of a number of possibilities will be indicated".

6. Conclusion

The three syntheses of 1937 vintage reviewed here all had an afterlife in the era of the Neoclassical Synthesis. Hicks' IS-LM skeleton became the latter's workhorse model, much to the dismay of the older Hicks who had become increasingly dissatisfied with his invention (Hicks 1980, Klamer 1989, Leijonhufvud 1994). As Haberler's *Prosperity & Depression* became the canonical text in business cycle theory, it was slowly acknowledged that he had anticipated the Pigou effect, thus enriching the debates about the stability of underemployment equilibrium. Lundberg's unit period survived, in a distorted form, as "the Lundberg lag" in standard multiplier analysis. Even though Lundberg amply demonstrated his capability of constructing formal model sequences, he did not attempt a formal generalisation. This was done by someone else in a reduced fashion in 1939:

> Harvard professor Alvin Hansen gave a talented young student with mathematical skills the assignment to formalize Lundberg's argument. The student, 23 years of age, was Paul Samuelson, and the result was the famous article about the interaction between the multiplier and the accelerator that led to Samuelson's international breakthrough. (Lindbeck and Persson 1990, p. 276 – my translation)

Multiplier–accelerator analysis à la Samuelson (1939) helped in turn to build bridges between business cycle theory and macroeconomics.

This brings us back to the question raised in Section 1: Did the authors of the three 1937 syntheses contribute anything to the turn of the

Neoclassical Synthesis towards nominal rigidities as the sole remaining explanation of persistent underemployment? The conclusion in this paper is that, if they did, it was done inadvertently, by leaving some loose ends. One of those could be detected in Hicks (1937a), where he starts with the conventional assumption of given money wages to demonstrate the effects of a change in the quantity of money. Next he assumes a rise in money wages at a *given* quantity of money; the concomitant rise in real wages would "necessarily diminish employment" (Hicks 1937a, p. 150). This was hardly controversial, not even with Keynes, and it was an outmoded scenario, as indicated by Hicks himself in his Wicksellian reference to a more elastic supply of money. Lundberg is even more critical of Keynes' assumption of a given money supply, and he deals with flexible prices in the analysis of inflationary gaps in sequence I(b). However Lundberg, too, left a loose end, as he did not analyse a deflationary gap or a full model sequence that ends in underemployment equilibrium; he was primarily interested in processes out of equilibrium. Haberler's loose end was his insistence that "an equilibrium with less than full employment can exist only if money wages are rigid" ([1939] 1964, p. 235, n. 1, similarly p. 390, n. 1). However, as pointed out in Section 5.2, Haberler also agreed with Keynes that a downward flexibility of wages could make a depression worse:

[A]lthough the classical theory is right in saying that an equilibrium with unemployment is incompatible with competition in the labour market, it does not necessarily follow that plasticity of wages would eliminate depressions. (Haberler [1939] 1964, p. 244)

Whatever one makes of those loose ends, it should be clear from the assessment of Hicks (1937a), Haberler (1937/1939), and Lundberg (1937) that nominal rigidities were inessential for their synthetic explanations of underemployment, business cycles, and other disruptions of steady-state growth. Their syntheses were centred on imbalances of investment and saving, largely conceptualised in terms of the "acceleration principle" and loanable-funds theory. They discussed problems of imperfect coordination of investment and saving decisions that are taken by different agents. Haberler and Lundberg paid attention to a variety of causes and effects of changes in elasticities of supply (of goods and finance) and in expectations. Those structural characteristics of imperfect information and coordination have been largely lost out of sight in the Neoclassical Synthesis and, even more so, in the New Neoclassical Synthesis.[17]

---

[17] Cf. Boianovsky and Trautwein (2006c), where the latter point is argued in greater detail and in direct dialogue with Woodford.

Acknowledgements

Helpful comments from Michaël Assous, Muriel Dalpont-Legrand, Harald Hagemann, Kevin Hoover, Jan Kregel, Axel Leijonhufvud, Rodolphe dos Santos Ferreira and two anonymous referees are gratefully acknowledged.

References

Backhouse, R. and Laidler, D.E.W. (2004). What was lost with IS-LM. In M. De Vroey and K.D. Hoover (Eds.), The IS-LM model: Its rise, fall, and strange persistence. History of Political Economy, 36 (Supplement), pp. 25–56.

Baumol, W. (1991). On formal dynamics: From Lundberg to chaos analysis. In L. Jonung (Ed.), *The Stockholm School of Economics Revisited.* Cambridge: Cambridge University Press, pp. 185–98.

Berg, C. (1991). Lundberg, Keynes, and the riddles of a general theory. In L. Jonung (Ed.), *The Stockholm School of Economics Revisited.* Cambridge: Cambridge University Press, pp. 205–28.

Blanchard, O. (2000). What do we know about macroeconomics that Fisher and Wicksell did not? *Quarterly Journal of Economics*, 115: 1375–409.

Boianovsky, M. (2000). In search of a canonical history of macroeconomics in the interwar period. Haberler's *Prosperity and Depression* revisited. In M. Psalidopoulos (Ed.), *The Canon in the History of Economics. Critical Essays.* London: Routledge, pp. 156–79.

Boianovsky, M. and Trautwein, H.-M. (2006a). Price expectations, capital accumulation and employment: Lindahl's macroeconomics from the 1920s to the 1950s. *Cambridge Journal of Economics*, 30: 881–900.

Boianovsky, M. and Trautwein, H.-M. (2006b). Haberler, the League of Nations, and the quest for consensus in business cycle theory in the 1930s. *History of Political Economy*, 38: 45–89.

Boianovsky, M. and Trautwein, H.-M. (2006c). Wicksell after Woodford. *Journal of the History of Economic Thought*, 28: 171–85.

De Vroey, M. (2004). The history of macroeconomics viewed against the background of the Marshall-Walras divide. In M. De Vroey and K.D. Hoover (Eds.), pp. 57–91.

De Vroey, M. and Hoover, K.D. (Eds.), (2004). The IS-LM model: Its rise, fall, and strange persistence. *History of Political Economy*, 36 (Supplement).

Haberler, G. (1936). Mr. Keynes' theory of the "multiplier": A methodological criticism. *Zeitschrift für Nationalökonomie*, 7: 299–305.

Haberler, G. (1937, 2nd ed. 1939). *Prosperity and Depression: A Theoretical Analysis of Cyclical Movements.* Geneva: League of Nations, quoted after 5th edition, London: George Allen & Unwin 1964.

Hagemann, H. and Trautwein, H.-M. (1998). Cantillon and Ricardo effects. Hayek's contributions to business cycle theory. *European Journal of the History of Economic Thought*, 5: 292–316.

Hayek, F.A. (1931). *Prices and Production.* London: Routledge & Sons.

Hicks, J.R. (1934). Review of *Monetary Equilibrium* by Gunnar Myrdal. *Economica*, 1: 479–83.

Hicks, J.R. (1935). Wages and interest: The dynamic problem. *Economic Journal*, 45: 456–68.

Hicks, J.R. (1936). Keynes' theory of employment. *Economic Journal*, 46: 238–53.

Hicks, J.R. (1937a). Mr. Keynes and the "Classics": A suggested interpretation. *Econometrica*, 5: 147–59.

Hicks, J.R. (1937b). *Théorie Mathématique de la Valeur en Régime de Libre Concurrence* (Mathematical Theory of Value under Free Competition). Paris: Hermann.

Hicks, J.R. (1977). Recollections and documents. In *Economic Perspectives – Further Essays on Money and Growth*. Oxford: Clarendon Press, pp. 134–48.

Hicks, J.R. (1980). IS-LM: An Explanation. *Journal of Post Keynesian Economics*, 3: 139–54.

Hicks, J.R. (1991). The Swedish influence on *value and capital*. In L. Jonung (Ed.), *The Stockholm School of Economics Revisited*. Cambridge: Cambridge University Press, pp. 369–76.

Keynes, J.M. (1930). *A Treatise on Money*, 2 vols. London: Macmillan.

Keynes, J.M. (1936). *The General Theory of Employment, Interest and Money*. London: Macmillan.

Keynes, J.M. (1937a). Alternative theories of interest. *Economic Journal*, 47: 241–52.

Keynes, J.M. (1937b). The "Ex-Ante" theory of the rate of interest. *Economic Journal*, 47: 663–9.

Keynes, J.M. (1940). *How to Pay for the War*. London: Macmillan.

Keynes, J.M. (1973). The collected writings of John Maynard Keynes. In D. Moggridge (Ed.), *The General Theory and After, Part 2: Defence and Development*, vol. XIV. Cambridge: Cambridge University Press.

Keynes, J.M. (1979). The collected writings of John Maynard Keynes. In D. Moggridge (Ed.), *The General Theory and After: A Supplement*, vol. XXIX. Cambridge: Cambridge University Press.

Klamer, A. (1989). An accountant among economists: Conversations with Sir John R. Hicks. *Journal of Economic Perspectives*, 3: 167–80.

Laidler, D.E.W. (1999). *Fabricating the Keynesian Revolution. Studies of the Inter-War Literature on Money, the Cycle and Unemployment*. Cambridge: Cambridge University Press.

Lederer, E. (1931). *Technischer Fortschritt und Arbeitslosigkeit* (Technical Progress and Unemployment). Tübingen: Mohr Siebeck.

Lederer, E. (1938). *Technical Progress and Unemployment. An Enquiry into the Obstacles to Economic Expansion*. Geneva: International Labour Office.

Leijonhufvud, A. (1968). *On Keynesian Economics and the Economics of Keynes*. New York: Oxford University Press.

Leijonhufvud, A. (1981). The Wicksell connection: Variations on a theme. In *Information and Coordination. Essays in Macroeconomic Theory*. New York: Oxford University Press, pp. 131–202.

Leijonhufvud, A. (1994). Hicks, Keynes and Marshall. In H. Hagemann and O. Hamouda (Eds.), *The Legacy of Sir John Hicks: His Contributions to Economic Analysis*. Abingdon: Routledge, pp. 143–58.

Lindahl, E. (1930). *Penningpolitikens medel*. Malmö: Förlagsaktiebolaget (trans. 1939: 'The Rate of Interest and the Price Level', Part II in *Studies in the Theory of Money and Capital*. London: George Allen & Unwin, pp. 137–268.

Lindbeck, A. and Persson, M. (1990). Erik Lundberg. In C. Jonung and A.-C. Ståhlberg (Eds.), *Ekonomporträtt*. Stockholm: SNS förlag, pp. 273–85.

Lundberg, E. (1930). Om ekonomisk jämvikt. *Ekonomisk Tidskrift* 32: 133–60 (trans. 1994a: On the concept of economic equilibrium, in Henriksson, R. (ed.) *Erik Lundberg – Studies in Economic Instability and Change*. Stockholm: SNS förlag, 13–47; for a translation of the underlying fil.lic. thesis: *Structural Change and Economic Dynamics*, (1996) 7: 361–90).

Lundberg, E. (1937). *Studies in the Theory of Economic Expansion*. London: King & Son.

Lundberg, E. (1994). Report on My Studies as a Rockefeller fellow of economics. In R. Henriksson (Ed.), *Erik Lundberg – Studies in Economic Instability and Change*. Stockholm: SNS förlag, pp. 48–66.

Modigliani, F. (1944). Liquidity preference and the theory of interest and money. *Econometrica*, 12: 45–88.

Myrdal, G. (1931). Om penningteoretisk jämvikt. En studie över den "normala räntan" i Wicksells penninglära. *Ekonomisk Tidskrift*, 33: 191–302 (German trans.: Der Gleichgewichtsbegriff als Instrument der geldtheoretischen Analyse, in Hayek, F.A. (ed.) *Beiträge zur Geldtheorie.* Vienna: Julius Springer, 1933, 361–487; English trans.: *Monetary Equilibrium.* London: William Hodge, 1939).

Ohlin, B. (1937). Some notes on the Stockholm theory of savings and investment. *Economic Journal,* 47: 53–69, 221–40.

Pearce, K. and Hoover, K.D. (1995). After the revolution: Paul Samuelson and the textbook Keynesian model. *History of Political Economy,* 27 (Supplement): 183–216.

Pigou, A.C. (1943). The classical stationary state. *Economic Journal,* 53: 343–51.

Samuelson, P.A. (1939). Interactions between the acceleration principle and the multiplier. *Review of Economics and Statistics,* 21: 75–8.

Snowdon, B. and Vane, H.R. (2005). *Modern Macroeconomics. Its Origins, Development and Current State.* Cheltenham: Edward Elgar.

Tamborini, R., Trautwein, H.-M. and Mazzocchi, R. (in press). Wicksell, Keynes and the New Neoclassical Synthesis: What can we learn for monetary policy? *Economic Notes – Review of Banking, Finance and Monetary Economics,* 43.

Tobin, J. (1956). The interest-elasticity of transactions demand for cash. *Review of Economics and Statistics,* 38: 241–7.

Tobin, J. (1958). Liquidity preference as behavior towards risk. *Review of Economic Studies,* 25: 65–86.

Trautwein, H.-M. (in press). The Stockholm school. In G. Faccarello and H.D. Kurz (Eds.), *The Handbook of the History of Economic Analysis,* vol. 2. Cheltenham: Edward Elgar.

Trautwein, H.-M. and Zouache, A. (2009). Natural rates in the New Synthesis: Same old trouble? *European Journal of Economics and Economic Policies: Intervention,* 6: 207–25.

Woodford, M. (2003). *Interest and Prices: Foundations of a Theory of Monetary Policy.* Princeton, NJ: Princeton University Press.

Young, W.L. (1987). *Interpreting Mr Keynes: The IS-LM Enigma.* Oxford: Polity–Blackwell.

Abstract

The 1920s and 1930s were years of intensive debate about economic dynamics and stabilisation policies. There was a large variety of explanations of cycles and depressions, and Keynes' *General Theory of Employment, Interest and Money* (1936) was pitched against them. In 1937, followed three different attempts to provide synthetic expositions of macroeconomic theory that would deal with the Keynesian challenge: Hicks' *Mr. Keynes and the "Classics"*, Haberler's *Prosperity and Depression*, and Lundberg's *Studies in the Theory of Economic Expansion.* This paper compares those 1937 syntheses and contrasts them with the "Neoclassical Synthesis" and the current "New Neoclassical Synthesis".

Lange's 1938 model: dynamics and the "optimum propensity to consume"

Michaël Assous and Roberto Lampa

1. Introduction

Oskar Lange's 1938 work "The Rate of Interest and the Optimum Propensity to Consume" is widely recognised as one of the earliest mathematical models of Keynes's *General Theory*. In light of its analytical content, it has usually been associated with the original IS-LM approach of Roy Harrod, James Meade, and John Hicks (Young 1987, Darity and Young 1995). However, Lange's article was not a reaction to Keynes's works but the first part of an ambitious project that included the development of a theory of economic evolution[1] (see Lampa 2014).

Indeed, Lange manifested his interest in dynamics very early in his career. For instance, both his doctoral dissertation and his thesis presented for the "docent" degree – that is, assistant professor – were devoted to the analysis of the business cycle in Poland. In several occasions, he also emphasised the close connection between his view and Karl Marx's ideas. Furthermore, he attached great importance also to the works of Joseph Schumpeter and Michal Kalecki[2]: from 1934 to 1936, he became tightly

---

1 Stated succinctly, Lange's project consisted of a theoretical generalisation (capable of guaranteeing *universality*) and an analysis of institutional data (in order to have *realism*), intended to separate economic theory from the tacit assumptions of a capitalist economy, as well as to generalise the economic theory for a "world to come", whose features were portrayed in a series of contemporary works about socialist theory (see Lampa 2011, 2014).

2 According to Kowalik, Lange's decision to study with Schumpeter stemmed from "Lange's wish to learn as much as possible from the universally recognized specialist in business cycles" (1994, p. xiii).

117

connected to the former at Harvard, whereas his interest in Kalecki's business cycle seems to have grown more important after the publication of the *General Theory*.[3]

Although Lange explicitly suggested that his 1938 static model might have been dynamised, he never devised any mathematical demonstration: he just stated, en passant, that this might have been done by means of a time lag à la Kalecki[4] (1937).

It may be recalled, however, that in the early 1940s, Paul Samuelson devised some "techniques" in order to dynamise what he called the "Keynesian system" (1941, p. 113). As he explicitly affirmed in his 1941 *Econometrica* paper, "I shall analyse in some detail the simple Keynesian model as outlined in the *General Theory*. Various writers, such as Meade, Hicks, and Lange, have developed explicitly in mathematical form the meaning of the Keynesian system" (1941, p. 133). He then proceeded to develop two dynamic systems: both a differential and a difference set of equations and he presented the condition that assured the stability of the equilibrium (1941, p. 120). Although Samuelson explicitly referred to Lange, his models were only loosely related to his.[5] First, Samuelson did not stress that the level of consumption was the key determinant of the investment function, as Lange repeatedly did. Second, and foremost, Samuelson paid no attention to the dynamics of the capital stock (which is the corner stone of Kalecki's theory of fluctuations) to which Lange explicitly referred.

---

3 Lange spent seven months at Cambridge in 1936 where he met Kalecki who, at that time, was working on a new version of his business cycle model, attempting to illuminate how his approach may be related to Keynes's theory. Given their proximity to the Polish socialist circle and their common friendship with their fellow countryman and economist Marek Breit, Lange might have certainly read Kalecki's 1933 *Essay*, published in Polish. It is, however, only after reading the *General Theory* that he really seemed to have come to grips with it.

4 According to Kalecki, there is, however, no doubt that Lange's 1938 paper was ultimately about dynamics. While discussing the scope of Lange's works, he claims:

Already in the early stage of Lange's work the versatility of his interests is apparent. I have in mind his three papers published in the years 1936–38: "On the Economic Theory of Socialism," "The Rate of Interest and the Optimum Propensity to Consume" and "Ludwik Krzywicki as a Theoretician of Historical Materialism" (in Polish). The first of these papers was concerned with the role of the quasi-market mechanism in a socialist system, the second with the dynamics of a capitalist economy (our emphasis), the third with historical materialism. These were the three directions in which Lange's work was to develop in its later stages. (Kalecki 1966, p. 431)

5 This is true also concerning Meade's (1937) model (see Rappoport 1992).

On the other hand, it might also be remarked that Timlin (1942) made an attempt to dynamise what she had defined as the "Keynes–Lange" system. Her method mainly consisted of developing a "system of shifting equilibrium" to determine how a monetary shock was likely to induce a transformation in Lange's set of structural functions, which were supposed to embed the "psychological–institutional complex" of the economy. Resorting to Lange's diagrammatic representation, Timlin showed how expectations in both the goods and the financial market became critical elements with respect to the dynamics of the economy. Furthermore, by extending Lange's analysis to the "long run", she was finally able to address the problem of the effects of a change in thriftiness upon the stationary level of the capital stock.[6]

Nevertheless, unlike Timlin and Samuelson, the present article focuses on Lange's (crucial) notion of the "optimum propensity to consume", whose importance is largely ignored in both the aforementioned analyses.

In particular, the aim of this paper is to suggest a consistent reconstruction of Lange's article in order to explore its potential implications in terms of dynamics. We are persuaded that such a reconstruction may be interesting from several perspectives. First, it may help us to better understand how Lange's notion of the "optimum propensity to consume" (on which he based his whole interpretation of the under-consumption theories) may operate in a dynamic context. Second and foremost, a similar reconstruction may be useful for making clear how close Lange's view on dynamics – expressed in a series of articles published between 1934 and 1943 – was to the "Keynesian" dynamic approach of both Kalecki (1939) and Kaldor (1940).

Consequently, Section 2 discusses Lange's early reflection on dynamics with the aim of highlighting its most outstanding features. Section 3 focuses on Lange's 1938 static model and indicates the effects of a change of saving on investment. Furthermore – by means of an unedited correspondence between Lange and Samuelson (dated 1942, see Samuelson, n.d.) recently discovered in the archives of Duke University by one of the authors – we clarify the meaning and the implications of the notion of "optimum propensity to consume". Section 4, by means of some additional assumptions concerning the introduction of a time lag, outlines the necessary and sufficient conditions for the generation of self-sustaining cycles. Finally, Lange's model (once dynamised) is compared to Kalecki's 1939 business cycle theory, and its consistency with Lange's view (expressed in a series of contemporary papers) is assessed.

---

6 See Young (2008) for a more extensive study of the attempts to make the IS-LM a dynamic system.

2. The foundations of Lange's endogenous dynamics: Marx and (a touch of) Schumpeter

According to a qualified judgement, the study of business cycles and the evolution of capitalism were Lange's chief research concerns from his early youth until the end of the Second World War (Kowalik 2008). This notwithstanding (and paradoxically enough), Lange did not publish any work explicitly dealing with these issues in the aforementioned period.[7] However, it is possible to reconstruct the essentials of his reflection on dynamics by means of a careful re-reading of his main articles. In "Marxian Economics and Modern Economic Theory" (1935), Lange advocated for an approach that could explain the "economic evolution" from "within" the economic process. In this field, modern economic theory was most likely to be misleading.[8] Lange's argument was that by resorting to a static theory of equilibrium, "bourgeois economists" – that is, all the economists ranging from the Austrian, Marshallian, and the Lausanne schools – were unable to depart from a framework in which all data related to preferences, institutions, and technology are supposed to be given so that the only possible explanation to fluctuations and crises was an exogenous one. In Lange's eye, this line of thought was likely to consolidate the unrealistic view that capitalist economies were intrinsically stable, whereas the 1930s contingency showed their destructive instability both in the United States and in Europe. Sarcastically enough, Lange wrote:

> It was very generally held among "bourgeois" economists both at the beginning of the twentieth century and in the years preceding 1929, that the economic stability of Capitalism was increasing and that business fluctuations were becoming less and less intense. Thus the Marxian claim that "bourgeois" economists failed to grasp the fundamental tendencies of the evolution of the Capitalist system proves to be true. (Lange 1935, p. 190)

However, it must remarked that the "real" superiority of Marxian economics was not supposed to stem from any specific analytical tool originally used by Marx. First, Lange considered that the labour theory of value, at best, can explain equilibrium's price and production, once a given amount of labour necessary to produce a commodity is known. On the other hand,

---

7 A possible explanation is the existence of an ambitious scientific project, to which Lange gave priority (see footnote 1).

8 Lange, however, recognised that the economic equilibrium approach, insofar as it precludes institutional data, has the merit of being abstract and, therefore, universal (since its basic notions hold true in any kind of economic system, included a socialist one). Consequently, it provides *a scientific basis* for current administrations of the economy in many respects, such as prices, market-structure, or the allocation of resources.

it is of no use to highlight how changes (particularly, technological changes) occur. (Lange 1935, p. 194) Second, he thought that also the original version of Marx's schemes of reproduction was of little help in the field of business cycle, because of its analytical backwardness[9]:

> The inability of Marxian economics to solve the problem of the business cycle is demonstrated by the considerable Marxist literature concerned with the famous reproduction schemes of the second volume of *Das Kapital*. This whole literature tries to solve the fundamental problems of economic equilibrium and disequilibrium without even attempting to make use of the mathematical concept of functional relationship. (Lange 1935, p. 196)

The alleged superiority of Marxian economics laid instead on the exact specification of the institutional datum within which the economic process was studied. Its merit, in particular, was to study the functioning of an economy made of two main social classes:

> [...] the consequences of the additional institutional datum which distinguishes Capitalism from other forms of exchange economy, i.e. the existence of a class of people who do not possess any means of production, is scarcely examined. Now, Marxian economics is distinguished by making the specification of this additional institutional datum *the very corner-stone of its analysis*, thus discovering the clue to the peculiarity of the Capitalist system by which it differs from other forms of exchange-economy. (Lange 1935, p. 192, emphasis added)

In Lange's eyes, it is thanks to this institutional datum that Marx could establish a theory of economic evolution which was conceptually consistent, despite its analytical faults: above all, it was certainly the only theory able to explain the origin of the changes in the economy and also in the extra-economic factors.[10] The specificity of this theory was supposed to come from the analysis of the interactions between the dynamics of income distributive shares and the dynamics of investment, in presence of

---

9 Lange's critique of Marx's reproduction schemes was also influenced by the Polish Marxist *milieu*, which on several occasions, since the well-known attempt of Rosa Luxemburg, had dealt with this issue trying to correct "Marx's error"(see Kowalik 2009).

10 Lange was especially aware that economic factors were likely to interact with extra-economic factors while the study of such interactions became the field of his application of historical materialism:

> [...] the full evolution of Capitalism in all its concreteness cannot be explained by a theory of economic evolution alone. It can be explained only by a joint use of both economic theory and the theory of historical materialism. The latter is an inseparable part of the Marxian analysis of Capitalism. (Lange 1935, p. 201)

technological progress.[11] In the first place, Lange recalled the essentials of Marx's analysis of the general law of capitalist accumulation of Volume I of "Das Kapital" (Lange 1935, Section 8)[12] emphasising how a high rate of capital accumulation was likely to trigger an increase in employment and in real wages and eventually to drive firms to introduce "labour-saving technical innovation". Once this tendency spreads throughout the economy, this process is accompanied by a fall in the profit rate that ceases only once new technological innovations are introduced:

> For Capitalism creates, according to Marx, its own surplus population (industrial reserve army) through technical progress, replacing workers by machines. The existence of the surplus population created by technical progress prevents wages from rising so as to swallow profits. Thus technical progress is necessary to maintain the capitalist system and the dynamic nature of the capitalist system, which explains the constant increase of the organic composition of capital, is established. (Lange 1935, p. 199)

By connecting the dynamics of investment to the dynamics of income distribution in the presence of two antagonistic social classes, Marx would hence have succeeded in developing a consistent theory of the causes of the intrinsic instability of capitalism. Of course, in Lange's eye, to emphasise the instability of capitalism implies that economic growth cannot be taken for granted:

> [...] the necessity of the fact that labour-saving technical innovations are always available at the right moment cannot be deduced by economic theory and in this sense the "necessity" of economic evolution cannot be proved. But *Marxian economics* does not attempt to prove this. All it *establishes is that the capitalist system cannot maintain itself*

---

11 On the other hand, Lange notes that a purely dynamic analysis would be "a poor basis" for solving more "ordinary" problems, such as monopoly prices, distribution of productive resources, etc. Therefore Lange concludes that a correct method of investigation presupposes both statics and dynamics, as clearly shown by business cycle theories.

12 The analytical tools used by Lange were quite different from the traditional Marxist approach because of the former's firm refusal of the labour theory of value:

In the Marxian system the labour theory of values serves also to demonstrate the exploitation of the working class under Capitalism, i.e. the difference between the personal distribution of income in a capitalist economy and in an 'einfache Warenproduktion'. It is this deduction from the labour theory of value which makes the orthodox Marxist stick to it. But the same fact of exploitation can also be deduced without the help of the labour theory of value. (Lange 1935, n. 3, p. 195)

Lange's rejection of the Marxian labour theory of value is expressed, even clearer, in the Appendix to "On the Economic Theory of Socialism" (1937).

> *without such innovations. And this proof is given by an economic theory which shows that profit and interest on capital can exist only on account of the instability of a certain datum i.e. the technique of production*, and that it would necessarily disappear the moment further technical progress proved impossible. (Lange 1935, pp. 199–200, emphasis added)

In other words, innovations and technological change represent, on the one hand, the endogenous driving forces of the economic "evolution". On the other hand, far from implying any enduring growth, they become a condition of instability (and eventually crisis), since changes in the (social) sphere of production induced by the innovations are uncoordinated, unplanned, and merely driven by the (individual) profit motive. Not coincidentally, in a subsequent work, Lange explicitly praised Schumpeter's 1939 *Business Cycles* precisely because of a certain proximity to Karl Marx's previous analysis:

> In intention and horizon Professor Schumpeter's book can be compared with *Das Kapital* of Karl Marx which set out to investigate the "law of motion" of capitalism (...) and found that *"crises" play the pivotal role*. This comparison is intended by the reviewer as highest praise. (Lange 1941a, p. 190. Emphasis added)

However, Lange firmly rejected Schumpeter's definition of "innovation":

> Professor Schumpeter says, "We will simply define an innovation as the setting up of a new production function". (...) This definition, however, is too wide. A large (possibly even infinite) number of ways always exists in which production functions can be changed. But an innovation appears only when there is a possibility of such a change, which increases the (discounted) maximum effective profit the firm is able to make. *All other possible changes are disregarded by the firms.* (Lange 1943, p. 21, n.8, emphasis added)

Stated succinctly, Lange is therefore persuaded (following Marx) that innovations are related to the maximisation of the rate of profit by means of *a most indissoluble tie*, which in turn refers to the distributive conflict, typical of any capitalist economy, and eventually to its unequal and anarchic *laws of development*.[13]

In the second place, in a series of parallel works written between 1934 and 1942, Lange also emphasised the close connection between the dynamics of the saving rate and the dynamics of income distributives

---

13 Therefore, Lange refers to a narrow economic and objective conception of innovation (i.e. traditional technical change), which contrasts with Schumpeter's vision of dynamics driven by the role of the entrepreneurs endowed with a different form of rationality and *subjective* motives, not exclusively based on discounted profits maximisation.

shares. Since the workers' saving must be considered negligible, the higher the profit share, the higher the saving rate. As a result, any innovation that comes with an increase in the profit share is accompanied by a rise in the saving rate. And since technical progress is a mere historical datum, the saving rate is most likely to be independent from "the requirements of the maximization of social welfare" (Lange 1937, p. 123).

> [...] saving is [...] in the present economic order determined only partly by pure utility considerations, and *the rate of saving is affected much more by the distribution of incomes, which is irrational from the economist's point of view.* (Lange 1937, p. 127, emphasis in original)

Along these lines, Lange firmly rejected the traditional idea (put forward by Schumpeter and Robertson) that the adjustment of the rate of interest may significantly affect saving and bring it into equilibrium with investment (see Toporowski 2012). In a series of seminars held in 1942 (and published posthumously in 1987), he emphasised, on the contrary, that in a capitalist economy saving and investment decisions were definitely uncoordinated. While saving depends on income distribution, investment, instead, depends partly on the rate of interest (which, in turn, depends on banking policy, i.e. on the banks' expectations about the safety of the investment) and partly on the profit expected by the entrepreneurs. However, these latter make their investments accordingly to poor and volatile expectations, as all that he is able to know is the current state of the market, so that any anticipation of the future inescapably becomes "a purely haphazard type or even ... subject to the quite erratic influences of mass psychology" (Lange 1987, p. 15).

In short, Lange was persuaded that *Capital* (meant as a social relation of production) was the key concept for treating satisfactorily the problem of capitalist dynamics. However, he was aware that this social relation had a dual dimension in dealing with both the struggle between capitalists and workers, and the competition among the capitalists themselves. Therefore, both the distributive conflict and the (un)coordination between saving and investment (which in turn affects technical progress and accumulation) represent the critical elements of capitalist dynamics. Thus, Lange does not share a widespread assumption among Marxists (e.g. Rosa Luxemburg) that entrepreneurs operate like an individual "collective capitalist" whenever they have to set out the level of investment. On the contrary, he is persuaded that crisis originates from the *individual decisions* of saving and investment. Along this line, capitalism's irremediable instability becomes strictly related to the separation between *social* and *individual*, in the sphere of both production and consumption.

Furthermore, it has to be remarked that Lange's endorsement of Marx's theory of economic evolution had at least another, crucial, implication. While analysing the role of time lags, Lange repeatedly insisted that they should in any case be considered the ultimate determinants of fluctuations and instability. At best, they could be considered the *phenomenal form* of deeper changes in the economic and institutional data. Lange denied neither their existence nor their theoretical relevance on certain occasions. He claimed simply that they could not, alone, suffice to justify a dynamic theory. For instance, it is for this reason that Lange rejected the analysis based on the "cobweb theorem" which, according to him, rested mainly on the existence of time lags:

> These theories deduce the impossibility of an equilibrium ... from the very nature of the adjustment mechanism, but they cannot deduce theoretically the changes of data responsible for the trend on which the fluctuations due to the process of adjustment are superimposed. (Lange 1935, n. 2, pp. 192–3)

Finally, it is worth considering to what extent Lange believed that also the analytical apparatus created by Keynes might be a useful tool to cope with the problems of capitalist dynamics originally raised by Marx. Such an interpretation has been suggested by Hyman P. Minsky (who was Lange's research assistant at University of Chicago). According to his memories, in the Spring of 1939 Lange's course explicitly dealt with such a topical issue:

> I took my quota of courses from him – including a memorable course in business cycle theory where Keynes, Marx and the connections between their frameworks was analysed. (Minsky 2009, pp. 201–2)

In particular, it is worth investigating if, in Lange's eyes, Keynes's theory of employment could serve as a basis for the theory of the business cycle. In our view, Lange's 1938 paper "The Rate of Interest and the Optimum Propensity to Consume" can help address this crucial issue.

3. Lange's 1938 static model

Lange developed in explicit mathematical form the meaning of the Keynesian system. He stated three fundamental relationships: (i) the consumption function relating consumption to income, and for generality, to the interest rate as well; (ii) the marginal efficiency of capital relating net investment to the interest rate and to the level of consumption (as for a level of capital equipment fixed for the short period under investigation);

(iii) the schedule of liquidity preference relating the existing amount of money to the interest rate and the level of income.[14]

At a first sight, Lange makes some assumptions similar to those previously made by Hicks (1937). First, Lange's analysis is static. Since net investment varies, so should total capital, eventually influencing output, investment, and savings. But these effects are ignored and the stocks of production factors and technology are treated as constant.[15] Second, like Hicks, Lange extended his model's assumption by allowing investment to depend on real income as well as the rate of interest.[16] However, he justifies such a choice recalling K. Marx's and T.R. Malthus's idea that investment must depend on the level of consumption itself related (also) to distributive shares, given the necessity to maximise profits:

> Mr. Keynes treats investment and expenditure on consumption as two independent quantities and thinks that total income can be increased indiscriminately by expanding either of them. But it is a common place which can be read in any textbook of economics that the demand for investment goods is derived from the demand for consumption goods. The real argument of the under consumption theories is that investment depends on the expenditure on consumption and, therefore, cannot be increased without an adequate increase of the later, *at least in a capitalist economy where investment is done for profit.* (Lange 1938, p. 23, emphasis added).

By introducing the level of consumption as an argument in the investment function, Lange aimed at emphasising that, in a market economy led by profit maximisation, any increase in the demand of consumer goods (as well as any favourable change in the expectations) was likely to affect the prospective yield of the investment projects:

> Investment per unit of time depends, however, (. . .) also on the expenditure on consumption. For the demand for investment goods is *derived* from the demand for

---

14 For a detailed analysis see Lange (1965), Kowalik (1994, 2008), and Lampa (2014).

15 "It also ought to be observed that the investment function holds only for a given capital equipment and for a given distribution of the expenditure for consumption between the different industries" (Lange 1938, p. 13).

16 The argument is close to that raised by Hicks who wrote:

> Surely there is every reason to suppose that an increase in the demand for consumers' goods, arising from an increase in employment, will often directly stimulate an increase in investment, at least as soon as an expectation develops that the increased demand will continue. If this is so, we ought to include *I* national income] in the second equation [investment function], though it must be confessed that the effect of *I* on the marginal efficiency of capital will be fitful and irregular. (Hicks 1937, p. 156)

One may also notice that it is assonant with Hobson's analysis, contained in his well-known 1910 book.

consumers' goods. The smaller the expenditure on consumption the smaller is the demand for consumers' goods and, consequently, the lower is the rate of net return on investment. Thus, the rate of interest being constant, investment per unit of time is the larger, the larger the total expenditure on consumption. (Lange 1938, p. 14 – emphasis in original)

Keynes, in Chapter 12 of the *General Theory*, considered that long-term expectations were merely exogenous, which amounts to assuming that investment was insensitive to current levels of output, consumption, or national income. In this respect, Lange's model evidently departs from Keynes's theory.[17]

In light of this premise, Lange's model can be summarised by the following four equations:

$$\frac{M}{P} = L(i, y) \qquad L_i \leq 0, \ L_y \geq 0 \tag{1}$$

$$c = \phi(y, i) \qquad 0 < \phi_y < 1 \quad \phi_i f\, 0 \tag{2}$$

$$I = F(i, c) \qquad F_i < 0 \ , \ F_c > 0 \tag{3}$$

$$y \equiv c + I \tag{4}$$

where M is the amount of money held by individuals or the real value of cash balances, y is total real income, i is the interest rate, c is total expenditure on consumption per unit of time, and I is investment per unit of time. According to Lange, M, y, c, and I are measured in wage units. Once the amount of money M (in wage units) is given, these four equations determine the four unknowns c, I, y, and i. Alternatively, i can be assumed to be given (i.e. exogenously set by the banking system) and M can be assumed to be endogenous.

In this case, the process of determination of the rate of interest is depicted by Lange in three diagrams. The first represents the relation between the demand for cash balances and the rate of interest. The quantity of money (in wage units) is measured on the axis OM and the rate of interest on the axis Oi, yielding a family of liquidity preference curves, one for each level of total income (measured in wage units). The greater the total income the higher positioned is the corresponding curve. We have a second family of curves (for each rate of interest) representing the relation between income and expenditure on consumption. Income is measured along Oy and expenditure on consumption along Oc. The relation

---

17 Kregel (1976, pp. 215–7) notes, however, that when dealing with money wage dynamics, and general policy, Keynes admitted that long-term expectations could be affected by current events.

between investment and the rate of interest is represented by the third graph. Measuring investment per unit of time along the OI axis and the rate of interest along the Oi axis we have a family of curves indicating investment corresponding to each value of the interest rate. These curves represent the marginal net return (marginal efficiency) of each amount of investment per unit of time. It is important to note that there is a separate curve for each level of expenditure on consumption. The greater the expenditure on consumption, the higher the position of the corresponding curve.

Having constructed this tool, Lange then determines interest rate, level of consumption, and investment in the economy. With a given amount of money, M_0 and a given initial level of income, say y, Equation (1) gives us a rate of interest of i_0. With y and i_0 given, Equation (2) determines total consumption, C_0, and Equation (3) provides the level of investment, i_0.

If we find that the sum of total consumption and investment precisely equals total income, then Equation (4) is confirmed. If not, we must start on a process of adjustment until an equilibrium position in the economy is established:

> This process of *mutual adjustment* goes on until the curves in our three diagrams have reached a position compatible with each other and with the quantity of money given, i.e., until equilibrium is attained. (Lange 1938, p. 17 – emphasis in original)

After having examined the *General Theory* of interest, Lange introduces the problem of under-consumption theorists (from Malthus onward) who believed that up to a certain point an increase in saving promotes investment, but beyond this point it would be harmful. To determine an optimal level of saving, Lange emphasised two effects working in opposite directions (Lampa 2014). First, an increase in the propensity to save induces a decrease in output which causes a negative "accelerator" effect on investment. Second, because of the fall in total income, as long as the money supply remains unchanged, the rate of interest falls, stimulating the level of investment. The optimality of the saving rate can be characterised by the condition that the decrease in investment brought about by decreasing income is just balanced by the increase in investment brought about by the pressure of lower income transaction monetary needs upon the rate of interest. Here is how Lange discusses both effects:

> Since investment per unit of time is a function of both the rate of interest and expenditure on consumption a decrease of the propensity to consume (increase in

the propensity to save) has a twofold effect. On the one hand the decrease of expenditure on consumption discourages investment, but the decrease in the propensity to consume also causes... a fall of the rate of interest which encourages investment on the other hand. The optimum propensity to consume is that at which the encouraging and the discouraging effect of a change are in balance. (1938, p. 34)

In an unpublished manuscript dated 1942 (see Samuelson, n.d.), Paul Samuelson attempted to determine whether Lange's model was conveying the essence of Keynes's ideas concerning the effects of an increase in saving or not. According to him, two critical propositions could be found in the *General Theory*: "(a) an increased desire to save serves merely to depress income" and "(b) the net result is actually less attained saving and investment". As a result, he stresses that the critical difference between Keynes and Lange appears to be that, notwithstanding the fact that Lange would surely agree with proposition (a), he would agree with (b) only up to the point of the optimum propensity to consume. If this were not to occur, emphasises Samuelson:

we would have a contradiction: income would then not have decreased, interest would not have fallen, and investment would not have risen. But then income must have fallen and not fallen simultaneously, which is an impossibility. Whether or not (b) is valid, it appears that Keynes contention (a) must hold. (1942, p. 23, see Samuelson n.d.)

A simple diagram of our own representing the saving and investment schedules may help illuminate this point (see also Lampa 2014). The marginal propensity to save $1 - \phi_y$ is assumed to be lower than the marginal propensity to invest $F_c\phi_y$.

Graphically, the negative "accelerator" effect of a fall in the marginal propensity to consume ϕ_y materialises in the rotation in the opposite direction of the saving and investment schedules whose slopes have respectively increased and decreased while the positive effect of the fall in the rate of interest comes with the upward shift of the investment schedule.[18] In the diagram (Figure 1), we have represented the situation in which the second effect balances the first one and the economy reaches a new equilibrium with a lower level of income but the same level of investment.

In his reply, Lange recognised the validity of Samuelson's interpretation and he clarified that the notion of "the optimum propensity to consume"

---

18 For sake of simplicity, we have left out the influence of the rate of interest on consumption.

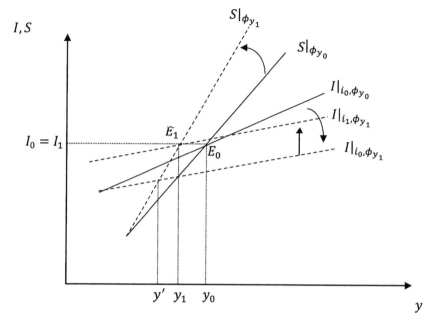

Figure 1. Samuelson on optimum propensity to save

is not the propensity which, for a given investment schedule, would guarantee a full employment level of national income:

> My optimum propensity to consume should in no way be interpreted as involving an "optimum" for policy. All it meant was maximizing the rate of investment. The policy optimum is in terms of maximum income and employment (plus stability considerations). In fact, when I wrote the article, I thought of writing another one on the propensity to consume which maximizes income, which I wanted to recommend as the optimum for policy. (1942, see Samuelson n.d.)[19]

Thus, he explicitly recognises that his theory of interest can be consistent with an analysis of both disequilibrium and under-employment equilibrium (Lampa 2014).

---

19 In a footnote added to the 1943 edition of his 1938 paper, he returned to this issue:

> Optimum means here merely "maximizing investment". This need not be the most desirable propensity to save from the point of view of social policy. From the latter point of view a propensity to save which maximizes real income may be more desirable. (Kowalik 1994, p. 211)

Although his article exclusively targets static analysis of the theory of interest and output with the aim of examining the effect of a change in thriftiness, Lange seems to recommend that an exhaustive approach to this topic should include dynamics as well. First, he explicitly cites Kalecki's 1937 business cycle model, thus suggesting a complementary as well as a consistent appendix to his own contribution.[20] In a cryptic footnote he explicitly states that in presence of time lags, the system might give rise to cyclical fluctuations:

> If this process of adjustment involves a time lag of a certain kind, a cyclical fluctuation, instead of equilibrium, is the result. Cf. Kalecki 'A theory of business cycle'….
> (Lange 1938, n. 1, p. 17)

Second, by way of conclusion, Lange pointed out that static investigation of how the optimum propensity to consume is attained was only part of the question, for:

> In a society where the propensity to save is determined by the individuals, there are no forces at work which keep it automatically at its optimum and it is well possible, as the underconsumption theorists maintain, that there is a tendency to exceed it.
> (Lange 1938, p. 32)

Unfortunately, Lange's 1938 article does not provide any further information on the role and characteristics of dynamics with respect to the change in the propensity to consume nor any elements illuminating how dependent the dynamics was to time lags.

In the following development, we try to shed some light on this issue by attempting a formal dynamic reconstruction along Kaleckian lines, as explicitly evoked by Lange in 1938.

4. The dynamisation of Lange's model: an interpretation

In order to both render effective and simplify our exposition, our starting point will be a general IS-LM model. First, it should be noted that such a general IS-LM model can be deduced easily from Lange's Equations (1)−(4)

---

20 According to Friedman (1946), such a methodology represented a typical example of "taxonomic theorizing", since formal and abstract analysis preceded (as well as determined) both the macroeconomic investigation and the economic policy proposals:

> …the ultimate test of the validity of a theory is not conformity to the canons of formal logic but the ability to deduce facts that have not yet been observed, that are capable of being contradicted by observation, and that subsequent observation does not contradict. (Friedman 1946, p. 631)

only on condition only that the equality (4) is assumed to be an equilibrium equation (whereas Lange emphasises that it is an identity).[21,22]

Second, the present analysis will adopt Kalecki's lag structure, as explicitly suggested by Lange himself in a footnote (1938). In a revised version of his 1937 business cycle model, Kalecki (1939) criticised Lange for not exploring the "fundamental importance" of this lag for analysing the dynamics of the economy. His point was that when a relatively long time is needed to complete investment projects, current investments are a result of former investment decisions and become a "datum inherited from the past like the capital equipment" (Kalecki 1937, p. 81). It follows that the "dynamic process" is similar to "a chain of short period equilibra" each of them prevailing as long as the actual level of investment remains unchanged. Naturally, in order to determine how "the links of the chains are connected" it becomes necessary to explain how investment decisions are related to the current economic situation.

With respect to this point, Lange's model did not suffer from the flaw identified by Kalecki (1936) in Keynes's analysis of investment. Kalecki was convinced that the development of a proper dynamic theory of employment implies the idea that the current rate of investment may itself, by means of current changes in profits, affect current investment decisions. In Lange's model, the influence of current profits (resulting from actual investments) on investment decisions is taken into account through the introduction of the level of real consumption (which is considered as a proxy of expected profitability in the investment function by Lange, as we have shown). It is true that the assumption of real variable (as Lange introduced the level of real consumption as an argument of the investment function) may obscure some important changes in prices that might influence investment decisions. In particular, any increase in investment which might improve profit expectations implies, at the same time, an increase in prices of investment goods that

---

21 One could add that also the shape of the LM curve is the result of a theoretical assumption, whereas in Lange it was "empirically determined". See: Boianovsky (2004, pp. 106–7).

22 The IS curve is therefore given by the following equation:

$$Y = \phi(y, i) + F(\phi(y, i), i)$$

whose slope is

$$\left.\frac{di}{dy}\right|_{IS} = \frac{1 - \phi_y - F_C\phi_y}{\phi_i + F_C\phi_i + F_i}$$

might reduce it. Although Lange's model does not allow disentangling these two effects, it helps highlighting, as we will see, how feedback effects of current investment on investment decisions, depending on the shape of the $F(.)$ and $\phi(.)$ functions, are likely to set off fluctuations.

A possible way to formalise Kalecki's time lag notion consists of assuming that actual investment changes according to the following equation:

$$dI/dt = \theta[I^d - I] \tag{5}$$

where I^d refers to the desired investment, I to actual investment, and θ to the speed of adjustment of the actual level of investment to the level of investment decisions.[23]

In contrast, it is assumed that the money market adjusts instantaneously through fluctuations in the interest rate. Solving the money market equation for i, we obtain

$$i = i(y, P, M)$$

To examine the dynamics, it is useful to introduce the following notation: F_x stands for the partial derivative of function F with respect to x: $i_y = -L_y/L_i > 0$, $i_P = -M/(P^2 L_i) \geq 0$, and $i_M = 1/L_i P \leq 0$.[24]

In the long run, the capital accumulation is defined as

$$dK/dt = I - \delta K \tag{6}$$

where $\delta < 1$, the rate of depreciation, is assumed to be proportional to the stock of capital.

The essential dynamic feature that enables the model to display cyclical behaviour is introduced by a Kaleckian assumption about the inverse relation between the capital stock and investment decisions: for any level of

---

23 The investment dynamics formalised by Kalecki was more complex since his analysis, by distinguishing three stages in the investment–production nexus: decisions to invest, the production period, and the time of delivery leads up to a mixed difference and differential equation.

24 Kalecki recognised in his 1937 paper that the coefficient i_y was likely to change during the business cycle:

We see that the rise of investment I increases the demand for cash and has in that way the tendency to raise the rate of interest. It is, however, not the only way in which the rate of interest is affected by a change in investment I. The investment I as we know determines (with a given capital equipment) the short-period equilibrium and thus the "general state of affairs." But the better this state of affairs the greater is the "lender's confidence" and, therefore, through this channel the rise of investment has a tendency to lower the rate of interest. (Kalecki 1937, p. 87)

consumption and income, an increasing capital stock lowers the marginal efficiency of capital, implying that investment decision is lower.[25] The investment curve is therefore, in the diagram drawn in Section 3, shifting downwards for high capital stock levels. Similar reasoning holds for a low level of the capital stock. The desired investment function is thus now

$$I^d = F(c, i, K)$$

In the short run, the actual level of investment, I, is given. So, as long as the consumption does not depend on the rate of interest, equilibrium in the goods market requires that $Y = (I + \bar{c})/(1 - \phi_y)$ where $\bar{c}$ is the autonomous component of consumption.[26] Replacing this expression in the equation and interest rate equations, we get

$$I^d = G(I, K)$$

where $G_I = (F_c\phi_y + F_i i_y)/(1 - \phi_y)$ and $G_K = F_K$.

Substituting the investment demand function in Equation (5), we get

$$\frac{dI}{dt} = \theta\Big(G(I, K) - I\Big) \tag{7}$$

The dynamics for this model therefore are given by Equations (6) and (7).

The long-run equilibrium values for I and K, obtained by setting $dI/dt = 0$ and $dK/dt = 0$ in Equations (6) and (7), are given by

$$I^* = \frac{\left(\frac{F_c\phi_y + F_i i_y}{1 - \phi_y}\right)\bar{c}}{1 - \frac{F_c\phi_y + F_i i_y}{1 - \phi_y} - F_K\delta}$$

and

$$K^* = \frac{1}{\delta}\frac{\left(\frac{F_c\phi_y + F_i i_y}{1 - \phi_y}\right)\bar{c}}{1 - \frac{F_c\phi_y + F_i i_y}{1 - \phi_y} - F_K\delta}$$

An increase in F_c and in ϕ_y increases the long-run equilibrium values of I and K by increasing effective demand due to an increase in consumption and investment, while an increase in F_K and δ reduces it by increasing the depressive effect of capital stock on investment, and by reducing the steady state level of investment.

---

25 Lange (1941b) attached great importance to this assumption.
26 Equilibrium between aggregate demand and aggregate output requires that $Y = I + C$ and thus $Y = (1 + \bar{c})/(1 - \phi_y)$.

To examine the local dynamics, we compute the Jacobian matrix evaluated in a neighbourhood of this steady state:

$$J = \begin{bmatrix} \theta(G_I - 1) & \theta F_K \\ 1 & -\delta \end{bmatrix}$$

The trace and determinant of this matrix are

$$T = -[\delta + \theta(1 - G_I)] \qquad D = \theta[-\delta(G_I - 1) - F_K]$$

Since the sufficient conditions for stability of the system are Tr $(J) < 0$ and Det $(J) > 0$, the condition $G_I < 1$ and so $F_c\phi_y + F_i i_y < 1 - \phi_y$ is sufficient to ensure stability and dampened oscillations. However, that it is not necessary is evidenced by the fact that $F_c\phi_y + F_i i_y = 1 - \phi_y$ still satisfies the stability condition. Explosive oscillations will occur if Tr $(J) > 0$ while Det $(J) > 0$. If $G_I > 1$ and so $F_c\phi_y + F_i i_y > 1 - \phi_y$, and θ is sufficiently large, so that $\theta \geq \delta [1 - \phi_y/(F_c\phi_y + F_i i_y - (1 - \phi_y))]$, the trace condition will be violated and persistent or explosive oscillations become possible. Thus the stable oscillations depend on the reaction coefficients F_c, ϕ_y, F_i, i_y, and the time lag represented by θ.

To further analyse the dynamic behaviour of this model we use the phase diagram for the two state variables I and K as shown in Figure 2.[27]

---

27 The isocline for $dK/dt = 0$ is seen, from Equation (6), to be given by the following equation:

$$I = \delta K$$

whose slope is equal to

$$\left. \frac{dK}{dI} \right|_{\dot{K}=0} = \frac{1}{\delta}$$

which is a positively sloped straight line. K rises below this line and falls above it, explaining the direction of the vertical arrows. The isocline for $dI/dt = 0$ is given by

$$I = \frac{F_K K}{1 - G_I}$$

whose slope is equal to

$$\left. \frac{dK}{dI} \right|_{\dot{I}=0} = \frac{1 - G_I}{F_K}$$

This shows that to the left of this isocline I is rising and to its right it is falling, explaining the direction of the horizontal arrows in the figure. If $F_c\phi_y + F_i i_y^m$ is lower than $1 - \phi_y$, this yields a downward-sloping straight line. As depicted in Figure 1, the cyclical behaviour is necessarily dampened.

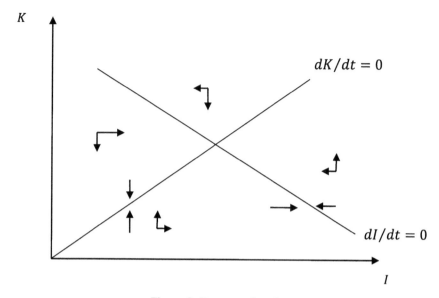

Figure 2. Dampened cycles.

If we have $F_c\phi_y + F_i i_Y > 1 - \phi_y$, the $dI/dt = 0$ isocline becomes positively sloped. In this case, we can distinguish between two possibilities. In one, in which the $dI/dt = 0$ isocline is flatter than the $dK/dt = 0$ isocline, we have $(G_I - 1) > \frac{F_K}{\delta}$, which implies that the determinant condition for stability is violated. This means that the dynamics of the system are saddlepoint-unstable, and there are no cycles. In the other case in which the $dI/dt = 0$ isocline is steeper than the $dK/dt = 0$ isocline, the determinant condition is satisfied, and the dynamics of I are unstable (leading I away from its null-cline) while those for K are stable. The result is cycles: explosive cycles if the trace becomes positive, and dampened ones if it is negative. Since the trace condition can be written as $\theta\left(\frac{F_c\phi_y + F_i i_Y}{1 - \phi_y} - 1\right) < \delta$, it is more likely to be satisfied the longer the investment lag or the smaller is θ.

When cycles do occur, their occurrence is related to both the slow adjustment of desired investment to actual investment and to the negative effect of capital stock on desired investment. If θ is infinitely large so that adjustment is very rapid, the economy will always be on the $dI/dt = 0$, so that adjustment to the long-run equilibrium will be smooth as long as the determinant condition is satisfied. If θ is large relatively to the rate at which the amount of equipment is increasing, the rate of investment decisions can change even though the level of profit and income remain stable. This happens at the peak and at the trough of the cycle when, for a given level of profit, the capital stock is increasing (or decreasing) and, the rate of profit goes down (up) causing investment decisions to decline (increase).

Thus introducing a time lag between the investment decision and the corresponding income may explain a cyclical movement even if the underlying situation is stable; although, in order that the cycle is not highly dampened (i.e. that it does not peter out too quickly in the absence of new disturbing factors), we need to assume that the effect of current investment on total equipment is relatively large, such that the equipment added during the period of the time lag has a considerable influence on the investment decision. It should be noted, however, that Lange's 1938 model, once dynamised along these lines, departs significantly from Kalecki's 1939 business cycle model. By resorting to his theory of profit, Kalecki aims at showing that the dynamics of the profit rate was completely independent from the functional distribution dynamics. This is because, in the presence of an investment time lag, the profit level remains uniquely determined by the actual level of investment and capitalists' expenditures. It follows that any change in the profit share which may happen during the business cycle will have no effect on total *current* profits, since they continue to be determined by actual investment and are themselves determined by past investment decisions. Hence, as long as investment remains constant there will be the same total amount of profits (i.e of saving). Naturally, while profits remain unchanged, the real wages and real national product will vary following the variations in aggregate demand, with a consequent fall or rise in output which will adjust as much as the new percentage share of profits in output renders an unchanged absolute amount of profits. We hence find the very striking Kaleckian proposition that capitalists (considered as a whole) cannot impinge the course of the cycle by raising their share in national income.[28] This does not mean income distribution does not affect the time path of national income, as a higher value of the profit share reduces the amplitude of output over the cycle. It means that the determinants of the profits share will have no effect on the current level of profit and thus on actual profitability. As a result, Kalecki's model breaks the connection between the dynamics of functional distribution and the dynamics of investment. On the contrary, in Lange's model, one can easily see that any change in the propensity to save that might result from a change in income distribution will directly change investment decisions and the dynamics of the economy.

---

28 See López and Assous (2010) for further details.

With this respect, Lange's model is closer to Marx's description of the business cycle than to Kalecki's.

Let us now examine the model when it is non-linear. Because of the introduction of non-linear reaction functions in I and K, the first derivatives of the model are non-constant and the sign of the trace can change. As a result, the model is likely to produce a self-sustained cycle in absence of any delay between actual investment and investment decisions (θ is infinitely large). This is the case when, for extreme values of the level of investment, $F_c\phi_y + F_i i_y$ is lower than $1 - \phi_y$ while for normal values of investment $F_c\phi_y + F_i i_y$ is higher than $1 - \phi_y$. Under this condition, the trace will be positive for very high and for very low levels of investment, and negative for normal levels of investment. Mathematically, these changes in the sign of the trace will allow the generation of self-sustaining cycles.[29] This is illustrated in Figure 2 by the fact that the $dI/dt = 0$ curve is decreasing for low and high levels of investment, and increasing for normal values of capital stock. In that case, the economy never reaches a stationary equilibrium. We saw earlier that the shape of the isocline for $dI/dt = 0$ because F_K is negative (negative capacity effect), depends upon the value of G_I.

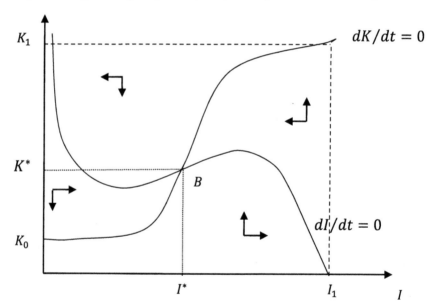

Figure 3. Self-sustained cycles.

---

29 The proof is a straightforward application of the Poincaré–Bendixson theorem.

Figure 3 shows that at very low and very high values of I, the isocline is negatively sloped; this corresponds to the areas where the savings function is steeper than the investment function. However, for normal values of I, the isocline is positively sloped, which corresponds to the region where the investment curve is steeper than the savings curve. Above the isocline, $dI/dt < 0$, and investment falls; below the isocline, $dI/dt > 0$, and investment rises. The directional arrows indicate these tendencies. Both curves are drawn such that the locus $dK/dt = 0$ intersects the ordinate at $K_0 > 0$ and that the curve $dI/dt = 0$ intersects the abscissa at $I_1 > I^*$. The curve $dI/dt = 0$ approaches the K-axis for $K \to \infty$.

When the $dI/dt = 0$ isocline is flatter than the $dK/dt = 0$ line at its intersection, the determinant of the Jacobian matrix is positive and limit cycles can exist. Indeed, if the trace condition is violated, that is, if $F_e \phi_y + F_i i_y > 1 - \phi_y$ is sufficiently large, the equilibrium B is unstable, and trajectories close to it will push the economy towards the limit cycle. The combination of the non-linear investment and saving curves, in absence of any delay between actual investment and investment decisions, is thus sufficient to produce limit cycles.

When there is no investment lag (θ is infinitely large) so that the economy is always on the $dI/dt = 0$ isocline, the economic dynamics is particularly interesting. Any high equilibrium will slowly decline due to the increase of the stock of capital until there is a catastrophic drop to a new low equilibrium, which now will slowly increase due to the decrease of the stock of capital until a new high equilibrium is reached, etc. Notice that during this catastrophic fall or rise, output is driven solely by the multiplier dynamic, the slower-moving capital dynamic is inoperative since, in moving from one equilibrium to another, capital is constant. Therefore, we show that cycles can exist without investment lags, which is perfectly consistent with Lange's idea that time lags represent the *phenomenal form* of capitalist dynamics and not its primary determinant.

With this respect, Lange's model offers an interesting framework for investigating the effects of structural changes that he wished for in his 1935 plea for Marxian economics. It is clear, however, that this model in itself, sheds no light on the origin of the "data" responsible for the trend (just like in Kalecki's 1939 and Kaldor's 1940 models) and, consequently, does not contain the solution to Lange's pursuit of a satisfactory "theory of economic evolution". The reason why is that Lange thought that this problem could be overcome only by developing a theory combining Schumpeter's analysis of innovation (and productivity) with either Kalecki's or Kaldor's trade cycle models, as evidenced by his 1941 review to Schumpeter's *Business Cycles*. On the one hand, he criticises Schumpeter's theory because it is not connected with the fluctuation of the level of employment (as well as the degree of utilisation of resources) and he praises both Kalecki's and Kaldor's analyses, based on what he defines "adaptive fluctuations of the rate of investment" (p.193). On the other hand, he stresses the limits of these latter contributions, as they both assume the unrealistic hypothesis that net disinvestment of capital during the recessions permits to turn the downswing to upswing, whereas Lange (following Schumpeter) is persuaded that the key factor is the higher productivity due to innovations. Therefore, he concluded:

> This raises the question of a possible synthesis between the 'adaptive fluctuations of investment' theories and that of Professor Schumpeter. The cycle in investment activity may prove to be a consequence of both adaptive fluctuations and fluctuations in the rate of innovation resulting from changes in the risk of failure.

Since:

> Professor Schumpeter's theory (...) provides us with a decisive element of any realistic explanation of the phenomenon. (Lange 1941b, p. 193)

Unfortunately, Lange did not highlight how waves of (profit-led) innovations were likely to cause changes in the parameters of the investment and saving function nor did he clarify how these changes would come through change in income distribution. Therefore, his 1938 analysis remains necessarily incomplete.

5. Concluding remarks

The analysis developed in this article can be interpreted as both a reconstruction of Oskar Lange's early beliefs on capitalist dynamics and (on such bases) a further development in terms of a dynamic analysis of his 1938 theory of interest, contained in "The Rate of Interest and the Optimum Propensity to Consume".

With respect to the first issue, we have shown that Karl Marx's (together with Joseph A. Schumpeter's) analysis of capitalist dynamics represented a crucial source of inspiration for Lange, because of the pivotal (as well as destabilising) role played by distributive conflict, technical progress (i.e. innovation), and accumulation of capital (i.e. uncoordination between investment and savings). Furthermore, we have also highlighted Lange's interest in Kalecki's (1939) and Kaldor's (1940) theories of the business cycle, because of their strict connection with the fluctuation of both employment and investment.

On the other hand – starting from an unedited correspondence between Lange and Paul Samuelson and from a sibylline footnote of Lange himself (1938) – we have clarified that his 1938 static model can easily be translated into a dynamic model in which the marginal propensity to consume (i.e. to save) plays a key role, as this latter may, by means of the investment, determine the stability property of the economy in a particular way. If there is a unique stationary equilibrium and the standard macro condition is globally satisfied, the unique equilibrium will be stable. If there are multiple equilibria due to varying marginal propensities to save, some will be stable and others will be unstable so that self-sustained cycles become possible. Naturally, any distribution policy that would modify the marginal propensity to save is likely to change the stability properties of the economy.

In turn, our results are able to capture some relevant aspects of Lange's (previous) reflection on dynamics. First, the functional distribution of income depends on the dynamics of the profit rate and it is related to saving, so that some of Marx's main ideas about the intrinsic instability of capitalism (i.e. about cycles and growth) are encapsulated.

Second, our results show that cycles can exist even without an investment lag, which is perfectly consistent with Lange's broader idea about the meaning and the role of time lags, as exposed in Section 2 of the article.

Finally – although our model could not capture the crucial interaction between technological progress and income distribution, since Lange (1938) largely ignores such implications – we have shown that Lange was persuaded that a synthesis between Kaldor's and Kalecki's theories and that of Schumpeter, in which the cycle in investment activity may prove to be a consequence of both adaptive fluctuations of investment and fluctuations in the rate of innovation resulting from changes in the risk of failure, might have been possible. In Lange's eye, such a synthesis precisely represented a "modern" and consistent reconstruction of the Marxist theory of the business cycle: unfortunately, probably due to his wide and ambitious scientific project, as well as due to his intense political and diplomatic career in the 1940s, he could not elaborate it.

Acknowledgements

For their many helpful suggestions and motivating advices, Michaël Assous and Roberto Lampa want to thank the three anonymous referees. Michaël Assous gratefully acknowledges the suggestions he received from the participants at the workshop "Crises, Business Cycles Theories and Economic

Policy", Les Treilles, 12–17 September 2011. Part of the research for this article was conducted during Michaël Assous's stay at Duke's Center for the History of Political Economy, where he profited from discussions with faculty and fellows, especially those from Marcel Boumans. For their professional support, Michaël Assous is also thankful to the archivists at the David M. Rubenstein Rare Book and Manuscript Library, Duke University.

Funding

Financial support for this project was provided by Procope (Partenariat Hubert Curie).

References

Boianovsky, M., 2004. The IS-LM model and the liquidity trap concept: from Hicks to Krugman. *History of political economy*, 36, 92–126.

Darity, W. and Young, W., 1995. IS-LM: an inquest. *History of political economy*, 27 (1), 1–41.

Friedman, M., 1946. Lange on price flexibility and employment: a methodological criticism. *American economic review*, 36 (4), 613–31.

Hicks, J.R., 1937. Mr. Keynes and the 'classics'; a suggested interpretation. *Econometrica*, 5 (2), 147–59.

Hobson, J.A., 1910 (1992). *The industrial system: an inquiry into earned and unearned income*. London: Routledge.

Julio López, G. and Assous, M., 2010. *Michal Kalecki*. London: Palgrave MacMillan.

Kaldor, N., 1940. A model of the trade cycle. *Economic journal*, 50, 78–92.

Kalecki, M., 1936. *Some Remarks on Keynes's Theory* translated by F. Targetti and B. Kinda-Hass in Kalecki, M., 1990. Collected Works of Michał Kalecki Volume I Capitalism: Business Cycles and Full Employment Oxford: The Clarendon Press.

Kalecki, M., 1937. A theory of the business cycle. *Review of economic studies*, 4 (2), 77–97.

Kalecki, M., 1939. *Essays in the theory of economic fluctuations*. London: George Allen and Unwin.

Kalecki, M., 1966. Oscar Lange 1904–1965. *Economic journal*, 76 (302), 431–2.

Kowalik, T., ed., 1994. *Economic theory and market socialism: selected essays of Oskar Lange*. Cheltenham: Edward Elgar.

Kowalik, T., 2008. Lange, Oskar Ryszard (1904–1965). *The new Palgrave: a dictionary of economics. First edition*. Eds. John Eatwell, Murray Milgate and Peter Newman. Palgrave Macmillan, 1987. The New Palgrave Dictionary of Economics Online. Palgrave Macmillan. 02 July 2014 <http://www.dictionaryofeconomics.com/article?id=pde1987_X001267> doi:10.1057/9780230226203.2923

Kowalik, T., 2009. Luxemburg's and Kalecki's theories and visions of capitalist dynamics. *In*: R. Bellofiore, ed. *Rosa Luxemburg and the critique of political economy*. London: Palgrave Macmillan, 102–15.

Kregel, J., 1976. Economic methodology in the face of uncertainty: the modelling methods of Keynes and the post-Keynesians. *Economic journal*, 86, 209–25.

Lampa, R., 2011. Scientific rigor and social relevance: the two dimensions of Oskar R. Lange's early economic analysis (1931–1945), thesis abstract. *Journal of the history of economic thought*, 33 (4), 557–9.

Lampa, R., 2014. A 'Walrasian Post-Keynesian' model? Resolving the paradox of Oskar Lange's 1938 theory of interest. Cambridge Journal of Economics, 38 (1): 63–86.

Lange, O., 1935. Marxian economics and modern economic theory. *Review of economic studies*, 2 (3), 189–201.

Lange, O., 1937. On the economic theory of socialism: part two. *Review of economic studies*, 4 (2), 123–42.

Lange, O., 1938. The rate of interest and the optimum propensity to consume. *Economica*, 5 (17), 12–32.

Lange, O., 1941a. Review: business cycles: a theoretical, historical and statistical analysis of the capitalist process. *Review of economic and statistics*, 23 (4), 190–3.

Lange, O., 1941b. Review: essays in the theory of economic fluctuations. *Journal of political economy*, 49 (2), 279–85.

Lange, O., 1943. A note on innovations. *Review of economic and statistics*, 25 (1), 19–25.

Lange, O., 1965. *On political economy and econometrics; essays in honour of Oskar Lange*. Oxford, New York, Pergamon Press.

Lange. O., 1987. The Economic Operation of a Socialist Society: II. *Contributions to political economy*, 6 (1): 13–24.

Meade, J.E., 1937. A simplified model of Mr. Keynes' system. *Review of economic studies*, 4 (2), 98–107.

Minsky, H.P., 2009. Beginnings. *PSL quarterly review*, 62 (248–251), 191–203.

Rappoport, P., 1992. Meade's 'general theory' model: stability and the role of expectations. *Journal of money, credit, and banking*, 24 (3), 356–69.

Samuelson, P., 1941. The stability of equilibrium: comparative statics and dynamics. *Econometrica*, 9 (2), 97–120.

Samuelson, P. n.d. Paul A. Samuelson papers, 1933–2010 and undated, Economists' Papers Project, Rare Book, Manuscript, and Special Collections Library, Duke University.

Timlin, M.F., 1942. *Keynesian economics*. Toronto: University of Toronto Press.

Toporowski, J., 2012. Lange and Keynes. *SOAS Department of Economics working paper series, No.170*. London: The School of Oriental and African Studies.

Young, W., 1987. *Interpreting Mr Keynes: the IS-LM enigma*. Cambridge: Polity-Blackwell.

Young, W., 2008. Is IS-LM a static and dynamic Keynesian model? *In*: R. Leeson, ed. *Archival insights into the evolution of economics, the Keynesian tradition*. London: Palgrave Macmillan, 126–34.

Abstract

Oskar Lange's 1938 article "The Rate of Interest and the Optimum Propensity to Consume" is usually associated with the original IS-LM approach of the late 1930s. However, Lange's article was not only an attempt to illuminate Keynes's main innovations but the first part of a wide project that included the development of a theory of economic evolution. This paper aims at showing that Lange's article can help in illuminating critical aspects of this project: in particular, Lange's idea that a synthesis between Kaldor's and Kalecki's theories and that of Schumpeter, might have been possible and that it represented (in intentions) a "modern" and consistent reconstruction of the Marxist theory of the business cycle. Section 2 clarifies Lange's early reflection on dynamics. Section 3 centres on Lange's 1938 static model and indicates the effects of a change of saving on investment. Section 4 suggests a dynamic reconstruction from which are addressed important arguments raised by Lange in a series of papers written between 1934 and 1942.

Toward a non-linear theory of economic fluctuations: Allais's contribution to endogenous business cycle theory in the 1950s

Alain Raybaut

1. Introduction

Most early post-war contributions to non-linear business cycle theory are credited to authors adopting a certain form of Keynesianism. Indeed, the approach initiated by Kaldor, Hicks and Goodwin contributed to the development of Keynesian macrodynamics within a non-linear perspective. Kaldor, Hicks and Goodwin's original approach is well-known and has been extensively studied following the renewed interest in non-linear dynamics in the 1980s (see e.g. Lorenz 1989). The pioneering mathematical formulations proposed by Yasui, Morishima and Ichimura are less known but are examined in detail in Velupillai (2008), which is dedicated to Japanese advances in non-linear dynamics in the 1950s. Therefore, we do not elaborate this approach further. We simply highlight that these contributions were the first to investigate closely the question of the existence and uniqueness of a limit cycle in the business cycle models of Kaldor, Hicks and Goodwin with Liénard or van der Pol equations and Levinson and Smith (1942) criteria resorting to controversial ad hoc assumptions (see Velupillai 2008). These findings were synthesised by Ichimura (1955) in his classical attempt to develop a general non-linear macrodynamic theory of economic fluctuations along Keynesian lines.

However, it would be misleading to attribute the pioneering research in the field of non-linear cycle theory exclusively to this first tradition. This paper attempts to shed light on the existence of another view expressed by Allais who published a less well-known but impressive number of contributions to non-linear cycle theory in the 1950s.

The paper focuses on different versions of Allais's non-linear model of endogenous monetary cycles. As in the first approach, Allais draws on the theory of non-linear dynamic systems in relation to limit cycles and relaxation oscillations. For Allais, relaxation oscillations are particularly relevant for modelling economic fluctuations as a lagged regulation process. The general formulation of the model based on his subtle theory of money is rather complex, and different approximations and simplifications are necessary to obtain analytical results. However, it can be shown analytically that the model admits a limit cycle provided, notably, that the stationary point is unstable and that the reaction functions of the agents are sufficiently non-linear. Allais also provides numerical examples and develops a prototype of the calibration procedure in his theoretical modelling of US data. The mathematical tools are similar to those used by Goodwin and the Japanese school, but the analytical frameworks are quite distinct. In particular, contrary to the emerging Keynesian macrodynamics, for Allais, the endogenous cycles are monetary and are explained by the gap between the desired cash balances and the actual stock of money.

As Allais pointed out in his 1988 Nobel Lecture, his experience of the major fluctuations associated with the Great Depression convinced him that "there can be neither economic efficiency nor equitable distribution of income in an economy with monetary instability" (Allais 1988, p. 6). By the 1940s, this conviction led him to think more about monetary phenomena and economic fluctuations. Thus, from the beginning, money was the key ingredient in Allais's view of economic dynamics. Accordingly, in the 1950s, he developed different versions of a non-linear model of business cycles. These models elaborate and extend the monetary explanation of economic fluctuations through variations in the desired cash balances in relation to the monetary policy outlined in Chapter VIII of his book *Economie et intérêt* published in 1947, and are completed by some macroeconomic accounting relations derived from his idiosyncratic macroeconomic treatise *Fondements comptables de la macroéconomie* (Allais 1954a). It should be noted that Allais was familiar with Fisher, and his theory follows some main Fisherian lines. Since the objective here is not to show what Allais borrows from various authors, we focus on the bare bones and results of his non-linear business cycle models.

The paper is organised as follows. The general framework supporting Allais's contribution to the analysis of endogenous fluctuations is outlined in Section 2. Section 3 presents the simplifications introduced by Allais and examines the conditions of existence of a limit cycle in this framework. Section 4 is devoted to Allais's comments on cyclical dynamics and its empirical verification. Section 5 offers some concluding remarks.

2. Money and endogenous cycles in Allais's contributions: the analytical framework

In 2001, Allais published the *Fondements de la dynamique monétaire*, devoted to the discussion of his main contributions to monetary dynamics. The introduction to this 1300-page volume provides an interesting synthesis of the genesis of Allais's monetary thinking over 50 years.[1] Indeed, Allais makes a distinction between two great periods in this research agenda, explaining that during the first period, 1947–1955, he characterised the fundamental principles and causal effects of the monetary dynamics and conceived his general theory of money, prices, interest, and economic fluctuations. On this basis, in the second period, 1961–1985, he developed his restatement of the quantitative theory of money and refined his "hereditary" theory of monetary dynamics and growth.[2]

During the first period, beside two major books, *Economie et intérêt* (1947) and *Les fondements comptables de la macroéconomie* (1954a), Allais published three lengthy essays on non-linear business cycle theory. First, in 1953, he contributed a paper to the European meeting of the Econometric Society in Innsbrück.[3] Second, in 1954, he wrote his major contribution to the issue, "Explication des cycles économiques par un modèle non linéaire à régulation retardée".[4] The third essay was written for the International Conference on Dynamics held in Paris in 1955. Allais (2001) indicates that these three formal contributions refer to the same theoretical framework. The first essay focuses on a simplified case of the general model which is analysed in the second and third essays.[5]

Allais explains that the theoretical framework and economic content of the model were discussed initially in Chapter VIII of *Economie et Intérêt*, in particular, the idea of the monetary origin of the dynamics and its endogenous type.[6] Accordingly, Allais makes a distinction between several

---

1 We are indebted to an anonymous referee for this point.
2 Allais explains that between 1955 and 1960, he dedicated his time to theoretical and experimental physics, and that after 1986, he worked essentially on European issues (see Allais 2001, pp. 27–38).
3 Only a short abstract of this 135-page essay and its discussion were published in *Econometrica* in 1954 (Allais 1954b). In his *Fondements de la dynamique monétaire*, Allais reproduced the first part and the conclusion to this text.
4 This paper was presented at the Econometric Conference in Uppsala in August 1954.
5 In the first model, the cyclical fluctuations are captured simply by the rate of variation of global expenditure, and formulation of the demand for and supply of money are not hereditary. In the complete version, Allais introduces his concept of "hereditary function," and the cycle is measured by a function of the previous rates of variation of global expenditure.
6 Especially, pp. 229–442 and pp. 318–68.

amplifying factors of the fluctuations, and the necessary and sufficient conditions accounting for their existence, the *sinequanon* factors.[7] For Allais, there are two and only two *sinequa* non-factors: the possibility for agents to hold the desired money balances and the capacity for managers in the banking system to create overdraft money.[8]

Starting with the traditional equation $D = PQ = M_S V$, where P is the general price level, M_S is the total stock of money, V is its average velocity, Q is an index of the level of activity, and D is the level of nominal global expenditures, Allais assumes a causative chain running from monetary variables to global expenditure. Indeed, he supposes that the variations in D are explained by the capacity of the banking system to modify the money supply, or by the variation in velocity V, which refers to hoarding behaviours and the "propensity to liquidity" of the agents.[9] In this perspective, an economy with neutral money is characterised by a constant level of global expenditure and cannot exhibit any form of cyclical fluctuations.[10]

Allais explains that in *Economie et intérêt*, he also introduced the key idea of a monetary cycle as a relaxation phenomenon, notably using the metaphor of a steam engine generating an endogenous cyclical dynamics with "lagged-regulation." However, he does not build a mathematical model of this endogenous cycle in *Economie et Intérêt*. Allais quickly realised that this type of "verbal reasoning" was unexciting and not sufficiently convincing, which according to him, might explain the many doubts and critiques of his explanation of cycles initially developed in *Economie et intérêt*.[11] Consequently, in his three 1950s' essays, his intention was to go further and propose the development of a fully fledged model based on certain advances in non-linear dynamics and numerical studies.[12]

---

7 The first ones refer to different elements traditionally mobilised in the business cycle literature such as the increasingly roundabout character of production, different market imperfections, and the role of expectations and errors. These factors play an important role, notably, in the intensity and amplitude of the fluctuations but they do not, for Allais, account for its existence. Here, Allais refers explicitly in his Innsbruck's paper to a passage in *Economie et intérêt* (see Allais 2001, p. 229).

8 For more details, see *Economie et Intérêt*, pp. 229–422.

9 Allais assumes that the monetary base remains constant.

10 Allais (1953), fn. 6, reprinted in Allais (2001), p. 229.

11 See Allais (2001, p. 235).

12 We will refer mainly to Allais (1956), which is the version of the communication in Uppsala, published in *Metroecomometrica*, which contains key features of Allais's views on business cycles. This 78-page long article, which details the variants of Allais's model and some numerical experiments, was submitted to *Metroeconomica* in 1954. Thus, it was written before Ichimura's classical contribution and was published in 1955, but Allais refers in his bibliography Ichimura's original mimeo written in June 1953. Allais (2001, p. 71) indicates clearly that he

The key factors in Allais's modelling of endogenous cycles are an equation describing the dynamics of global expenditures described by him as the fundamental equation of monetary dynamics, and the "hereditary" formulations of the demand for and the supply of money that depends nonlinearly on lagged expenditures. This analytical framework is considered in detail next.

The starting point of the model is a simple relation which explains the dynamics of global expenditure, defined as the sum of all funds spent by the agents within a period of time. This relation states that the global expenditure $TD(t + T)$ in period $t + T$ is equal to the nominal income in the preceding period $TR_T(t)$ augmented by the gap between the actual and desired money balances in the period t, $M(t) - M_D(t)$. That is,

$$TD(t + T) = TR_T(t) + M(t) - M_D(t) \qquad (1)$$

where T denotes the agents' delayed reaction. Accordingly, this delay measures the length of the period existing between the creation and the expenditure of the global income.[13]

A second relation specifies the desired level of money balances $M_D(t)$ as the product of the current nominal expenditure $D(t)$ and a function f which encapsulates the agents' decisions to hold money balances:

$$M_D(t) = D(t)f\left(u(t)\right) \qquad (2)$$

The economic justification for this assumption is as follows. When global expenditure decreases during bad times, Allais supposes that the economic agents tend to increase their monetary balances beyond their normal or strictly necessary levels. Indeed, with falling prices, the agents postpone their purchasing decisions, and because of the global atmosphere of economic insecurity, they increase their stock of liquid balances. However, Allais explains that they will not continue to hoard indefinitely if the purchasing power of their balances exceeds a certain value. Conversely, during good times when global expenditure is increasing, the agents are confident, the propensity to liquidity declines, and the agents reduce their monetary balances below their normal levels. However,

---

considered his Paris communication to be an extension of his 1954 article. Among the modifications which do not include the qualitative initial conclusions, he mentions the possibility of the money base varying during periods of hyperinflation, the introduction of a more complex hereditary function with endogenous delays as a function of the rate of psychological expansion, and the addition of exogenous perturbations.

13 We reproduce here the notation in Allais (1956).

despite the inflationist tendency, it is necessary to maintain a minimum amount of money balances. Allais captures these modifications to the propensity to liquidity over the cycle, by a non-linear relation f as a function of the indicator of the level of economic prosperity.

Therefore, this function f bounded from above is positive monotonous and decreasing in $u(t)$, the indicator of economic prosperity in the period computed by the agents.[14] This key function encapsulates Allais's theory of liquidity preference, and the indicator $u(t)$ is described by Allais as the "individual psychological rate of economic expansion" (Allais 1956, p. 9). Indeed, this idiosyncratic formulation of the demand for cash balances is one of the major innovative and distinctive features of Allais's business cycle model compared to the Keynesian underpinnings of macrodynamic models of the period.[15] Accordingly, Allais assumes in the formula that

$$u(t) = \chi' \int_{-\infty}^{t} \frac{1}{D(\theta)} \frac{dD(\theta)}{d\theta} e^{-\chi'(t-\theta)} d\theta \qquad (3)$$

where the coefficient χ' is a positive constant. This variable is defined as the weighted average of the previous rates of variation of global expenditure assuming that the weighting coefficient declines exponentially over time. Allais mentions that this formulation is analogous to the fading and forgetfulness functions in physics, developed by Boltzman and Volterra. For Allais, this assumption means simply that the individual agents estimate the current economic situation in period t on the basis of the past observations in periods θ, with an exponential fading memory or forgetfulness captured by $t - \theta$. According to Allais, this assumption is a "natural hypothesis" (Allais 1956, p. 10) which corroborates "the immediate data of our introspection"(Allais 1956).[16] It is beyond the scope of this paper to discuss Allais's monetary theory and sources of inspiration – notably

---

14 The economic justification for the shape of this function was notably refuted by Hahn. First, Allais speaks in nominal terms and, not as usually, in real terms. Second, unlike Allais, Hahn believes that consumers and producers tend to behave in opposite directions during the cycle. For Hahn, Allais's assumptions are true only for consumers in downswings and not for producers. However, Baumol disagrees with Hahn, contending that producers try both to postpone their purchases and to sell more, and that on the whole, they also increase their balances. See the discussion following Allais's 1955 presentation in Paris, reproduced in Allais (2001, pp. 1037–54).

15 As noted by an anonymous referee, it is interesting that this formulation differs from the analysis developed by Allais in *Economie et intérêt* which made it possible to conclude that the demand for transactions depended on the interest rate.

16 For a discussion of some psychological foundations and introspective elements in Allais's work, see especially Lenfant (2005).

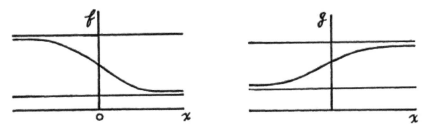

Figure 1. The two reaction functions f and g (Allais 1953, p. 116)

Fisher and Pareto. Let us note simply that this formulation introduces the notion of hereditary function which plays a crucial role in Allais's restatement of the quantity theory of money, and his psychological theory of the rate of interest.[17]

In relation to the total quantity of money in circulation, $M(t)$, with a constant level of the monetary base, it varies between a minimum level and a maximum level during the cycle.[18] Global expenditures increase during the time of prosperity, the banking system is inclined to supply more credit and more easily, the economic agents are confident, and the level of deposits increases. Consequently, the total quantity of money rises but this process must halt when the reserve coefficients fall below the legal limits or become too low for the bankers, then the money supply has reached its maximum.[19] Conversely, during a downturn, the banking system adopts a more prudent policy and restricts its credit supply, and consumers and producers reduce their deposits. Consequently, by an inverse mechanism, the total quantity of money contracts and tends to its minimum. Thus, this process can be described by a non-linear function. Accordingly, Allais assumes that

$$M(t) = g[v(t)] \qquad (4)$$

where g is a positive, monotonous, increasing, and bounded-from-above function in $v(t)$, an index of average general business activity computed by

17 See, in particular, the critical reviews of *Economie et interêt*, e.g. by Schakle (1949), Boulding (1951), and Allais (2001). Allais admitted later that in the early fifties, Cagan and he independently developed the same formulation, albeit from different starting points and using different terminology. Allais added that Cagan's work was brought to his attention by Friedman in July 1954 at the precise time that Allais was presenting the results of his framework for the analysis of the business cycles.
18 Its variation is introduced by Allais in 1955 in a complement to his model dedicated particularly to the case of hyperinflation.
19 See *Monnaie et Intérêt*, pp. 277–79.

the banking system. This variable is called "the psychological bank rate of economic expansion" (Allais 1956, p. 11), and is explained by the same forgetfulness mechanism as the rate $u(t)$ defined above for other agents.[20]

On the basis of these elements, the two key functions f and g, encapsulating demand for money balances and the behaviour of the banking system, respectively, can be depicted as shown in Figure 1.

Then, referring to his book *Les fondements comptables de la macroéconomie* for a complete demonstration, Allais asserts that at the macroeconomic level, global income $R_T(t)$ and global expenditure $D(t)$ are necessarily equal. Next, derivation of the dynamic equation "which explains the fundamental mechanism of economic evolution" (Allais 1956, p. 12) is a simple question of algebraic manipulation as follows:

$$D(t+T) - D(t) = \frac{1}{T}\{g[v(t)] - D(t)f[u(t)]\} \tag{5}$$

Before analysing the stability properties of his equation, Allais conducts some simplifying manipulations. First, he considers "a permanent equilibrium regime" (Allais 1956, p. 12) associated with a stationary solution D_e to this equation. This solution, which is not necessarily unique, satisfies $D_e = \frac{g(0)}{f(0)}$ and $D_e = M_e V_e$, where $M_e = g(0)$ and $V_e = \frac{1}{f(0)}$ refer, respectively, to the money stock and the velocity of circulation in equilibrium. Second, he replaces the reaction function f and g by the respective ratio $\phi = \frac{f}{f(0)}$ and $\gamma = \frac{g}{g(0)}$.[21] Third, more importantly, in order to deal with the business cycles proper and to facilitate the statistical verification of his theory, Allais replaces total expenditure $D(t)$ by national nominal income $R(t)$. Thus, he makes the simplifying assumption that expenditure is proportional to income, that is, $D(t) = \delta R(t)$, where δ is a constant. Finally, Allais introduces the ratio of global income to its equilibrium value, $r(t) = \frac{R(t)}{R_e}$, where R_e denotes equilibrium or stationary income.[22] With these assumptions, and "without no loss of generality" (Allais 1956, p. 13), the fundamental dynamic equation (5) becomes

$$r(t+T) - r(t) = \frac{1}{V_e T}\{\gamma[v(t)] - r(t)\phi[u(t)]\} \tag{6}$$

This reduced form of the model displays the dynamics of $r(t)$, the ratio of global income to its stationary value, a standard indicator of business cycles. For any arbitrary delay T, this relation determines the variation of this ratio

---

20 The formula differs only in the coefficient χ'' instead of χ'.
21 Which implies that $\phi(0) = 1$ and $\gamma(0) = 1$
22 Let $d(t) = \frac{D(t)}{D_e}$, then, it is clear that $d(t) = r(t)$.

between t and $t + T$. Both the behaviour of the banking system $\gamma[v(t)]$ and the demand for money balances $r(t)\phi[u(t)]$ are explained by the behaviour of the ratio $r(t)$ in the preceding periods, which is used by the agents to compute their psychological rates of economic expansion, $v(t)$ and $u(t)$. Indeed, as noted by Munier (1991, p. 195), Allais believed that the behaviour of the agents "is determined by their memories, in contrast with most authors who relate it to some form of expectation of the future".[23] In addition, the re-scaling of the variables allows the formulation to be dimensionless, which facilitates its mathematical and statistical treatment.

From a formal point of view, by definition of the two psychological rates of economic expansion, $u(t)$ and $v(t)$, this relation is both a finite non-linear difference equation and an integral equation with one variable $r(t)$.[24] This type of formalism is widely applied to various issues involving oscillation problems in mathematical physics.[25]

In this perspective, another connection with physics refers to the notion of relaxation oscillations. The origin of this approach is generally attributed to Le Corbeiller and Hamburger.[26] It is now acknowledged that this formalism is at the root of the non-linear cycle theory of pioneering Keynesian macrodynamics (see. e.g. Lorenz 1987, ,1989; Velupillai 2008). In this perspective, economic fluctuations have been modelled by relaxation oscillations using either Rayleigh's formalisation such as Goodwin (1951), or van der Pol's equation which was adopted by the "Japanese connection," to use the expression coined by Velupillai (2008).[27] In France, independent of Allais's research, the theory of non-linear motions,

---

23 However, this formulation may, to some extent, also refer to a kind of adaptive expectation process.

24 In mathematics, an integral equation is an equation in which an unknown function appears under an integral symbol.

25 Allais mentions in his biography that before the Second World War, he was fascinated by physics and mechanics at the Ecole Polytechnique, and as a young engineer, he spent his leisure time reading in this fields.

26 As we know, at the 1931 Lausanne Meeting of the Econometric Society, Le Corbeiller suggested the possibility of analysing business cycles by applying the theory of relaxation oscillations developed by Lord Raleigh in 1883, Van der Pol in 1928–1930, and Lienard in 1928 (Le Corbeiller 1933). In a note in *Ecometrica*, Hamburger (1934) contends that the applicability of relaxation oscillations to economic cycles was first emphasised by him in 1928 in a discussion of a paper by Van der Pol and J. van der Markas.

27 Notice that it is possible to derive a form of integral equation from the mixed differential equation proposed by Goodwin (1951) in his non-linear accelerator model. Using Goodwin's notation, one of his equations is written as $\dot{y}(t) + (1 - \alpha)y(t) = \Phi[\dot{y}(t - \theta)]$, and we obtain $y = y_0 e^{r(t_0 - t)} + e^{-rt}\int_{t_0}^{t} e^{rt}\Phi[\dot{y}(t - \theta)]d\theta$, where $r = 1 - \frac{\alpha}{}$, θ is a lag, and Φ is Goodwin's sigmoid non-linear accelerator function.

relaxation oscillations, and van der Pol equations was diffused notably by Yves Rocard (1941) in his book *Théorie des oscillations* published in 1941. Accordingly, in a paper delivered at the Washington Meeting of the Econometric Society, Rocard (1949b)develops a series of integral equations of the type $\dot{y}(t) + \alpha \int_0^\infty f(\theta)y(t - \theta)d\theta = 0$ with some economic applications, albeit limited to microeconomic issues.[28] Allais was obviously aware of these advances which he includes in the abundant bibliography in his 1956 article.[29] Indeed, for him economic fluctuations and relaxation phenomena in physics have a lot in common. On the one hand, as shown below, for Allais endogenous cycles develop in the neighbourhood of an unstable equilibrium. Each time the system reaches some threshold sufficiently close to its unstable equilibrium position, the monetary mechanisms captured by the two non-linear functions f and g disturb it with inputs of energy. Hence, economic oscillations are characterised by long periods of dissipation followed by short impulses. The period of the cycle then is defined by the time it takes for the economy to relax from each disturbed state. This type of dynamics refers to what Allais describes as a "lagged-
regulation" illustrated with the van der Pol equation (Allais 1956, p. 58). Moreover, Allais, in *Economie et interêt*, uses the metaphor of a steam engine with two regulators which generate a cyclical dynamics.[30]

However, mathematical discussion of stability conditions, and the existence of a limit cycle and the possibility of a statistical illustration of the dynamics in the non-linear integral equation obtained above, at this stage remained too difficult. In face of this, Allais resorted to different simplifications of his model which are examined in the next section.

3. The different simplifications and the endogenous cycles

Allais discusses at length five different types of potential simplifications. A first possibility (model M_1) is to assume identical forgetfulness functions for the bank sector and the other agents. Letting $\chi' = \chi'' = \chi$, we have in

---

28 See also "Les oscillateurs des théories économiques" (1941) and Quelques problèmes élémentaires d'économie dynamique"(1948).
29 However, as usual in Allais's works, there is no direct reference in the text.
30 "Les circonstances qui jouent sont analogues à celles qui seraient observées dans la marche d'une machine à vapeur si elle était munie de deux régulateurs à boule, l'un puissant mais ne jouant qu'à partir de deux limites déterminées (mécanisme régulateur), l'autre faible mais jouant en sens inverse (mécanisme accélérateur). Dans de telles conditions, il est facile de démontrer que la marche de la machine au lieu d'être régulière serait cyclique." (Economie et interêt, p. 367).

this case $u(t) = v(t) = y(t)$. The second and third versions (models M_2 and M_3) consist of replacing the integral forgetfulness functions by simpler formulations with only two delays T and T_0. The fourth possibility (model M_4) is to consider a model with a unique delay T. Finally, the fifth possibility is to approximate the continuous derivable functions ϕ and γ by a piecewise linear function (model M^T). This simplification can apply to each of the other four and to the initial model. Consequently, Allais finally obtains 10 potential versions of his model, that is, M, M_1, M_2, M_3, M_4 and $M^T, M_1^T, M_2^T, M_3^T, M_4^T$. We do not go through the details of these different versions. For simplicity but also because this version was presented by Allais and discussed at the Econometric Society meeting in 1953, we focus on the model with one delay.

3.1. The model with a unique delay T

In this simplified framework, Allais supposes that the dynamics of r, the ratio of the global income to its equilibrium value, is for any arbitrary delay T, totally determined by two consecutive values of this ratio. This assumption means that the agents' computations of their psychological rates of economic expansion are very simplified. First, the banking system and the other agents share the same rate, that is, $u(t) = v(t) = y(t)$. Second, the integral forgetfulness functions are replaced by the rate of variation of global income between two periods.

Let us make the change of variables $r_n = r(t)$ and $r_{n-m} = r(t - mT)$.[31] Then, the reduced form (6) becomes a simple second-order difference equation in r_n:

$$r_{n+1} - r_n = \frac{1}{V_e T} [\gamma(y_n) - r_n \phi(y_n)] \tag{7}$$

where $y_n = y_t = \frac{r_n - r_{n-1}}{T r_{n-1}}$ is the simplified psychological rate of economic expansion.

As discussed above, the two reaction functions ϕ and γ (or equivalently f and g)[32] are non-linear and bounded from below and above (see Figure 1). Thus, they are easily approximated by three tangents with steeper slopes K_0 and K_0' in the central interval than for the extreme values. Recall that this class of continuously differentiable or linear piecewise functions plays a crucial role in the conditions for the existence of limit cycles in the

---

31 We have $r_n = r(t)$, $r_{n-1} = r(t - T)$ and $r_{n+1} = r(t + T)$.
32 Since ϕ and γ are defined by the ratios of f and g to their stationary values $f(0)$ and $g(0)$.

endogenous business cycle models of the period.[33] The importance of this assumption is confirmed also in Allais's framework. In particular, Allais shows that the model cannot generate closed trajectories with constant or linear functions. In the non-linear case, when the functions are shaped as above, there is a unique singular point E with $r = 1$. This solution is globally stable for $K_0 + K_0' < V_e T^2$ and the singular point is a stable node if $K_0 + K_0' < T(1 - \sqrt{V_e T^2})$ or stable otherwise. Conversely, the equilibrium is unstable for $K_0 + K_0' > V_e T^2$ and a limit cycle may then exist.

3.2. The existence of a limit cycle

Next, Allais proceeds to determine the sufficient conditions for the existence of a relevant limit cycle with positive values of r. These conditions can be summarised as follows.[34] First, the two reaction functions ϕ and γ are non-linear positive functions of y with sufficiently small first derivatives with respect to y for small and large values of y. Second, the fixed point is unstable, that is, $V_e T^2 < K_0 + K_0'$. Third, the delay T satisfies $1 < V_e T$. The first and the second conditions mean simply that the reaction of the agents in relation to liquidity preference should be sufficiently strong near equilibrium and more sluggish for larger deviations from the equilibrium value.[35] Finally, the third condition guarantees that the cycle remains economically relevant with positive values.

The heuristic of proof of existence of a limit cycle is formulated by Allais as follows. He considers a sequence of point M_n in the plan (r_n, ϕ_n).[36] For any arbitrary initial condition M_0, M_0' or M_0'', the proof supports the idea of a closed orbit C distinct from the singular point E which is unstable, such that the limit of the distance between M_n and C reduces to zero as time tends to infinity. We reproduce the phase diagram and the corresponding evolution of the variable r_n over time in Figure 2. In these two diagrams, the discrete-time model is represented by continuous lines. On the right-hand side of the figure, θ is the period of the cycle which can be approximated by an increasing function of $K_0 + K_0'$.

---

33 See, in particular, Goodwin's non-linear accelerator model and/or Ichimura's reformulations of the Kaldor−Hicks−Goodwin models.

34 As in the case of the complete stability analysis of different versions of his model, Allais mentions a major contribution from two young engineers in Ecole des Mines, Lessourne J. and Mathieu M., "Note sur les propriétés mathématiques utiles dans l'étude des cycles économiques", Mimeo, May 1953.

35 Consequently, this assumption becomes a kind of non-linear reaction function similar to the sigmoid type used by Kaldor (1940) in a different theoretical framework.

36 As mentioned by Allais, the same reasoning can be applied alternately with the couples (r_n, y_n) or $(\frac{y_n}{r_n}, y_n)$.

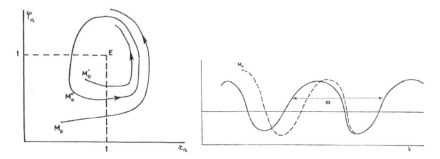

Figure 2. Phase diagram and cyclical dynamics

Finally, notice that the delicate question of the limit cycle's uniqueness is not addressed directly by Allais. Allais indicates that his findings refer to the conditions for the existence of at least one limit cycle but his discussion assumes a unique cycle. However, this assumption is supported by the numerical examples provided in the appendix to the model and by some empirical regularities.[37]

4. The meaning of the cycle and its empirical verification

To sum up, qualitative study of the model shows that for a limit cycle to exist, the singular point must be unstable. If this condition is fulfilled, it is sufficient that the functions γ and ϕ are positive and upper bounded. Moreover, we have shown that the singular point is likely to be unstable if the functions γ and ϕ are, respectively, sufficiently decreasing and increasing in the neighbourhood of the stationary point. Accordingly, for Allais, these conditions are "extremely simple and we realise through observation that they can be met in many circumstances" (Allais 1956, p. 55). For this reason, Allais devotes a long section to empirical verification of the model. However, before examining these developments, we need to examine the unfolding of the cycle and its economic interpretation.

4.1. The monetary cycle

However, briefly, Allais endeavours to include in his theory the main aspects characterising business fluctuations. First, he reminds us that he is dealing

---

37 Allais (1956, p. 28). See also Lessourne and Mathieu, "Note sur les propriétés mathématiques utiles dans l'étude des cycles économiques", Mimeo May 1953. Allais and his two collaborators were aware of the Japanese advances (mentioned in the bibliography) on this issue. Unfortunately, the question was addressed in the different framework of continuous-time systems of the so-called generalised Liénard equation. See Lorenz (1987) and Velupillai (2008).

with global phenomena which affect almost all industries. This cycle is classically characterised by covariations in aggregate prices and quantities, and is defined by "alternate movements of increase and decrease in the overall expenditure and the national income in nominal value" (Allais 1956, p. 61). Second, he makes a clear-cut distinction between the *sinequanon* and the *accelerating* factors of the business cycles. The *sine – quanon* factors are "the necessary and sufficient conditions of cycles" (Allais 1956, p. 62), while accelerating factors are all other elements which amplify instability and modify the duration or intensity of an initial cycle.

Allais underlines that there are two and only two *sinequanon* factors, "the variability of the function ϕ, i.e. the variability of the propensity to liquidity" (Allais 1956, p. 62) and "the variability of the function γ, i.e. the variability of the quantity of money" (Allais 1956, p. 62.). As a consequence, with constant ϕ and γ, the equilibrium is stable, expenditure D remains constant, and cycles are ruled out.[38]

On this basis, Allais analyses the influence of money in his setting, as follows.[39] He begins with a reminder that the functions ϕ and γ are decreasing and increasing with respect to the rate of economic expansion. With the onset of prosperity, the total quantity of money in circulation M increases and the level of desired balances M_D decreases. Agents holding excessive amounts of money tend to spend more, and total expenditure D increases. If expenditure is growing fast enough, that is, if the delay in agents' adjustments T is sufficiently small, the difference $M - M_D$ will continue to increase, which enhances prosperity. The reverse mechanisms apply to a downturn.

Next, Allais provides an intuitive rationale for the shape assumed by the functions γ and ϕ. For the desired balances, he argues that on the basis of the intuition and the statistical data, it is inconceivable that agents infinitely increase their cash to national income ratio $\frac{M}{R}$. Similarly, when this ratio decreases, it must remain finite and positive, or at least tend to zero. Allais develops similar reasoning for the function γ. As a consequence, simple specification of the above two functions explains endogenously the occurrence of an upper-turning point, and a revival is highly plausible.

The preceding arguments make it easy to understand some of the main aspects of the cyclical pattern of economic activity.

---

38 This conclusion is illustrated by the basic accounting relation $D = MV$, while velocity V provides a rough approximation of the inverse of the propensity to liquidity ϕ since we have $\frac{1}{V} = \frac{M}{D}$ and $f = \frac{M_D}{D}$.
39 Allais refers to his book *Économie et intérêt*, Chapter VIII, for further explanations.

During prosperity when aggregate spending increases, production finds an outlet at a purchasing power superior to its cost. This results in higher prices, a reduction in the size of inventories, higher profits, and a general process of growth activity and investment. During a depression when aggregate expenditure decreases, production finds an outlet at a purchasing power that is less than its cost. As a consequence, we observe the same sequence of events as during prosperity with the difference that rises become declines and underemployment. However, these phenomena – and the role of errors or confidence generally – should be regarded as byproducts of the triggering factor, the sluggish adjustment between desired and actual balances, rooted in the psychological monetary mechanisms. Allais does not elaborate further on the mechanisms underpinning the upper and lower turning points. Clearly, this conception of the cycle contrasts with explanations based on the role of the divergence between the real and monetary rates of interest, and the process of adjustment between saving and investment. These considerations prompted Allais to claim that his approach was "classical" and "incomplete opposition to the Keynesian and neo-Keynesian theory, based on saving and investment" (Allais 1956, p. 60), which he regarded as fundamentally flawed.

Reactions to Allais's model included several critical comments. For instance, Hahn at the 1953 meeting of the Econometric Society, pointed out that "Professor Allais has no doubt constructed an elegant model of the trade cycle and solved a number of mathematical problems" (Allais 1954b, p. 117). However, several commentators expressed doubts about his assumptions and his explanation of the cycle. Hahn was critical also of the microfoundations of the non-linear functions assumed in the model. For him, "having regard for the great difficulties of subjecting such models to econometric tests, it is most important that they should be firmly based on a proper micro-theory of decision making" (Allais 1954b, p. 117). According to Hahn, it was clear that this theory was almost absent from Allais's model. Other commentators, such as R. Roy and G. Lutfalla, expressed considerable skepticism about Allais's exclusive focus on the monetary aspects of the cycle. In this context, Hahn also argued that all Allais's variables were measured in money terms, and "this seems to be a very great drawback since it is difficult to believe, for instance, that individual reactions will be the same when money national income rises irrespective of whether such rise is due to an increase in production or in prices. Surely the real and monetary variables must be disentangled" (Allais 1954b).

There was also an interesting discussion of Allais's model that took place in Paris in May 1955. Ichimura, arguing from a different standpoint to Hahn, expressed serious reservations about the foundations of Allais's global functions. For Ichimura, Allais's reference to certain empirical features was not convincing enough for a new theory which would require more plausible arguments, notably in relation to the institutional framework. More generally, referring to the Keynesian approach of the cyclical fluctuations, he questioned the reasons put forward by Allais to discard the usual apparatus on saving and investment, liquidity, and global expenditure. Along these lines, Hahn again, and Baumol to some extent, emphasised the similarities between Allais's approach and the traditional investment-saving view, pointing out that the main innovation in Allais's approach lay in his specific behavioural functions. Goodwin agreed with this assessment. He saw clearly the complexity introduced in the model by the concept of a rate of psychological expansion, recalling that the main difference with the Keynesian models lay in Allais's specific theory of desired monetary balances, and his non-linear liquidity function replacing the role of interest rate in the liquidity preference theory.[40]

4.2. The empirical verification

This section is concerned with the statistical and numerical verification of the model. Allais proposes an interesting and detailed calibration of his theoretical findings. To begin with, Allais approximates the actual value of the key parameters, functions, and variables in his theoretical model. This preliminary econometric step is based mostly on US data for the period 1909–1951.[41]

The average duration of the cycle Θ is quite well documented and varies between 2 and 10 years, which in months is $24 < \Theta < 120$. To determine V and V_e, Allais retains the average value of the velocity of money in the USA, which according to his own calculation gives $V = V_e = 1.75$ per month. Concerning the delay in adjustment to the balances T, in Allais's view, this should be relatively short – between one week and four months, that is, $0.25 < T < 4$. It is obviously impossible to compute directly the original shape of the functions ϕ and γ. Thus, Allais proceeds to estimate their approximation on three tangents, which for the critical coefficients K_0 and K_0' gives the values $6 < K_0 < 24$ and $4 < K_0' < 16$, respectively.

The next step is to compare these statistical findings with the qualitative findings from the theoretical part. In the case of the simple model M_4 with

---

40 Discussion of Allais's model in Paris in May 1955, reproduced in Allais (2001, pp. 1040–51). Fléchet, Frisch, and Klein also contributed to this discussion particularly in relation to the statistical methods and status of empirical verifications of the model.
41 Here, Allais refers explicitly to the works of Mitchell and the National Bureau of Economic Research (NBER). He also draws on Davis's (1941a, 1941b) book on econometrics and time-series analysis.

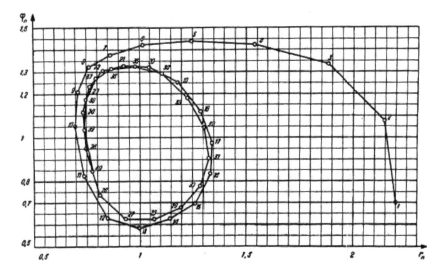

Figure 3. An example of numerical integration of the model with one delay (Allais 1956, Annex 1)

one delay, the conclusion is straightforward. Recall that a limit cycle exists if $V_e T^2 < K_0 + K_0'$ and $1 < V_e T$. With V_e equal to 1.75, these conditions imply that $2.1 < T < 4.8$. Simple comparison with the actual interval $0.25 < T < 4$ justifies the conclusion that "this verification must be seen as remarkable" (Allais 1956, p. 49).[42] The same conclusion applies to the computed duration of the cycle Θ. However, the model with one delay overestimates the difference between ϕ_n and $\frac{Y_n}{r_n}$, which logically is explained by the relative high values of T required in this simple framework. Indeed, it can be shown that this difficulty disappears in more complex configurations with two delays.[43] Then, Allais refers to long and tedious calculations. He mentions that 55 models, M_4^T with one delay, and 17 models, M_3^T with two delays, are numerically integrated. We reproduce in Figure 3 below, a representative example of these numerical findings. Figure 3 gives an example of the phase diagrams obtained by Allais through numerical integration of the model M_4^T with the empirically relevant parameters. Here, Allais assumes that $V = 1.75$, $T = 3$, $K_0 = 9$, and $K_0' = 9$. Where the numbers refer to the successive months that unfold during the cycle, a unique limit cycle of duration $\Theta = 43.5$ is obtained.

---

42 With the qualification that the estimate of the actual interval for T is highly questionable.

43 See notably Allais (1956, p. 54).

To sum up, what this empirical investigation shows is that the necessary conditions for the existence of a limit cycle "are exactly met by the values of the constants suggested by the observation and that, for these values the period of the limit cycle is actually of the magnitude observed."(Allais 1954b, p. 116). In that sense, the theoretical explanation of the endogenous monetary cycle is for Allais confirmed by the observation.

5. Concluding remarks

This paper focused on the impressive, although not well-known, contribution to non-linear monetary cycle theory provided by Allais in the 1950s. In this framework, the existence of at least a limit cycle is mathematically proved and its existence is confirmed by empirical evidence.

Not surprisingly, Allais concludes that the unique difficulty with this theory of endogenous business cycles "is mathematical and not economic. Nobody can remain indifferent to its great power of suggestion and its undeniable esthetics" (Allais 1956, p. 69). Despite several criticisms, Allais persists with his position. The endogenous cycles are monetary and are explained by the gap between desired cash balances and the stock of money. This is Allais's monetarism, in which money supply management can stabilise or destabilise the economy. As in the models suggested by Friedman, and, to some extent, by Lucas in the 1970s, money is the main source of business cycles. However, there is an important difference in the frameworks. In the framework suggested by Lucas, the cycle is triggered by exogenous monetary shocks, and the transmission mechanism is rooted in imperfect information and expectations errors; there is no room for monetary shocks or expectations errors in Allais's endogenous business cycle model in which the behaviour of the agents is determined by their memories, although there is an analogy between this assumption and the hypothesis of adaptive expectations adopted by Friedman and the Keynesian's in the 1950s and the 1960s. This may explain the absence of any reference in modern equilibrium business cycle theories to Allais's attempts.[44] Indeed, contrary to the pioneering advances in the Hicks−Kaldor−Goodwin perspective which influenced a whole tradition in non-linear macrodynamics,[45] Allais's contribution remains isolated, a position that is attributable mainly to Allais himself. His approach was often idiosyncratic and not

---

44 This applies also to the endogenous approach with money where Allais is credited only for invention of the overlapping generation model, not for his endogenous business cycles theory (see e.g. Grandmont 1985).
45 This tradition persists but culminated in a renewal of non-linear dynamics in the 1980s and 1990s with the development of a series of business cycle models inspired by Goodwin, Keynes, Kaldor, Kalecki, and Minsky.

always easy to penetrate. Indeed, as Boulding points out in the context of Allais's work, "Reading Allais is rather like going for a walk with a highly intelligent and active fox terrier. No alley is left unexplored and no rabbit unchased...The net result is a certain mental exhaustion and a somewhat confused picture" (Boulding 1951, p. 69). By the mid-1950s, Allais's interest had shifted to different applications of his non-linear hereditary theory of the demand for money, notably, inflation and growth. However, he never totally abandoned his business cycles theory. For example, he resumed his model of monetary endogenous cyclical fluctuations in the late 1960s, and in 1982, introduced some exogenous factors and, finally, in 2000, produced several additional graphics and numerical examples for publication in his 2001 *Fondements de la dynamique monétaire.*[46]

Overall, despite some flaws in the economic underpinnings of his model, Allais's contribution to the theory of endogenous cycles is an interesting input to the 1950s pioneering field of non-linear dynamics. The model contains several innovative insights, particularly on the relations between the magnitude of perturbations, global instability, and the existence of limit cycles and their empirical verification. From this perspective, as Grandmont (1989, p. 25) emphasises, some aspects "of modern business cycle theory had already been anticipated in Allais (1956)," albeit in a specific theoretical framework.[47]

Acknowledgements

This research benefited from the support of the PHC (Programmes Hubert Curien) Procope and Germaine de Stael. I am also indebted to the anonymous referees for their valuable comments and suggestions. The usual caveat applies.

References

Allais, M., 1947. *Economie et interêt.* Paris: Imprimerie Nationale.
Allais, M., 1953. Illustration de la théorie monétaire des cycles économiques par des modèles non linéaires, *Communication au Congrès de la Société Européenne d'Econométrie,* September 1953 Innsbrück. Reproduced in Allais (2001), 221–51.

---

46 See Allais (2001, pp. 969–1026).
47 Grandmont (1989) also somewhat ambiguously attributes to Allais' paternity of the "Leijonhufvud corridor." From a technical point of view, the notion of a stability corridor is presented in Allais (1956), but the theoretical framework is obviously different, particularly because of Leijonhufvud's Keynesian underpinnings.

Allais, M., 1954a. *Les fondements comptables de la macroéconomie.* Paris: PUF. Reprinted in 1993.

Allais, M., 1954b. Illustration de la théorie monétaire des cycles économiques par des modèles non linéaires, *Econometrica*, 22 (1), 101–22. Compte rendu du Congrès d'Innsbrück 1953.

Allais, M., 1955. Explication des cycles économiques par un modèle non linéaire à régulation retardé: mémoire complémentaire, *Colloque International sur la Dynamique de Paris*, Paris, May. Published in *Les modèles dynamiques en économétrie*, Vol LXII, CNRS, 1956, 259–308 and in Allais (2001), 341–74. Discussion reproduced in Allais (2001), 1035–54.

Allais, M., 1956. Explication des cycles économiques par un modèle non linéaire à régulation retardée. *Metroeconomica*, 8(1), 4–83.

Allais, M., 1988. An outline of my main contributions to economic science, *Nobel Lecture*, December 9. Reprinted in *The American Economic Review*, 87 (6); *Nobel Lectures and 1997 Survey of Members*, December 1997, 3–12.

Allais, M., 2001. *Fondements de la dynamique monétaire.* Paris: Editions Clément Juglar.

Boulding, K.E., 1951. M.Allais' theory of interest. *Journal of Political Economy*, 59(9), 69–73.

Davis, H.T., 1941a. *The analysis of time series.* Bloomington: The Principia Press.

Davis, H.T., 1941b. *The theory of econometrics.* Bloomington: The Principia Press.

Goodwin, R., 1951. A nonlinear theory of the cycle. *The Review of Economics and Statistics*, (4), 316–20.

Grandmont, J.M., 1985. On endogenous competitive business cycles. *Econometrica*, 53, 995–1045.

Grandmont, J.M., 1989. Report on Maurice Allais' scientific work. *The Scandinavian Economic Journal*, 91(1), 17–28.

Hamburger, L., 1934. Note on economic cycles and relaxation oscillations. *Econometrica*, 2, 112.

Ichimura, S., 1955. Towards a general nonlinear macrodynamic theory of economic fluctuations. *In:* K. Kurihara, ed. *Post Keynesian economics.* London: Allen and Unwin, 192–226.

Kaldor, N., 1940. A model of the trade cycle. *The Economic Journal*, 50(197), 78–92.

Le Corbeiller, P., 1933. Les systèmes autoentretenus et les équations de relaxation. *Econometrica*, 1 (3), 328–32.

Lenfant, J.S., 2005. Psychologie individuelle et stabilité d'un équilibre général concurrentiel dans le Traité d'Economie Pure de Maurice Allais. *Revue Economique*, 56(4), 855–88.

Levinson, N. and Smith, O.K., 1942. A general equation for relaxation oscillations. *Duke Mathematical Journal*, 9, 382–403.

Lorenz, H.W., 1987. On the uniqueness of limit cycles in business cycle theory. *Metroeconomica*, 38, 281–93.

Lorenz, H.W., 1989. *Nonlinear dynamical economics and chaotic motion.* Berlin: Springer Verlag.

Munier, B., 1991. The many other Allais paradoxes. *The Journal of Economic Perspectives*, 5(2), 179–99.

Rocard, Y., 1941. *Théorie des oscillations.* Paris: Editions de la Revue Scientifique.

Rocard, Y., 1949a. *Dynamique générale des vibrations.* Paris: Masson.

Rocard, Y., 1949b. Les modèles économiques dynamiques. *Econometrica*, 17, 328–29.

Shackle, G.L.S., 1949. Review of *Economie et intérêt* by M. Allais. *Economic Journal*, 59(233), 86–8.

Velupillai, K.V., 2008. Japanese contributions to nonlinear cycles theory in the 1950. *The Japanese Economic Review*, 59(1), 54–74.

Abstract

In this framework, the existence of a limit cycle is mathematically proved and its existence confirmed by empirical evidence. The mathematical tools are similar to Keynesian pioneering non-linear macrodynamic advances but the theoretical framework is obviously totally distinct. In particular, for Allais, the origin of endogenous cycles is monetary, and explained by the interplay between two key elements: the agents that hold the desired money balances and the banking system that can create money.

The "Treasury View": An (un-)expected return?

Pascal Bridel

One often attributes to Marx the apocryphal opinion according to which "history does not repeat itself, it stutters". The recent (un-)expected resurrection of a policy debate around the old *Treasury View* is a splendid demonstration that economic theory – and/or might it be economists themselves – do more than stammering: they seem in fact to suffer from a serious speech impediment.

Once again, and nearly 80 years after the 1929 great recession, the unexpected character and brutality of the 2008–2009 crisis have put in great difficulties the economic profession and the credibility of their models. The return of old theoretical arguments most thought forgotten, but also the way discussions between some economists rapidly took place in 2009 in the press are strangely reminiscent of the early 1930s. Pigou and Hawtrey are no longer politely but firmly arguing with Keynes, but Cochrane and Fama angrily inveigh Krugman; the debate is no longer taking place in the *Times* of London but in the *New York Times* (or, even better, in the more sophisticated *New York Review of Books*; Soros et al. 2009); the *Treasury View* is replaced by the *crowding out effect*; and, even if the pseudo classical model attributed by Keynes to Pigou has been replaced by a dynamic stochastic general

This paper has greatly benefited from comments from participants at presentations at the *Treilles* Foundation in Southern France (Meeting on "Crises, business cycles theories and economic policy", 12–17 September 2011), in Lausanne, Nice, Paris ("75 years of *General Theory*" Conference, 2–3 December 2011) and Nice again ("XIVème colloque de l'Association Charles Gide – Histoire de la macro-économie", 7–9 June 2012). The present version has also greatly benefited from the wise and sometimes sharp comments offered by three referees. Despite strenuous efforts to make this essay sounds more academic, the final version inevitably retains some of the oral flavour of the Nice conference where it was presented at a keynote speaker session.

equilibrium model (DSGE) of the *n*th generation, one cannot be but flab-bergasted by the economists' inability to organise and carry out a reasonable debate on such fundamental questions of economic theory and policy.

Before turning to the core of this debate, two obvious but important issues must be dealt with first: on the one hand, the very different nature of the economic policy decisions taken by policy makers during the 1930s compared with those taken between 2009 and 2012. On the other, the cru-cial question of the exact measure of the multiplier effects of budget defi-cits during these two episodes.

In June 1933, most industrial countries (including the Soviet Union and China) gathered in London to examine various possible ways out of the crisis already in its fifth year. Perfectly analysed by Kindleberger (1986), the central difficulties was to avoid a vicious spiralling recession initiated by uncoordinated deflationary economic policies reinforced by *beggar-thy-neighbour policies* based on competitive devaluations and creeping protectionism. Characterised by the gold-exchange standard (the anchor *par excellence* of price stability) and the balanced budget canon (the *Treasury View*), this theoretical framework would by definition hinder any systematic countercyclical economic policy. In particular, the crowding out effect makes sure that consumption (via price rises and substitution effects) and private investment (via rises in interest rates) would be altered by an amount equivalent to any increase in public spending. Behind this twin argument, Say's law is obviously looming large (in fact a primitive version of a Walrasian general equilibrium then surprisingly fallen into oblivion).

Even if the United Kingdom (during the Summer of 1931) and the United States (in June 1933) eventually gave up the gold-exchange stan-dard, the Hoover administration kept alive the *Treasury View* until 1931 (the Federal budget for 1931 even registered a *surplus*). The same argu-ment reigned supreme for HM Treasury against which Keynes battled fero-ciously. To make a complicated argument temporarily simple, and to paraphrase Jean-Claude Trichet (who, in… 2010, like in Molière was speaking *Treasury View*, and did not even know it!), during a recession, a balanced budget is supposed to ease the recovery by freeing resources for private investments strengthening thus the private sector's confidence.

Conversely, 75 years later, in November 2008, The Washington G-20 summit worried that "1929 could happen again" asserted with great clar-ity to have understood how not to commit twice the same mistakes: a hyper-expansionist monetary policy coupled with substantial budget defi-cits were the order of the day. As a 2008 IMF Staff Position Note judi-ciously explained: "the optimal fiscal package should be timely, large, lasting, diversified, contingent, collective and sustainable" (Spilimbergo et al. 2008, p. 2). Less than two years later, most European countries adopted some version of the *Treasury View* in an attempt to solve the euro crisis.

The heated discussion between US economists to be examined later took precisely place during this two-year interval. And, of course, to try to understand the part, if any, played by the economic profession in the (un-) expected resurrection of the *Treasury View*.

Second qualification to the present discussion: the question of the measure of the multiplier effects of budget deficits. In the same 2008 Staff Note, the IMF economists asserted that multiplier effects is much weaker than postulated by Keynesian economists, and that "existing studies provide a range of fiscal multipliers from less than zero to larger than four" (p. 17). Five years later, and still within a deep recession, Blanchard as the IMF chief economist has produced several papers arguing unexpectedly that the fiscal multipliers have been considerably stronger, at the zero lower bound, than previously thought (see e.g. Blanchard and Leigh 2013).[2] In what follows, nothing is said about this crucial issue. At that stage of the discussion, even if most economists would readily admit the weakness of the multiplier effect, most of them would also admit that, during a recession, deficit reduction (or even engineering a surplus) is not the best solution to support a potential recovery.

On the other hand, a majority of economists is well aware today that, unlike during the late 1920s when most countries had a recent record of balanced budgets, during the first decade of the twenty-first century, most countries have a long, sometimes very long, history of systematic and recurrent structural budget deficits reaching – some of them being saddled with hard-to sustain debt levels. Hence, the underlying argument recently has been much more on the unsustainable development of the stock of debt, i.e. a potential exponential increase in the debt/GDP ratio.

This contribution is organised in three parts. With the help of the so-called Chicago Cannon-Cochrane-Fama (CCF) model, part one is an attempt at a critical inventory of the resurrection process of a simplified version of the *Treasury View* during this 2008–2009 debate. Part two investigates some of the parallels between pre-Keynesian modelling and the logic of modern dynamic stochastic general equilibrium models (DSGE); it discusses the possible part played in that debate by the history of recent economic thought. A discussion of the nature and genealogy of the models used is also put forward. Part three suggests more briefly some parallels between Keynes's suggestions in the *General Theory* and modern models on the level of public debt, the distribution of this debt between agents, the

---

[2] As a result, they argue that fiscal consolidation plans have had a much more recessionary impact that previously anticipated.

risk transfer from private agents to the government and the opportunity to stimulate an economy in recession by ... increasing the level of the public debt. Some conclusive remarks round up the contribution.

A last warning is plainly not out of place here: in terms of economic theory, the level of sophistication of this contribution is extremely modest. As a matter of fact, it does not report on careful discussions in top-tier journals but on the rhetoric used by some economists to sell their favourite theoretical conclusions to a large public. Hence, this paper is neither a scholarly history of the interwar *Treasury View* nor a sophisticated (or polemical) critique of current economic policy. By examining the rhetorical use of an old piece of economic theory by some modern economists, it simply intends to report on "how today's economists conduct a public debate". For once, the interest of the discussion does not lie in its level of sophistication but in the way it is conducted.

1. The return of the *Treasury View*

1.1. The Cannon-Cochrane-Fama model (2008–2011)

Initiated with a round table organised in June 2009 by the *New York Review of Books*, and extensively discussed in the American press (in particular in the *New York Times*), this all-American debate has progressively invaded the numerous blogs fed by American economists to end up with a few rather inconclusive articles in professional journals. Among the participants to a still unfinished debate, famous and diverse names like Cannon, Cochrane, Fama, Krugman, Mankiw, Sargent, Taylor, Bradford de Long (Bradford de Long 2009) and even Niall Ferguson can be found. During this dispute, and in parallel to the resurrection of a *Treasury View*-type of argument, strange and long-forgotten theoretical issues, which only survived in obscure articles written by historians of economic thought, reappeared front-stage. Who in his/her right mind would be still familiar today with the quasi-theological debate on the respective merits of a liquidity preference theory of interest vs. that based on a loanable funds approach? Which economist could reasonably within a DSGE framework inquire about the adjustment between saving and investment by way of a change of the level of output? While most countries experienced substantial (if not catastrophic) output gap, who could still deny the stimulating effect of budget deficits? And more generally, who could not question the use of equilibrium models to analyse a crisis such as the one Western economies are still tottering through?

As strange as it might look, among many others, most of these theoretical arguments resurfaced during this still unfinished debate on the *Treasury View*.

Finally, needless to say that neither side in this debate has a deep knowledge of the 1920s and 1930s debates. They both share a minimal understanding of the old *Treasury View* more akin to the standard modern textbook crowding out effect. Once again, dismissive about the history of economics (as most modern economists are), participants to this debate cannot help but rush to rummage in a slipshod way the attic of economic theory to find intellectual support for their argument. The result is a very selective and biased reading of a much more sophisticated argument.

To start with, a small anthology of five of the most pregnant quotations should provide an interesting starting point to the discussion.[3]

(i) Michael Cannon (2009) Cato Institute:

> The only way Congress can spend money is to extract it from the private sector – either by taxing it, borrowing it, or seigniorage ...

(ii) John Cochrane (2009a) University of Chicago:

> ... the money has to come from somewhere. If the government borrows a dollar from you, that is a dollar that you do not spend, or that you do not lend to a company to spend on new investment. *Every dollar of increased government spending must correspond to a dollar less private spending.* Every job created by stimulus spending is one job not created by the private spending it must displace. And hiring construction workers to build a road in Nevada is not going to help an unemployed mortgage officer in New Jersey.

And a few lines further:

> This isn't fancy economics. This is simple arithmetic. Why are so many economists said to support fiscal stimulus? Am I some sort of radical? No, in fact economics, as written in professional journals, taught to graduate students and summarized in their textbooks, abandoned fiscal stimulus long ago.

(iii) Eugene Fama (2009) University of Chicago:

> There is an identity in macroeconomics ... private investment [PI] must equal the sum of private savings [PS], corporate savings (retained earnings) [CS], and government savings [GS] ...

$$Pl = PS + CS + GS \tag{1}$$

> The equation ... must hold in the world as a whole. The quantities in the equation are not predetermined from year to year, and government actions affect them.

---

[3] All italics added.

Government bailouts and stimulus plans seem attractive when there are idle resources – unemployment. Unfortunately, bailouts and stimulus plans are not a cure. *The problem is simple: bailouts and stimulus plans are funded by issuing debts that absorbs savings that would otherwise go to private investment. In the end, despite the existence of idle resources, bailouts and stimulus plans do not add to current resources in use.*

They just move resources from one use to another. . . . The added debt absorbs savings that would otherwise go to private investment . . . which means private investment goes down by the same amount . . . "Stimulus" spending must be financed, which means it displaces other current uses of the same funds, and so does not help the economy today.

This last quotation recalls statements of the *Treasury View* Keynes attributed to what he called the "Classical economists" to which naturally belonged those working in HM Treasury during the 1930s.

Eventually, with Niall Ferguson, and already dear to Robertson (1940), the inevitable loanable funds connection resurfaces as the predictable complement to the *Treasury View*.

(iv) Niall Ferguson (in Soros et al. 2009) Harvard University:

Now we're in the therapy phase. And what therapy are we using? Well, it's very interesting because we're using two quite contradictory courses of therapy. One is the prescription of Dr. Friedman – Milton Friedman, that is – which is being administered by the Federal Reserve: massive injections of liquidity to avert the kind of banking crisis that caused the Great Depression of the early 1930s. I'm fine with that. That's the right thing to do. But there is another course of therapy that is simultaneously being administered, which is the therapy prescribed by Dr. Keynes – John Maynard Keynes – and that therapy involves the running of massive fiscal deficits in excess of 12 percent of gross domestic product this year, and the issuance therefore of vast quantities of freshly minted bonds.

There is a clear contradiction between these two policies, and we're trying to have it both ways. You can't be a monetarist and a Keynesian simultaneously – at least I can't see how you can, because if the aim of the monetarist policy is to keep interest rates down, to keep liquidity high, the effect of the Keynesian policy must be to drive interest rates up.

At that intermediate stage, it seems useful to take stock of the argument:

(a) This CCF model does attempt to swallow more than it can chew: if an increase in public spending cannot increase output and employment, in good logic, private investment cannot succeed either.
(b) The equality between saving and investment mentioned by Fama is only a bookkeeping equality that would hold in any model (including those allowing for stimulating effects of increased government spending). To reach such conclusions, Fama is clearly in need of extra hypotheses.

(c) In joining the debate, Mankiw (2009) immediately noticed that Fama's conclusions only hold in a model Keynes would have called "classic" in which there are neither unused resources, nor output gap, nor unemployment. Obviously, this is the extra hypothesis; but, nevertheless ...

(d) Fama asserts very explicitly (see above) that his model does also apply "when there are idle resources-unemployment".

(e) Rapidly, during this debate, Peterson (2009) reached the logical conclusion that the CCF model is nothing else but the good old Hicksian IS-LM (1937) in which LM is vertical; which is nothing else but a moderately sophisticated version of the *Treasury View* (total inefficiency of fiscal policy at full employment).

Intermediate conclusion no. 1: The Cannon-Cochrane-Fama model does not support the hypothesis that fiscal policy can never influence the level of output and employment.

Intermediate conclusion no. 2: The implicit model behind Cannon, Cochrane and Fama's conclusions is probably some sort of general equilibrium model from which disequilibrium positions are excluded (and hence any unused resources and unemployment).

1.2. The CCF model: a vintage 1930s approach? Or, how, for some modern theorists, the ignorance of the history of economic thought is bliss

1.2.1. The saving-investment equality: $S(Y) = I(i)$. Bearing in mind the 1920–1930s debate leading to Keynes's *General Theory*, is it possible to outline what seems to have been forgotten or even lost in the CCF model?

At the root of the famous principle of effective demand, Keynes's functional relationship S(Y) is, after all, nothing else but a Marshallian equilibrium concept (as argued in chapter 3 of the *General Theory*). This approach has no connection whatsoever with Barro's contribution to the debate (2009) in which rigidities on prices and wages are introduced. Again, the discussion evolves around the confusion between bookkeeping identities and causal relationships between saving and investment.

In 1936, Keynes disposed of this confusion (clearly already present in the "classical" model) by introducing under a shower of criticisms (notably from Schumpeter) consumption and savings as functions of income. Like in modern neo-Keynesian models, increased desired spending (by private sector investment *or* by government spending) induces an increase in the level of production, income and saving (the old Samuelson 45° line).

1.2.2. The theory of interest (loanable funds vs. liquidity preference). Since changes in the level of income determine changes in the level of saving, and that, according to Keynes, the principle of effective demand ensures the equality between saving and investment, an alternative to the Marshallian "productivity and thrift" theory of interest has to be provided. Hence, a bloody intellectual debate took place (and lasted at least for 30 years) around the theory of interest.[4] With the CCF model a whole range of long-forgotten pre-1936 arguments reappeared. Like for Hawtrey (1937, p. 62), for Fama, the demand for money is a function of income only (*cash-in-advance*): the rate of interest already introduced by Keynes in the *Treatise on Money* (1930) is totally absent. And this interest inelasticity of the demand for money is even already part and parcel of Hawtrey's (1925) case in favour of the *Treasury View*.[5] Without surprise, the parallel theory of interest is of the loanable funds variety (*productivity* and *thrift*) and the LM curve is, by definition, vertical. Hence, one and only one conclusion can be safely drawn: any increase in public spending crowds out an equivalent amount of private investment.

Such an argument in favour of the *Treasury View* (or is it some sort of naivety or even false innocence?) tends to demonstrate a level of knowledge in economic theory inferior to that of the economists of the 1930s. Again, chapter 3 of the *General Theory* gives an answer to such a statement: the supply and demand curves for loanable funds can only be drawn under the hypothesis of a *given* level of output/income. Any rise in the level of income would shift the saving curve to the right, reducing the rate of interest and shifting in turn the investment curve. In other and simpler words, the argument falls back on the IS curve: for a given rate of interest, what is going to be the level of income (a conjunction between loanable funds and IS)? At the time of the debate, as during the 1930s, many economies (including first and foremost the US economy) were suffering from an excess of desired saving over the level of desired investment and, of course, at an extremely low (close to zero) rate of interest.

All this can be easily illustrated with the old (and sadly forgotten) Klein (1949, p. 85) diagram in which the supply and demand of loanable funds intercept at a negative rate of interest (a point which nevertheless, and by definition, is on the IS curve). Forgotten by Ferguson et al., the subtlety here is that any point on the IS curve implies an equality between the supply and the demand for loanable funds *and* that liquidity preference and

---

[4] On the early phase of this debate immediately before and after the publication of the *General Theory*, see e.g. Presley (1979) and Bridel (1987).

[5] See also the famous 1928 Treasury Memorandum apparently largely written by Hawtrey (Davis 1983, addendum and Peden 2004). Clarke (1988) and Peden (1996) are extremely valuable sources to understand fully in historical context Hawtrey's own version of the Treasury View.

loanable funds theories of interest are *simultaneously* verified (the LM section relevant here is horizontal).

Hence, and even faced with massive government borrowing, there is no reason why the rate of interest should rise (unless of course this extra borrowing is so colossal as to shift the IS curve to the right of full employment output).

Keynes, like most modern post-Keynesians, shows beyond doubts that, in a deep recession, even massive government borrowing does not imply a rise in the rate of interest (Krugman 2011).

2. Some tentative explanations

This second section offers some tentative methodological and theoretical explanations of this renewed debate around this simplified version of the *Treasury View*.

2.1. Answers to some methodological remarks

Using Cochrane's (2009b) answer to Krugman, joined somewhat later by Sargent (2010), this section intends to demonstrate that this debate goes well beyond a discussion of the *Treasury View*.[6] This section also sends the reader back to the fundamental question of the choice of the relevant model and brings to the forefront some fundamental questions on the relationships between theoretical models and economic policy, between models and "reality", and on the difficult bridge remaining to be built between theoretical models and economic policy.

2.1.1. The efficient market hypothesis.
To give credit where credit is due, Cochrane starts with a defence of the efficient market hypothesis so much vilified by critiques of the dominant model. Should this hypothesis be verified, it would go without saying that the counter-cyclical role of fiscal policy would be much reduced if not completely eliminated. Bearing probably in

---

[6] Incidentally, it does also illustrate how the tone of the debates has radically changed since the 1930s. While Keynes's critiques of and answers to, e.g. Hayek and Haberler could be sharp, to the point, and somewhat even brutal, the intellectual exchanges between these leaders of the profession never departed from an exquisite urbanity beset with old-world academic courtesy. Judging by the tone used by the leading proponents in the 2007–2009 debates, exchanges between leading modern theorists have sunk to a level of discourtesy seldom encountered in the groves of Academe.

mind that the current crisis in no way put this hypothesis into question, Cochrane writes:

> The central empirical prediction of the efficient market hypothesis is precisely that nobody can tell where the markets are going – neither benevolent government bureaucrats, nor crafty hedge-fund managers, nor ivory-tower academics. (2009b)

Is it really the case? Fama's central idea (Fama et al., 1969) is clearly that markets evolve within a dynamic defined by the CAPM. In other words, risky assets should exhibit higher earnings than less risky ones (the risk being measured by way of the ß factor which determine the degree of correlation between a particular asset and the whole market). And from this assertion, and despite the proviso introduced by Fama and French (1992), finance professors have been successfully selling to Wall Street stockbrokers that risks on financial markets could not only be computable but also easily controllable. The subprime crisis should thus never have happened . . .

In passing the efficient market hypothesis illustrates in a remarkable way John Austin's principle of performativity.[7] The efficient market hypothesis not only intends to describe and predict the functioning of financial markets but also, and above all, to create the social reality within which it is supposed to operate. As a matter of fact, a strictly theoretical construction seems to be so well adapted to what stockbrokers are experiencing that they end up systematically adapting their own behaviour to a piece of theoretical equipment they might never have heard about (see Callon 1998, p. 30).

2.1.2. The origins of the crisis. Hence, the current crisis cannot have originated on the financial markets:

> The centrepiece of our crash was not the relatively free stock or real estate markets, it was the highly regulated commercial banks. (Cochrane 2009b)

Even if the crisis started in the Californian real-estate and then moved on to the under-regulated shadow banking system to finally nearly destroyed the "classical" banking system, and even if the stock market was relatively less incoherent than the rest of the economic system, it is hard to accept Cochrane's hypothesis about the origins of the crisis resting with bank regulations.

---

[7] Austin (1962). On the application of the principle of performativity to the efficient market hypothesis, see Callon (1998).

2.1.3. ... and back to the Treasury View.

> Macroeconomists have not spent 30 years admiring the eternal verities of Kydland and Prescott's 1982 paper. Pretty much all we have been doing for 30 years is introducing, flaws, frictions, and new behaviours, especially new models of attitudes to risk, and comparing the resulting models [DSGE ?], quantitatively, to data. (Cochrane 2009b)

Well and good. But this statement seems to reflect only fairly accurately the strategy of the CCF-type of macroeconomists. However, when turning to the influence exercised by such an approach during the past three decades on economic policy, one is forced to conclude that it has been very modest – if not non-existent. Of course, some immediately suggested that such a poor record might well be the politicians' fault. But since the doxa of these macroeconomists in terms of economic policy is to minimise or even to exclude any government's intervention to smooth the cycle, one can eventually admit such an opinion if dealing only with modest and well-behaved fluctuations. However, what should be done when faced with a financial cataclysm of the 2008 order of magnitude? Most macroeconomic models then available largely neglected the influence of the financial sector. One of the most fastidious theorists in this debate, Thomas Sargent, easily accepts this distinction:

> These models were designed to describe aggregate economic fluctuations during normal times when markets can bring borrowers and lenders together in orderly way, not during financial crises and market breakdowns. (2010)

Faced with such an intellectual disaster, and without delay, the profession could have invoked Keynes (the economics of depression), Kindleberg and, of course, Minsky (and his famous "moment").

But nothing of the sort happened.

2.1.4. More, much more of the same.... Cochrane and, behind him, most of the Chicago-led economists could not have harsher words to criticise what they consider as an intellectual regression:

> Science that moves forward almost never ends back where it started. Einstein revises Newton, but does not send you back to Aristotle. At best you can play the fun game of hunting for inspirational quotes, but that does not mean that you could have known the same thing by just reading Keynes once more. (2009b)

Such a reaction makes us come closer to the heart of the problem: are not there two types of generic models behind pro- and anti-*Treasury View*?

To compare, like Cochrane, the evolution of economic theory with that of physics is not only absurd but also completely outdated. "Economic facts" are not of the same order than physical or even biological phenomena; they are infinitely more complex and economists will never be in a position to define in their integrality, the permanent properties of any social reality – should such concepts exist at all.

Despite the usual suspicion shown by economists towards other social sciences, it seems doubtful to be a reasonable macroeconomic theorist today without having some clear ideas about the connections this discipline has with political philosophy and the dominant intellectual fashions. Such an explicit connection would help bridge the gap between macroeconomic theory and the resulting economic policies. In fact, economic theory (and not only macroeconomics) seems to be short of a proper ... theory of the link between theoretical models and the type of economic policy these models are able to support.

A return to the Smithian synthesis advocated by Sen (1987) between *economics as ethics* and *economics as engineering* is particularly relevant to macroeconomics and economic policies. But, of course, given the complexity of such an exercise, an historical and philosophical contextualisation of macroeconomics could not be conducted within the traditional formal modelling which is too often the economist's methodological alpha and omega.

This logic of linear progress of an economic theory little sister of physics naturally brings Cochrane not to question the capacity of various "frictions" within his models to explain the recent crisis but rather to complain about the lack of the right mathematical instruments to carry on such a programme:

> The problem is that we do not have enough maths. Math in economics serves to keep the logic straight, to make sure that the "then" really does follow the "if", which is so frequently does not if you just write prose. The challenge is how hard it is to write down explicit artificial economies with these ingredients, actually solve them, in order to see what makes them tick. Frictions are just bloody hard with the mathematical tools we have now. (2009b)

Such an approach implies, of course, that, without frictions, the underlying model is perfectly stable, and, moreover that the passage from such a model to "real world" economic policy is a quiet postprandial stroll. Nothing could be further from the truth. Whatever Cochrane's opinion might be, behind his Chicagoan smokescreen, one will inevitably stumble on a competitive general equilibrium model. And any reasonably trained economist knows that, since the 1970s, it has been demonstrated within the mathematical logic of this model's model that its stability is mathematically impossible to prove; furthermore, Walras (1898) himself already solemnly warned his students about the limits of his general equilibrium model: a "realistic utopia" which "expects no confirmation from reality". After a brief excursion (Section 2) within the logic of modern DSGE models used today in most economic policy discussions, Section 3 below returns on this distinction between formal models and their interpretative contents which seems to separate the methodology behind the *Treasury View* from that which does not accept a permanent confirmation of this crowding out effect.

2.2. DSGE models: fallacies of composition and transversality conditions

Dynamic stochastic general equilibrium models form today the backbone of theoretical thinking in most ministries of finance and central banks. Without entering a detailed critical discussion of the logic of these models, this section recalls nevertheless some brief remarks on their underlying theoretical structure. This exercise should help convince the reader that the resurrection of the *Treasury View* is the logical consequence of such models. And this should be no surprise that such models leaving no room to short-term economic policy and to its arbitrages (including fiscal policy) have been vigorously criticised by numerous economists (including Nobel Prize winners such as Krugman, Sims, Solow and Stiglitz).

The key logic of this DSGE approach is to adopt a (by definition) stable general equilibrium model, to introduce then a collection of "frictions" in order to give microeconomic foundations to instable processes detected in the "real world" (in order of course to escape the "Lucas critique"). The central difficulty is that, unlike traditional Walrasian general equilibrium models, these DSGE models pretend to be both dynamic (in theoretical time at least) and stochastic (i.e. including random shocks). Is it thus reasonable to use such models to analyse real, and above all financial instabilities?

From their very inception, DSGE models have been vigorously criticised by economic policy makers for not including either financial markets, or financial intermediaries or, even, financial assets. The burst of the financial bubble in 2008 and its deadly overflows on the real sector were naturally excluded. Eventually, and once again, and despite massive stimulating packages and high levels of unemployment, these models have only very lately come to term to the idea of introducing in a rather awkward manner such elements which are contrary to their inner logic.

Initially suggested by Leijonhufvud (forthcoming) and extensively discussed with him, the fallacy of composition and the transversality condition are two central weaknesses of DSGE, at least for the generation of economists, which still make a distinction between micro and macroeconomics.

(i) Fallacy of composition:
   - The representative agent, or even better the quasi-Rousseauist representative household used in these models send the reader back to pseudo-heterogeneity hardly compatible in models including financial markets. In particular, the total absence of non-rational (or at least moderately rational) financial agents goes hand in hand with the lack of financial disequilibria.
   - When, in these models, frictions on the labour market only explain unemployment (e.g. a change in the work-leisure preferences or a mark up on wages), one wonders if there is not here confusion between the respective logics of partial and general equilibrium?
(ii) Stability and transversality:
   The stability of these DSGE models is explained by means either of a linearity condition around the solution point or by multiple equilibria with sunspots. One might here sensibly wonder if this is not another way to formulate (whatever the state of the world) the Arrow-Debreu market completeness condition?

Should it be the case, this would imply a resurrection of old arguments linked to the "trading at false prices" excluded, by definition, by *tâtonnement*: a possible bankruptcy by one agent and the resulting violation of the intertemporal budget constraint would also logically exclude strictly linear fluctuations. In other words, the confidence crisis on the interbank market, the credit rationing or the massive budget deficits, in short most of the characteristics of the crisis since 2008 are nothing but splendid ... non-linearities. The introduction into a DSGE model of any of these elements would imply a zero probability for the system to reach one of its multiples equilibria.

As suggested, tongue in cheek, by Leijonhufvud, in terms of monetary policy, the transversality condition imposed by these DSGE models would be equivalent to modern central banks to the nineteenth-century gold standard framework.

At the risk of overdoing the case, and for fear of any misunderstanding, there are no good reasons to give up the use of such DSGE models (unless one is ready to give up the entire general equilibrium approach). But, one should be constantly aware of their limits and, above all, of using them for anything else but their heuristic value when one intends to move from purely theoretical models to economic policy.

Without arguing in terms as brutal as those used by Buiter (as quoted in Kay 2011, DSGE models are "a privately and socially costly waste of time and resources"),[8] it seems appropriate to rally to Charles Goodhart who asserts not to be very interested by models, which, by definition, eliminate all the economic policy problems he is interested in. Or, even more sarcastically, to adopt Solow's statement delivered to a House of Representative Committee in 2010:

> I do not think that the currently popular DSGE models pass the smell test. They take it for granted that the whole economy can be thought about as if it were a single, consistent person or dynasty carrying out a rationally designed, long-term plan, occasionally disturbed by unexpected shocks, but adapting to them in a rational, consistent way ... The protagonists of this idea make a claim to respectability by asserting that it is founded on what we know about microeconomic behaviour, but I think that this claim is generally phony. The advocates no doubt believe what they say, but they seem to have stopped sniffing or to have lost their sense of smell altogether.

As recently elaborated by Carré (2011), and despite a temporary drop in the popularity of DSGE with Central Banks during 2009 and 2010, it seems that the window of opportunity, which would have made possible a toning down of the importance of this approach, has recently been closed. In 2010, Trichet had already suggested that Keynes, not DSGE, could give "keys to understand the crisis" (quoted by Fox 2010); there were even rumours about the *beauty contest* replacing rational expectations and some sarcastic commentators were quipping that DSGE supporters were "slaves of some (not quite) defunct economists". Judging by the very recent scientific output (vide Cochrane), the internal theoretical coherence seems once again to have won over the external coherence of these models.

In order to take to its logical end the path initially used to discuss the return of the *Treasury View*, it is necessary now to turn to the opposition which seems to exist between formal developments of a model and its interpretative content (or what Blaug used to call internal vs. external coherence). Does the DSGE's formal beauty lead to a skeletal or even inexistent interpretative content? Or, conversely, does not the ability of a model to mobilise its theoretical conclusions to properly working policy conclusions rely on a somewhat more rustic analysis?

2.3. Formal developments and interpretative contents

The founding father of general equilibrium already warned his students about the strictly abstract nature of his model – a realistic utopia to use Jaffé

---

[8] With various degrees of sophistication, Colander et al. (2008), De Grauwe (2010) and Mirowski (2010), just to name but a few, made very similar comments to those suggested by Buiter.

felicitous expression – "which does not expect any confirmation from reality". Simultaneously, Walras hastened to add that "the economist should not be fooled by his abstractions" to finally conclude that "a state of crisis is not an accident but the permanent and regular state" of an economy (1898).

A century later, Debreu is keen to put as an epigram to his collected writings Bacon's famous sentence according to which "truth emerges more readily from error than from confusion". For his part, Hicks links this self-same problematic with the link between economic theory and mathematical logic:

> There is much of economic theory, which is pursued for no better reason than its intellectual attraction; *it is a good game.* We have no reason to be ashamed of that, since the same would hold for many branches of pure mathematics. (1979, p. viii; italics added)

Be it between Walras and the German historical school, or between the numerous children of Debreu's axiomatic and most modern development economists or socio-economists, economic theory, by its very nature, cannot escape from this duality already discussed in terms of ideal types by Max Weber. Sophisticated theorists like Arrow and Hahn readily admit that the importance of the main theoretical results brought about by modern general equilibrium models stem from the distance (and not from the proximity) between the model and some kind of "real" world (Arrow and Hahn 1971, pp. vi–vii).

And the few contemporary economists still interested in these questions usually consider themselves as pure instrumentalists in the Paretian tradition. Of course, there is the complex case of theorists who, like Debreu, are adepts of a topologic approach to price theory. In this good "bourbakiste" tradition, theory is "logically entirely disconnected from its interpretation" (1959, p. viii). In fact, for more than half a century, "pure theory" of the general equilibrium type has completely ceased to pretend to any external coherence: for these theorists, the logical point of reference is no longer some loosely defined competitive economic system, but exclusively and solely the mathematical logic (Ingrao and Israel 1990).

Even if it may come as a surprise to some, this position is adopted by Lucas, the founding father of contemporary macroeconomics: "I think general discussions ... of whether the system is in equilibrium or not are almost entirely nonsense. You can't look out of this window and ask whether New Orleans is in equilibrium. What does that mean? *Equilibrium is a property of the way we look at things, not a property of reality*" (Lucas as cited in Snowdon and Vane 1998, p. 127; emphasis added).

Economic theory (or at least general equilibrium theory used by New Classical and DSGE economists) became eventually consistent with the Bourbaki position and language: an empty schema of "possible realities". The model (not historical facts or some sort of abstract idealised "real world") is the laboratory within which theorists conduct their experiments.

Ever since at least Ricardo, this vision ultimately rests on the necessity experienced by economic theory to undergo first a process of knowledge rationalisation discarding most, if not all, practical necessities linked to these abstract representations. But, it seems that this ignorance of the practical side of economic policy might have gone too far. And in this field, and ever since the beginning of the current crisis, the majority of theorists has been seized by a deafening silence! Eventually, is the discipline not badly lacking a proper theory of the links between our theoretical models (à la DSGE) and the conduct of economic policy? The discussion around the resurrection of the Treasury View seems to be a perfect example of this growing divorce, which has finally reached a breaking point.

Underlining this entire debate between formal developments and interpretative contents, the very old question of the operational function of any model in social sciences finds the beginning of an answer in a methodology suggested long ago by ... John Maynard Keynes, the critique *par excellence* of the *Treasury View*.

In the 1930s, most economists (including both Keynes's friends and foes) shared radically different ideas about the connections between formal models and interpretative contents. Models were mere scaffoldings, which had to display a maximum of "realism". The analytical rigour should always yield to any possible interpretative contents: "facts" and "empirical references" were the criteria against which the validity of a model should be tested. Dating back at least to Marshall's disparaging judgements on general equilibrium, Cambridge partial equilibrium tradition was no more, but no less, than "a study of mankind in the ordinary business of life" (Marshall 1890, p. 1).

In the same tradition, in his *Treatise on Probability*, Keynes refined in a more subtle way the idea of economic theory being simultaneously empirical and rational. Within a process of knowledge acquisition, observation (relative knowledge) and formalisation (rational knowledge) are necessary. Both elements are, for Keynes, indispensable. In his own terms:

> That part of our knowledge, which we obtain directly, supplies the premises of that part which we obtain by argument. From these premises we seek to justify some degree of rational belief about all sorts of conclusions. (1921, p. 121)

However, for Keynes (and for most of his closest disciples), intuition was always more important than analytical skills. In his famous essay on Malthus, Keynes (1933) claimed for him "a profound economic intuition and an unusual combination of keeping an open mind to the shifting picture of experience and of constantly applying to its interpretation the principle of formal thought" (JMK 1972, p. 108). Even if overrating Malthus's analytical skills, Keynes was considering such a combination of intellectual qualities as ideal for a great economist.[9] In his capacity of Keynes's authorised biographer, Harrod was also of the opinion that "it is the combination of theoretical power with his great sense of realism that gives Keynes perhaps a unique position as an economist" (1970, p. 617).

This brings in the last stage of this contribution. The central idea of a lack of a theory of the links between economic theory and economic policy and the need to use Keynes's rational *and* relative knowledge is illustrated with some recent research that brings the argument back to the *Treasury View*.

3. Keynes's current policy relevance: debts, distribution of debts, banking system and risk transfers

These two sets of questions are not only highly topical today but refer to problems already mentioned long ago by Keynes. Their modern reformulations are a breath of fresh air away from the conventional DSGE structure underpinning the resurrection of a *Treasury View*-like argument.

3.1. Debts and distribution of debts between agents (Eggertsson and Krugman 2010)

Even a casual reader of Keynes's great book knows that there is no financial sector in the *General Theory*, even if the great depression went through a pretty spectacular banking crisis. To ponder further on the integration of the financial sector within Keynes's logic is precisely what Eggertsson and Krugman have recently suggested. Moreover, such an approach seems to be a step towards a better connection between theory and economic policy.

In a 1929–1936 or 2008–2012 situation, one might reasonably wonder if more debts are really the solution. It is clearly not necessary to justify again the importance of a question so obviously at the centre of the policy

---

[9] Similarly, in his usual paradoxical and sarcastic mood, Hahn kept repeating to his students that if Keynes had been a better theorist he would not have been such a great economist! Lack of intuitions cannot be replaced by a wealth of technical devices!

debate in most if not all countries today. What is, however, less obvious is the link that one could establish between a possible increase in public debt and the definition of the entity who owns the debt. It is an extremely old question, dating back at least to the Italian Renaissance city-states and the progressive construction of financial markets to finance public debts within the famous Anglo-Dutch model.

Obviously, within a closed economy, the overall level of debts makes no difference to aggregate net worth (one person's liability is another person's asset). In other words, more debt does not make the country poorer.

The level of debts matters, however, if the *distribution* of net worth between agents matters. If the levels of leverage that were considered as tolerable are suddenly (like in 2007–2008) deemed unacceptable following a sharp revision of conventional views (*à la* Keynes, *General Theory*, chapter 12), debtors are faced with a brutal deleveraging (and reduced spending) while creditors have no reason to spend more.

In other words, if highly indebted agents face different constraints than agents with low debt levels, borrowing by some agents today can help cure problems created by excess borrowing by another class of agents in the past. Again, absolute level of debts matters only if the distribution of wealth matters.

And, as a matter of course, in today's zero interest lower bound situation, government could precisely be the agent borrowing to invest to put to work resources that would otherwise be unemployed. In other words, debts are not equal.

Moreover, increased government spending would also help highly indebted agents (like banks) to reduce their debt level leading them to a situation in which they would no longer be severely balance-sheet constrained. They would start spending again and further deficit spending would be unnecessary. The *Treasury View* is clearly here a *non sequitur*.

Public would *temporarily* (insist: temporarily) replace private debts. The overall level of debt is not reduced but redistributed from balance-sheet constrained agents to government and the level of output and employment increased: debt can cure debt via a temporary (repeat: temporary) risks transfer.[10]

Without altering in the least the essence of such an argument (at the antipodes of the *Treasury View*), two central questions cannot be begged (if not answered here): on the one hand, what is the government's own constraint? In particular, this transfer of debts and risk can only be temporary: decades of systematic structural budget deficits would obviously make such

---

[10] The 2008 UBS rescue by the Swiss Federal Government is nothing else but such a temporary risk transfer mechanism.

a policy inoperative.[11] On the other, to what use could be put this debt transfer? Clearly, the answers to these twin questions would widely differ depending of the geographical location of the government.

3.2. Banking system: risks transfer and Central Bank as the "dealer-of-last-resort" (Mehrling 2010)

This Eggertsson-Krugman argument can be directly, and briefly, linked with Mehrling's novel idea of a Central Bank as not only the lender-of-last-resort, but also, and above all, as the dealer-of-last-resort.

Mehrling's idea is the financial complement to the risk transfer scheme from a balance-sheet constrained private sector to the government. By becoming the "dealer-of-last-resort", the Central Bank would backstop the financial system by being the ultimate market maker or, the expression is particularly cunning, "the insurer-of-last-resort". As it is done today in various countries according to the local idiosyncrasies of their respective financial markets, the Central Bank would put a floor to the value of some collateral in the system (some? the best? or even an exchange rate). The Central Bank would thus insure freely (and not only lend freely) at what would naturally be a penalty rate. And since the government is the only entity, which can freely create new financial assets, it can always cover (at a cost) the potential liabilities during a crisis.

4. Conclusive remarks

The modest argument offered in this contribution seems to demonstrate that the (un-)expected return of a simplified version of the *Treasury View* has (fortunately) nothing to do with decision-making processes in economic policy but is a purely academic dispute linked to modelling preferences. Hence, for some participants to the debate this return was to be expected, while, for others, it was fully unexpected! And, once again, this debate sends the economic profession back to the difficult connection between formal developments and interpretative contents of these various modelling strategies.

Accordingly, this article has also shown that economic theory (or economists?) seems to be short of a proper theory of the link between theoretical models and the types of economic policy these models are able to support. And, above all, looming in the background, an old but fundamental

---

[11] The very recent discussion has progressively moved from a budget deficit flow issue to a debt stock question and the concomitant implications of unsustainable debt levels.

question should be tackled again: what is the operational function and the intellectual respectability of models which, in social sciences, do not *also* take the trouble to link their formal developments with their interpretative content?

In connection with these central questions, it is not out of place to conclude here with Goethe's old but famous dictum: "To think is easy. To act is hard. But the hardest thing in the world is to act in accordance with our thinking".

And eventually, and closing this still un-conclusive round of the debate around the *Treasury View*, Krugman remarked wisely that "the economics profession went astray because economists, as a group, mistook beauty, clad in impressive-looking mathematics, for truth" (2009).

And this last remark could easily be extended to much broader fields in economics than the modest *Treasury View* . . .

References

Arrow, K. and Hahn, F. (1971). *General Competitive Equilibrium.* Amsterdam: North Holland.

Austin, J. (1962). *How to Do Things With Words.* Cambridge, MA: Harvard University Press.

Barro, R.J. (2009). Government spending is no free lunch; now the democrats are peddling voodoo economics. *Wall Street Journal,* 22 January 2009.

Blanchard, O. and Leigh, D. (2013). *Growth Forecast Errors and Fiscal Multipliers.* IMF Working Paper N° 13/1.Washington: International Monetary Fund.

Bradford de Long, J. (2009). *The Modern Revival of the 'Treasury View'.* Berkeley University. January 18, 2009 draft <http://s3.amazonaws.com/files.posterous.com/braddelong/TgsNS29JSegEsIXdnpVbdzJnhpaASoWVXlq6OvesGtTb5DUpmDU2BSxAj9nf/20090118_treasury_view.pdf?>.

Bridel, P. (1987). *Cambridge Monetary Thought. The Development of Saving-Investment Analysis from Marshall to Keynes.* London: Macmillan.

Callon, M. (1998). The embeddedness of economic markets in economics. In M. Callon (Ed.), *The Laws of the Markets.* Oxford: Blackwell.

Cannon, M. (2009). *"Contribution" to John Boehner, ed. (2009), "Stimulus Spending Skeptics: Economists Express Doubts About Trillion Dollar Spending lan".* <http://republicanleader.house.gov/UploadedFiles/stimulusskeptics.pdf>.

Carré, E. (2011). 'DSGE', l'art des banques centrales au défi de la crise financière. *Economie appliquée,* 64: 171–89.

Clarke, P. (1988). Keynes, Buchanan and the balanced budget doctrine. In P. Clarke (Ed.), *The Keynesian Revolution an its Economic Consequences.* Cheltenham: Elgar.

Cochrane, J. (2009a). *Fiscal Silliness.* University of Chicago. <http://faculty.chicagogsb.edu/john.cochrane/research/Papers/fiscal2.htm>.

Cochrane, J. (2009b). *How did Paul Krugman Get It so Wrong?.* Chicago University. <http://faculty.chicagobooth.edu/john.cochrane/research/Papers/krugman_response.htm>

Colander, D., Howitt, P., Kirman, A., Leijonhufvud, A., and Mehrling, P. (2008). Beyond DSGE models: Toward an empirically based macroeconomics. *American Economic Review,* 98: 236–40.

Davis, E. (1983). *The Macro-models of R.G. Hawtrey. Carleton Economic Papers, 4.* vol. 83. Ottawa: Department of Economics, Carleton University.

Debreu, G. (1959). *Theory of Value: An Axiomatic Analysis of Economic Equilibrium.* New Haven: Yale University Press.

De Grauwe, P. (2010). The scientific foundations of dynamic stochastic general equilibrium (DSGE) models. *Public Choice,* 144: 413–43.

Eggertsson, G. and Krugman, P. (2010). *Debt, Deleveraging, and the Liquidity Trap: A Fisher-Minsky-Koo Approach.* New York and Washington: Federal Reserve Bank of New York and Federal Reserve System.

Fama, E., Jensen, M.C., and Roll, R. (1969). The adjustement of stock prices to new information. *International Economic Review,* 10: 1–21.

Fama, E. and French, K.R. (1992). The cross-section of expected stock returns. *Journal of Finance,* 47: 427–65.

Fama, E. (2009). *Bailouts and Stimulus Plans.* University of Chicago. <http://www.dimensional.com/famafrench/2009/01/bailoutsand-stimulus-plans.html>.

Fox, J. (2010). The (many) things macroeconomists don't know. *Harvard Business Review,* http://blogs.hbr.org/fox/2012/03/the-many-things-macroeconomist.html.

Hawtrey, R.G. (1925). Public expenditure and the demand for labour. *Economica,* 13: 38–48.

Hawtrey, R.G. (1937). *Capital and Employment.* New York: Longmans, Greens & Company.

Harrod, R. (1970) [1951]. *The Life of John Maynard Keynes.* London: Macmillan, 1970.

Hicks, J.R. (1937). Mr. Keynes and the 'Classics', A suggested interpretation. *Econometrica,* 5(2): 147–15.

Hicks, J.R. (1979). *Causality in Economics.* Oxford: Blackwell.

Ingrao, B. and Israel, G. (1990). *The Invisible Hand. Economic Equilibrium in the History of Science.* London: MIT Press.

Kay, J. (2011). *Financial Times,* 19 October 2011.

Keynes, J.M. (1921). A treatise on probability. In *The Collected Writings of John Maynard Keynes.* vol. VIII. London: Macmillan, 1973.

Keynes, J.M. (1930). A treatise on money. In *The Collected Writings of John Maynard Keynes.* vols. V and VI. London: Macmillan, 1971.

Keynes, J.M. (1933). Essays in biography. In *The Collected Writings of John Maynard Keynes.* vol. X. London: Macmillan, 1972.

Keynes, J.M. (1936). The general theory of employment, interest and money. In *The Collected Writings of John Maynard Keynes.* vol. VII. London: Macmillan, 1973.

Kindleberger, C.P. (1986). *The World in Depression, 1929-39.* Berkley: University of California Press.

Klein, L.R. (1949). *The Keynesian Revolution.* 2nd ed. London: Macmillan, 1966.

Krugman, P. (2009). How did economists get it so wrong?. *Wall Street Journal,* 2 September 2009.

Krugman, P. (2011). *Mr Keynes and the Moderns, Plenary Lecture for the 75th Anniversary of the General Theory.* Cambridge. http://www.econ.cam.ac.uk/keynes-conf-2011/Plenary-Lecture.pdf.

Leijonhufvud, A. (forthcoming). The economic crisis and the crisis in economics. *European Journal of the History of Economic Thought,* forthcoming.

Mankiw, N.G. (2009). *Fama on Fiscal Stimulus.* Harvard. <http://gregmankiw.blogspot.com/2009/01/fama-on-fiscal-stimulus.html>.

Mehrling, P. (2010). *The New Lombard Street: How the Fed Became the Dealer of Last Resort.* Princeton: Princeton University Press.

Mirowski, Ph. (2010). The great mortification: Economists' responses to the crisis of 2007–(and counting). *The Hedgehog Review*, 12.

Peden, G.C. (1996). The treasury view in the interwar period: An example of political economy? In B. Corry (Ed.), *Unemployment and the Economists*. Cheltenham: Elgar.

Peden, G.C. (2004). *Keynes and His Critics: Treasury Responses to the Keynesian Revolution 1925-1946*. Oxford: Oxford University Press for the British Academy.

Peterson, T. (2009). *I Have Thought About the Fama Article a Bit More....* <http://delong.typepad.com/sdj/2009/01/famas-fallacy-v-arethere-ever-any-wrong-answers-ineconomics>.

Presley, J. (1979). *Robertsonian Economics*. London: Macmillan.

Robertson, D.H. (1940). *Essays in Monetary Theory*. London: Staples Press.

Sargent, Th. (2010). *Interview with Thomas Sargent*. Banking and Policy Issues Magazine. The Federal Reserve Bank of Minneapolis.

Sen, A. (1987). *On Ethics and Economics*. Oxford: Blackwell.

Snowdon, B. and Vane, H.R. (1998). "Transforming macroeconomics: An interview with Robert E Lucas Jr." *Journal of Economic Methodology*, 5: 115–45.

Solow, R. (2010). "Statement", house committee on science and technology subcommittee on investigations and oversight. *Building a Science of Economics for the Real World*.

Soros, G., Ferguson, N., Krugman, P., Robin Wells, P., and Bradley, B. (2009). The crisis and how to deal with it. *The New York Review of Books*, 56, 11 June 2009. <http://www.nybooks.com/articles/archives/2009/jun/11/the-crisis-and-how-to-deal-with-it/>.

Spilimbergo, A., Symansky, S., Blanchard, O., and Cottarelli, C. (2008). *Fiscal Policy for the Crisis, IMF Staff Position Note, SPN/08/01*. Washington, DC: International Monetary Fund.

Walras, L. (1898). *Etudes d'économie appliquée*, in *Auguste et Léon Walras Oeuvres économiques complètes*. vol. X. Paris: Economica.

Abstract

By examining the rhetorical use of an old piece of economic theory by some contemporary economists, this paper intends to report on "how today's economists conduct a public policy debate". This paper is neither a scholarly history of the interwar debate nor a sophisticated critique of current economic policy. It is an attempt to link the policy and theoretical arguments of two similar debates separated by nearly 80 years. The second part of the paper demonstrates that the (un-)expected return of the *Treasury View* is a case study illustrating two very different modelling strategies.

Index

Note: Page numbers in **bold** represent figures

Acceleration Principle 1, 96–8, 111, 128–9; Goodwin's sigmoid non-linear 153
accelerator processes 13; and effect 128
accordion effect 13
accumulation 39
adaptive behaviour 13
Aftalion, A. 107
agents 38–40, 55; debts distribution 183 5; heterogeneous 38; individual 38
aggregation 53–7, 134; demand function 13, 57–9, 69, 73; expenditure 159; over agents 55; price index 39; real income 69; supply function 57–9
Allais, M. 145; analytical framework 147–54; cycle meaning and empirical verification 157–62; different simplifications 154–7; endogenous business cycle theory contribution 147–63; equations/formulae 148–61; hereditary theory 147, 163; limit cycle existence 156–7; monetary cycle 157–60; Nobel Lecture (1988) 146; non-linear functions f and g 149–55; one delay model 160–1, **161**; phase diagram 156, **157**; psychological theory of rate of interest 151–3; reaction functions 150–2, **151**; unique delay T model 155–6

AltA mortgages 10
amplification: endogenous 10
animal spirits 72
Arena, R. 2, 21–46
argumentation styles 106
Arrow, K. 181
Arrow-Debreu market completeness 179
Assous, M.: and Lampa, R. 4, 117–44
Austin, J. 175
Austrian School 120

Bacon, F. 181
bailouts 171
balance sheet 6; recession 6
Banca Italiana di Sconto 34
banking systems 151–3; British evolutionary 41; Central Bank as dealer-of-last-resort 185; conglomerate 11–12; crisis 34; finance and industry relationship 34; German 41; mixed 34, 41; and risk transfers 185
bankruptcy 179
bargaining: collective 64
Barro, R. 172
Baumol, W. 150, 160
bears 73–4
bifurcation 12–14; financial 14
Blanchard, O. 168; and Kiyotaki, N. 50

Blankenburg, S.: *et al.* 23
Boltzmann, L.: and Volterra, V. 150
bonds 73–5; prices 73–7
bootstrap theory 88
Boulding, K. 163
bourbakiste tradition 181–2
Bradford de Long, J. 169
Breit, M. 118
Bridel, P. 4, 166–88
British evolutionary banking systems 41
Brookings Institution 100
budget 18; intertemporal constraints 18
Buiter, W. 16, 179–80
bulls 73–4
Business Cycles (Schumpeter) 123, 139

Cagan, P.D. 151
Cannon, M. 169–70
Cannon-Cochrane-Fama (CCF) model
    168–76; saving-investment equality
    172; theory of interest 172–4
capital 55, 124–6; goods 55; marginal
    efficiency 66, 72
Capital Asset Pricing Model (CAPM) 175
capitalism 34–5, 40, 121–2; concept 124;
    instability 122–3; law of motion 123
Carré, E. 180
cash-balance effect 91
Cassel, D.: and Cassel, L. 23, 100, 103,
    106–7
Cato Institute 170
Central Bank 33, 180, 185; as dealer-of-
    last-resort 185
Champernowne, D. 48, 90
Chicago University 170–1
Citigroup 9
Clark, J.M. 28, 96
class 33
classical economics *see* postulates of
    classical economics
Cobb-Douglas function 59
cobweb theorem 125
Cochrane, J. 166, 169–70, 174–7
Colander, D.: *et al.* 180

collective bargaining 64
competition 9, 50; free 28, 60; given
    degree 50–1; imperfect 49, 89;
    monopolistic 50, 54–6, 61; perfect
    theory 28–9; semi-monopolistic
    26–30
consumption 55, 102, 127–9; classes 52,
    68; future 71; optimum propensity
    to 119, 129–31; propensity 66;
    under- 103
contagion 8
coordination failures 4
corporate savings (CS) 170
Corridor Hypothesis 12–14
crisis of economics 6–19, 166, 171;
    agent models and fallacies of
    composition 16; balance sheet
    troubles 6; bifurcation 12–14; budget
    constraint violations 17–18; complex
    dynamical system 12–13; DSGE
    unemployment 15–16; economic
    logic 9–10; financial markets 8; GE
    with frictions 17; leverage dynamics
    8–10; macroeconomics and financial
    economics 15–19; network structures
    11–12; ontology 18–19; origins
    175; produced goods markets 7–8;
    stability and instability 6–17

Das Kapital (Marx) 121–2
Davis, H. 160
De Cecco, M. 31
De Grauwe, P. 180
De Vroey, M. 64, 89
Debreu, G. 181
debt: and distribution between agents
    183–5; legacy 9
debt-deflation 10, 16; black hole 13
deflation 32–3, 54, 79, 98
deleveraging 16
demand 29; aggregate 134; effective 58,
    66–71, 173; elasticity 56; function
    expression 57
depreciation 55, 66

depression 97–9, 107
development: laws of 123
deviation-amplifying processes 10, 13
deviation-counteracting processes 13
Dimand, R. 48
disequilibrium 101, 130
Dixit, A.: and Stiglitz, J. 50
Domar, E. 103
Dos Santos Ferreira, R. 2, 47–84; and Michel, P. 51
Duke University 119
Dunlop, J. 61
Dunlop-Tarshis observation 51
Dynamic Stochastic General Equilibrium (DSGE) 2, 7, 15–19, 86; composition fallacies and transversality conditions 178–80; core model 87; and Treasury View 166–9, 182; unemployment 15–16

Ecole des Mines 156
Ecole Polytechnique 153
Econometric Society 90, 147, 159; Lausanne Meeting (1931) 153; Washington Meeting (1949) 154
Econometrica 90, 109, 118, 147, 153
economic evolution 139, 143, 177
Economic Journal 29, 33, 89–90, 97, 110
economic sociology 22
economics crisis 6–19
Economics of Industry (Marshall) 27
Economics and Reality (Lawson) 19
Economics (Samuelson) 86
Economie et intérêt (Allais) 146–51, 154; Chapter VIII 147–8, 158
Economisk Tidskrift 100
Edgeworth, F.Y. 90
Edgeworth-Bowley box 17
effective demand principle 68–71
Eggertsson, G.: and Krugman, P. 185
employment 57–80, 92; effective demand principle 68–71; financial market coordination failures 49, 71–7; full 62–80, 63, 99, 107;

fundamental postulates 57–65; labour demand 57–9; labour market coordination failures 49, 77–80; labour supply and wage setting 59–62; obstacles 72; theory generalisation 67–80, 125; under 70, 70, 88, 101, 108, 111–13, 130; volume 68, see also Keynes
endogenous amplification 10
eponomy: law of 99
equilibrium 17–19, 49, 76, 102, 155–6, 180–2; dynamic 103; economic 120; full employment 99; loanable-funds 93, 97; partial 15, 53, 107, 182; shifting 119; short and long-period 53, 72; steady-state 76; temporary 49; underemployment 50, 68, 70, 70, 101, 108; values/equations 134–6; Walrasian models 18, see also general equilibrium (GE) systems
European Journal of the History of Economic Thought (EJHET) 1–5
Eurozone 10
expenditure 127

fallacy of composition 178–9
Fama, E. 166, 169–75; and French, K. 175
Fascism 35
Federal Reserve Bank 100
feedback 7, 133; negative 7; positive 9, 13
Fergusson, N. 169–73
financial market coordination failures 49, 71–7
fire sales 10
Fisher, I. 13, 66, 88, 146, 151; and debt-deflation 16; quantity theory of money 31
Flechét, J.F.: Frisch, R. and Klein, L. 160
flexibility 9
fluctuations 147–8
Fondements comptables de la macroéconomie (Allais) 146–7, 152

Fondements de la dynamique monétaire (Allais) 147
fraud 8
free markets 6–7
French, K.: and Fama, E. 175
frictions 7, 17, 177–8; labour market 15; stable GE vs. instability 17
Friedman, M. 16, 65, 131, 162, 171
Frisch, R. 107; Klein, L. and Flechét, J.F. 160

G-20 meeting (Washington 2008) 167
Gali, J. 15
gambling 26
Garegnani, P. 42–3; and core concept 42–3
general equilibrium (GE) systems 7, 13–16, 86; non-monetary 7; Paretian theory 21, 89
General Theory of Employment, Interest and Money (Keynes) 3, 39, 47–56, 64, 77, 80, 129; aggregation 53–6; Book I 48; Book II 51; Chapter 16 postponed dinner parable 71; Chapter XII 127; coordination failures 71–2; draft (1934) 55; expectations 52–5, 68; of interest 128; as Lange's model 117–18; and macroeconomic syntheses 87–101, 105–10; modelling 51–6; and Treasury View 168, 172, 183
Germany: banking systems 41
given quantities assumption 23–6
Glass-Steagall Act (1933) 10
Goethe, J.W. 186
Goodhart, C. 180
goods 55; consumption and capital 55
Goodwin, R. 145, 153, 160; Hicks-Kaldor models 156, 162; sigmoid non-linear accelerator function 153, 156
government savings (GS) 170
Gram, H.: and Walsh, V. 21
Gramsci, A. 36

Grandmont, J. 163
Great Depression 8–10, 14, 95, 146, 171

Haberler, G. 3, 86–9, 94, 105–13, 174; content 96–100; context 95–6; Synthetic Exposition 96, *see also Prosperity and Depression* (Haberler)
Hahn, F. 21, 150, 159–60, 181–3
Hamburger, L. 153
Hansen, A. 96, 100, 107, 112
Harrod, R. 48, 90, 103, 117, 183
Harvard University 171
Hawtrey, R. 71, 79, 107, 166, 173
Hayek, F. 37–8, 88–90, 95–7, 101–13, 174; conception of money 39; individual agents conception 38; investment boom scenario 104
hereditary function 147
Hicks, J. 3, 47–8, 69, 72, 80, 100, 105–6, 145, 181; content 91–4; context 89–91; crude model 91, 109; Kaldor-Goodwin models 156, 162; and Lange 117–18, 126; temporary equilibrium 49, *see also IS-LM* model; *Mr Keynes and the Classics* paper (Hicks)
Hobson, J. 126
Hoover, K. 56
How to Pay for the War (Keynes) 110
Hubert Curien programme 1
hyperinflation 151

Ichimura, S. 145, 159; Mimeo 148
income 32, 102–3, 127; concept 94; distribution 32; global ratio 152; ratio 158
industry (company/firm) 39–42; banking and finance 39–42; personification 40; and union bargaining 60–1
Industry and Trade (Marshall) 27–8
inflation 11, 31–3, 37, 92, 99, 104, 150, 163; cumulative 111; gap 104; high 13; hyper- 151

innovation 123–4, 141
instability 6–17, 123, 146, 149;
    capitalism 122; and economic logic
    9–10; and network structures 11–12;
    representative agent models and
    fallacies of composition 16; vs.
    stable GE with frictions 17
institutions 23–31; organisation forms
    and social conventions 23–31;
    ownership, management and control
    30–1, 40; role in Sraffa's conception
    31–42
Interest and Prices (Woodford) 86
interest rates 14, 25, 39, 42, 68, 74–5,
    103, 128, 133; Allais' psychological
    theory of 151–3; determination
    process 127; natural 111; nominal
    71; and optimum propensity to
    consume 117–44; real 62–3, 67, 70,
    159; rigidity 78; sacrifice 92; zero
    lower bound 14, 184
interests 33; conflicting 33; group 33;
    theory 109, 130
International Conference on Dynamics
    (Paris 1955) 147
International Monetary Fund (IMF) 167;
    Staff Position Note (2008) 167–8
investment 66, 88, 102–3, 127–9, 140,
    159; adjustment effects 136–7;
    boom 104; demand function 133–4;
    feedback effects 133; inducement
    66; lag 118, 132–3, 139; levels 132;
    maximising 130; savings (IS) 66, 88,
    93; traps 87
investment function 4, 36–7, 133–4;
    non-linear 4
IS curve 69, 132, 173–4; equation 132;
    imbalances 111
IS-LM model 3, 47, 74, **75**, 80–1, 117,
    131, 172–4; general 131–2, 143;
    Hicks' generalised relation 93, **93**,
    97; Hicks' Wicksellian model 94, **94**;
    and macroeconomics 86–7, 92–3,
    108, 112; theory 3

isoclines 135–6, 139
Italy 34–5; Lira devaluation 35

Jacobian matrix 135, 139
Jaffé, A. 180; realistic utopia 178–81
Japan 6, 13; crisis (1992–3) 6, 74
Johnson, H. 2

Kahn, R. 64
Kaldor, N. 119, 139–41, 144–5, 156–8;
    Goodwin-Hicks models 156, 162
Kalecki, M. 107, 117–19, 162; business
    cycle model (1937) 131, 137–41;
    dynamic process 132–4; lag structure
    118, 132–3, 139
Kaufmann, H. 95
Kay, J. 179
Keynes, J.M. 1–3, 29, 32, 35–9, 117–19,
    127–9; bootstrap theory 88; classical
    doctrine and New Keynesians 47–81;
    and classical economics 56–7; essay
    on Malthus 183; finance motive 110;
    first fundamental postulate (labour
    and price setting) 57–9, 62–3, 71;
    on full employment 62–80, **63**;
    macroeconomic syntheses 4, 85–113;
    multiplier concept 69, 87, 97–8, 104,
    112; psychological reaction functions
    101–2; and Say's law 56, 65–8,
    71, 75–7, 81; second fundamental
    postulate (labour supply and
    wage setting) 59–62, 65, 71; slump
    economics 111; and Treasury View
    166–8, 171–6, 180–3; *Treatise on
    Money* 36–9, 48, 110, 173; *Treatise on
    Probability* 182–3, *see also General
    Theory of Employment, Interest and
    Money* (Keynes); *Mr Keynes and the
    Classics* paper (Hicks)
Keynes-Lange system 119
Keynesianism 12, 145, 159–62, 168;
    literature theme characteristics 49;
    monopolistic competition model
    55–6; New 47–81, 85

Kindleberger, C. 167, 176
Kiyotaki, N.: and Blanchard, O. 50
Klamer, A. 112
Klein, L. 48, 173; Flechét, J.F. and
    Frisch, R. 160
Koo, R. 6
Kowalik, T. 117
Krugman, P. 50, 75, 166, 169, 174, 186;
    and Eggertsson, G. 185
Kurz, H. 37
Kuznets, S. 100

labour 25, 57–80; *a posteriori*/*a priori*
    division 28–9; demand function
    57–62; disutility 68; imperfect
    mobility 79; marginal product 59;
    marginal product of (MPL) 59;
    market coordination failures 77–80;
    market frictions 15; social division
    integrating force 30; supply function
    60–2; supply and wage setting
    59–62, *see also* employment
labour theory of value 54, 120–2
lagging 118, 132–3, 146–8; and
    Lundberg 87, 102, 112; regulation
    processes 146, 154
laissez-faire 3, 41
Lampa, R.: and Assous, M. 4, 117–44
Lange, O. 4, 48, 117–44; dampened
    cycles 135–6, **136**; directions 118;
    dynamics foundations 120–5;
    equations 127–8, 131–5; model
    dynamisation interpretation 131–40;
    1938 static model 125–31; non-linear
    investment function 4; self-sustained
    cycles **138**, 139, *see also* optimum
    propensity to consume
Lausanne School 120
Lavington, F. 92
laws of development 123
Lawson, A. 19
Le Corbeiller, P. 153
League of Nations 95; Economic
    Intelligence Service 95

Lectures on Continental Banking
    (Sraffa) 34, 41
Lectures on Industry (Sraffa) 25–6, 30,
    33, 40–1
Lederer, E. 103, 107
Leijonhufvud, A. 2, 6–20, 47–9, 86, 91,
    105, 178–9
lender confidence 133
Leontief, W. 23
Lerner, A. 97
Lessourne, J. 156
Levinson, N.: and Smith, O. 145
Liénard 145, 153; continuous-time
    systems 157
Lindahl, E. 88, 91, 100, 109–11
liquidity 13, 76, 110; balances 149;
    constraint 73; preference 74, 92,
    101, 127, 150; trap 75, 109–11; vs.
    loanable funds 172–4
Lira devaluation 35
LM curve 74, 92, 132, 174; liquidity trap
    109
loanable-funds 93, 97, 169; equilibrium
    93, 97; vs. liquidity preference 172–4
London School of Economics (LSE)
    33, 90
Lucas, R. 64, 162, 181; critique 178
Lundberg, E. 3, 86–9, 94, 105–13;
    content 101–5; context 100–1;
    core 102–3; fundamental dynamic
    relations 102; lag 87, 102, 112;
    model sequences 103–4; multiplier-
    accelerator tool 87; toolkit 106–7,
    *see also Studies in the Theory of
    Economic Expansion* (Lundberg)
Lutfalla, G. 159

machinery pricing 36
macroeconomic theory 4–5, 15–19,
    176; business cycle groups and
    phases 96–8, 105, 110–11; common
    ground 110–12; crude model 91;
    divided paths 105–8; equations
    91–4, 101; and financial economics

15–19; Haberler on Prosperity and Depression 86, 95–100; Hicks on Keynes 89–94; Keynesian challenge 108–10; Lundberg's Studies in Theory of Economic Expansion 86, 100–5; vintage syntheses (1937) 85–113

macroeconomics: and *IS-LM* model 86–7, 92–3, 108, 112

Malthus, T.R. 126, 183

Manchester Guardian Commercial 33

Mankiw, N. 169, 172

marginal product of labour (MPL) 59

Markas, J. Van der 153

markets 72; financial 49, 71–7; forces 7, 12; free 6–7; imperfections 7, 49; incompleteness 72; labour and output 76; output 76; private 30; spot 72

Marshall, A. 27–30, 88–92, 107, 172, 182; symmetric theory of prices 29; symmetric theory of value 27

Marshallian School 120

Marx, K. 4, 117, 120–6, 138–41, 166; class 33; underconsumption argument 103

Marxian Economics and Modern Economic Theory (Lange) 120

Marxism 36

Mathieu, M. 156

Meade, J. 48, 90, 117

Mehrling, P. 185

Metroeconometrica 148

Michel, P.: and Dos Santos Ferreira, R. 51

micro-foundations 37

Mimeo 148, 156–7

Minsky, H.P. 10, 125, 162; moment 176

Mirowski, P. 180

Mises, L. von 95

Mitchell, W.C. 100, 160

Modigliani, A. 48, 86–7

Molière 167

Monetarism 12

monetary cycle theory, non-linear 145–63; different simplifications and endogenous cycles 154–7; limit cycle existence 156–7; meaning and verification 157–62; reaction functions 138; unique delay *T* model 155–6, *see also* Allais

monetary theory and policy 31–5, 54; balances 149–50, 153; Sraffa's early contributions 31–5

money 39; Keynes on 36–9, 48, 110, 173

monopoly: pricing 122; semi- 26–30

Morgenstern, O. 96

Morishima, M. 145

mortgages 10

Mr Keynes and the Classics paper (Hicks) 86, 89–94, 105–6; content 91–4; context 89–91

multiplier concept 69, 87, 97–8, 104; accelerator 104, 112; processes 13

Munier, B. 153

Mussolini, B. 35

mutatis mutandis application 79

Myrdal, G. 18, 91, 100, 109–11

Naldi, N. 35–6

Nash, J.F. 60; solution 60–1

National Bureau of Economic Research 100, 160

necessity concept 24–6; costs 26

Neo-Walrasian GE theory 21

Neoclassical Synthesis 22, 85–113; New 3, 85–9; one-commodity model 54

network connectivity 12

New York Review of Books 166, 169

New York Times 166

Newman, P. 23

Ohlin, B. 96–7, 110

optimum propensity to consume notion (Lange) 119, 129–31; and to save 129–30, **130**

organisation forms 23–31; institutions and social conventions 23–31;

ownership, management and control
30–1, 40; role in Sraffa's conception
31–42
output 57; aggregate 134; markets 76

Panico, C. 31–4, 42
Pareto, V. 21, 89–90, 151, 181; optimal
general equilibrium 89
Patinkin, D. 48
Peden, G. 173
Penrose, E. 28
performativity principle 175
Peterson, T. 172
Phillips curve 51
Pigou, A. 64, 91–2, 166; effect 70, 77,
99, 112
Pol, B. Van der 145, 153–4
Political Economy Club (Stockholm)
100, 105
Popper, K. 95
postulates of Classical economics
56–65, 71; demand for labour and
price setting 57–9; labour supply and
wage setting 59–62
Price, C. 9
prices: bonds 73–7
Prices and Production (Hayek) 37
pricing 29–30, 57, 85, 88; aggregate
index 39, 50; as closed system 43;
full-cost 29; machinery 36; monopoly
122; securities 37; staggered 49
private markets 30
private savings (PS) 170
probability 73; Keynes on 182–3
production 102
*Production of Commodities by Means of
Commodities* (PCMC) (Sraffa) 21–7,
42; and societies (systems) 25
profit maximisation 57, 66, 137
Prosperity and Depression (Haberler)
86, 95–100, 105–6, 110–12; basic
facts 96–7; business cycle theory
groups 96; content 96–100; context
95–6; Synthetic Exposition 96

quantity theory 14; Cambridge equation
91; and indices 50; of money 39

*Rate of Interest and the Optimum
Propensity to Consume* (Lange)
117–44
rates of interest *see* interest rates
rates of return 8
Raybaut, A. 4, 145–65
RBC framework 89
real economy 8
realism 52, 178–82
recession 6, 37
Reddaway, W. 48, 90
Ricardo, D. 32, 92, 182
Richardson, G. 28
rigidity 7
risk transfers 185
Riskbanken (Swedish central bank) 100
Rist, C. 96
Rivot, S. 80
Robbins, L. 90, 96
Robertson, D.H. 39, 96, 101, 171;
golden rule 26
Robinson, A. 110
Robinson, J. 21
Rocard, Y. 154
Rockefeller Foundation 95; fellowship
100
Roncaglia, A. 23, 29
Rotemberg, J. 50
Rousseau, J-J. 179
Roy, R. 159

Samuelson, P. 86–7, 110–12, 118–19,
129–30, 141
Sargent, T. 169, 174–6
savings 102, 159; corporate (CS) 170;
investment (IS) 66, 88, 93; private
(PS) 170
Say's law: failure 68, 81; and Keynes 56,
65–8, 71, 75–7, 81
Schumpeter, J. 22, 107, 117, 123–5,
139–40, 144; innovation definition 123

securities: pricing 37
self-stabilisation 3
semi-monopoly 26–30
Sen, A. 177
sinequanon factors 148, 158
Smets, F. 15
Smith, A. 177
Smith, O.: and Levinson, N. 145
social conventions 23–31; and
    inequalities in Sraffa's conception
    31–42; institutions and forms of
    organisation 23–31, 40
Solow, R. 180
speculative gains 26
Spence, M. 50
Spiethoff, A. 107
spirits: animal 72
spot markets 72
Sraffa Archives 21–3, 26–8, 31–3, 37
Sraffa, P. 2, 21–44; on banking, finance
    and industry 39–42; on business
    cycles 35–9; early contributions to
    monetary theory and policy 31–5;
    economic institutions role 31–42;
    given quantities assumption 23–6;
    institutions and organisation forms
    23–42; *Lectures on Continental
    Banking* 34, 41; *Lectures on Industry*
    (Sraffa) 25–6, 30, 33, 40–1; monetary
    theory and policy 31–5; ownership,
    management and control 30–1;
    price entrepreneurial decisions and
    real-world competition 26–30;
    *Production of Commodities by Means
    of Commodities* (PCMC) 21–7, 42;
    social conventions and inequalities
    23–42
stability 6–17, 135–6; corridor and
    bifurcation 12–14; equation
    properties 152; with impediments
    7–8; policies 13, 99; self 3; and
    transversality 179
Stigler, G.J. 99; law of eponomy 99
Stiglitz, J.: and Dixit, A. 50

stimulus plans 171
Stockholm: Political Economy Club
    100, 105
Stockholm School 88, 97, 100, 109–10
Strutt, John William Lord Rayleigh 153
*Studies in the Theory of Economic
    Expansion* (Lundberg) 100–8;
    Chapter IX 102–3; content 101–5;
    context 100–1
Svensson, L. 50
Sweden: Business Cycle Research
    Institute 101; *Riskbanken* 100,
    see also Stockholm
Switzerland 10
symmetric forces 27–9

Tasca, A. 34–5
tâtonnement 179
taxonomic theorising 131
Théorie des oscillations (Rocard) 154
Theory of the Individual Industry or
    Firm 54
Theory of Output and Employment 54
Times 166
Timlin, M. 119
Tinbergen, J. 96, 107
Tobin, J. 86
Tract on Monetary Reform (Keynes) 32,
    35–6
transversality 17–18, 179
Trautwein, H-M. 3, 85–116
Treasury View 4, 166–86; banking
    system and risk transfers 185;
    Cannon-Cochrane-Fama (CCF) model
    169–74; crisis origins 175; debts and
    distribution between agents 183–5;
    DSGE 166–9, 182; DSGE models
    178–80; efficient market hypothesis
    174–5; formal developments and
    interpretative contents 180–3;
    and Keynes 166–8, 171–6, 180–3;
    Keynes' current policy relevance
    183–5; Memorandum (1928) 173;
    methodological remarks 174

Treatise on Money (Keynes) 36–9, 48, 110, 173
Treatise on Probability (Keynes) 182–3
Treilles Foundation 1, 166; Scientific Committee 1
Trichet, J-C. 167, 180

underconsumption 103
underemployment 70, **70**, 88, 101, 108, 111–13, 130
unemployment 15–16, 48, 99, 109; frictional 63–4; natural rate 65; voluntary/involuntary 48, 59, 63–5, 71, 80
unions 60–1, 78–9; monopoly model 61
United Kingdom (UK) 10
utopia: realistic 178–81

Value and Capital (Hicks) 89
velocity 148, 160
Velupillai, K. 145
Volterra, V.: and Boltzmann, L. 150

wages 25, 49, 62, 85; adjustments 49; cut therapy 99; and first fundamental postulate 57–9; movements 51, 109; pure economic determination 43; real 68, 79; rigidity 78, 81, 88; units 50, 77, 80; utility 61
Wages and Interest (Hicks) 108
Walras, L. 17–18, 23, 90–1, 181; realistic utopia 178
Walrasian model 49–50; auctioneer 49; equilibrium 18; modes 89; realistic utopia 178–81
Walsh, V.: and Gram, H. 21
Weber, M. 181
Weitzman, M. 50
Wicksell, K. 90–1, 101, 106–9, 113; connection 88; cumulative changes scenario 104; inflation gap 104; *IS-LM* model 94; natural rate of interest concept 111; process 111
Wittgenstein, L. 26–7
Woodford, M. 86
Wouters, R. 15

Yasui, T. 145

Zappia, C. 37

For Product Safety Concerns and Information please contact our EU representative GPSR@taylorandfrancis.com Taylor & Francis Verlag GmbH, Kaufingerstraße 24, 80331 München, Germany